£4.99

# THE PIRATE WARS

**Peter Earle** formerly taught at the London School of Economics and is now Emeritus Reader in Economic History at the University of London. He is the author of over a dozen books on English social and maritime history, including two on different aspects of piracy, *Corsairs of Malta and Barbary* and *The Sack of Panama*.

D0532634

Also by Peter Earle

*Corsairs of Malta and Barbary*
*The Sack of Panama*
*The Wreck of the* Almiranta
*The Last Fight of the* Revenge
*Sailors: English Merchant Seamen 1650–1775*

# THE PIRATE WARS

PETER EARLE

Methuen

Published by Methuen in 2004

5 7 9 10 8 6

Copyright © 2003, 2004 by Peter Earle

The right of Peter Earle to be identified as the author of this
work has been asserted by him in accordance with the
Copyright, Designs and Patents Act 1988

First published in Great Britain in 2003 by Methuen

This edition published in 2004 by
Methuen Publishing Ltd
11-12 Buckingham Gate,
London SW1E 6LB
www.methuen.co.uk

Methuen Publishing Limited Reg. No. 3543167

ISBN 10: 0 413 75900 8
ISBN 13: 978 0 413 75900 9

A CIP catalogue for this title is available from the British Library.

Printed and bound in Great Britain
by Cox & Wyman Ltd, Reading, Berkshire

This book is sold subject to the condition that it shall not, by way
of trade or otherwise, be lent, resold, hired out or otherwise circulated
in any form of binding or cover other than that in which it is
published and without a similar condition, including this condition,
being imposed on the subsequent purchaser.

# Contents

# Preface

# *Preface*

Blackbeard and the pirates boarded the naval sloop under cover of the smoke and 'were not seen by Lieutenant Maynard until the air cleared. He then gave a signal to his men, who all rose in an instant and attacked the pirates with as much bravery as ever was done upon such an occasion. Blackbeard and the lieutenant fired the first pistol at each other, by which the pirate received a wound; and then engaged with swords, till the lieutenant's unluckily broke, and he stepping back to cock a pistol, Blackbeard, with his cutlass was striking . . .'[1]

It is this dramatic moment in the fight between the notorious pirate Blackbeard and sailors of the Royal Navy that is depicted in the cover illustration of this book. Blackbeard stands poised on the left with his cutlass raised to strike. Lieutenant Maynard of the Royal Navy, with his broken sword blade on the deck before him, flinches in anticipation of the blow as he desperately tries to cock his pistol. Things look bad for the navy, as the artist J.L.G. Ferris teasingly wants us to believe, but of course they are not really so bad as they seem since this is a painting of *Blackbeard's Last Fight*. The key to the picture is the stout sailor standing behind the two main protagonists with his eyes on Blackbeard and his cutlass raised to strike a backhand blow. It is difficult to tell which side he is on, as he is not wearing uniform, but he was in fact one of Maynard's men and he struck at the same moment as Blackbeard, giving 'him a terrible wound in the neck and throat' and deflecting the pirate's cutlass, 'by which the lieutenant came off with a small cut over his fingers'. This was by no means the end of the fight, but it proved a turning point and Blackbeard and most of his men were eventually killed in this battle against royal sailors on 22 November 1718.[2]

This bloody fight was just one incident, albeit a very dramatic one, in a series of wars or near wars fought against pirates by the navies of Britain and other countries from the early seventeenth century until the third decade of the nineteenth century. These conflicts varied in intensity, but on occasion could involve considerable numbers of naval ships and men sent out specifically to hunt down pirates and capture or kill or otherwise drive them from the seas. These pirate wars are the principle subject of this book and the aim is to examine both sides in this long conflict. Some chapters focus on the pirates and uncover their changing nature as they gradually acquired the attributes, customs and lifestyle which we associate with the word pirate today. Others examine the changes in government attitudes and policy towards pirates and look in detail at the many anti-piracy campaigns conducted with varying success by navies, campaigns whose unsung heroes are not remembered today while the pirates themselves have entered into fable.

The book starts in the late sixteenth century, a time when piracy was rife in the Mediterranean and endemic in many parts of Western Europe, such as Cornwall and south-west Ireland. We then follow the pirates across the oceans, to America and the Caribbean, to West Africa and the Indian Ocean, seas where they were chased by naval vessels at first with little success but finally with a remorseless efficiency which appeared to have eradicated European and American piracy as a serious problem by 1730. This, however, turned out to be a false dawn, for the end of the Napoleonic Wars in 1815 ushered in a little known but devastating epidemic of piracy, more intense and much crueller than any other considered in the book, a period of maritime mayhem which ended in 1835 when the last true pirate captain to ply his trade in the Atlantic was hanged in Boston.

Pirates and piracy have retained a perennial fascination and books on the subject are legion, though they tend to repeat each other and draw on the same rather limited range of source materials. This study necessarily makes use of these same materials, but also draws on previously unused sources, especially the records of the British Admiralty which have been surprisingly neglected by historians of piracy. These and other government records provide plenty of information on the pirates themselves and are of course central to an understanding of the long and ultimately successful story of how European and American governments and navies managed to rid the seas of these bold predators. This story has never been told before in its entirety and it is the main task of this book to fill this surprising lacuna in naval and pirate history.

It would be tempting to see the story as a moral fable in which the forces of good ultimately overcome the forces of evil, the precursor of other campaigns in which nations have united to eradicate what they saw to be sinful, such as the long campaign to abolish the slave trade or today's 'war' against international terrorism. Such moral convictions certainly existed in the minds of some of those who were contemporaries of the pirates, but there were also many who had more ambiguous attitudes towards these daring seafarers. It will be seen in early chapters that many governments supported or at least condoned piracy committed by their own subjects, seeing it as a cheap and effective way of advancing trade and empire, a policy which can be called piratical imperialism. And many individuals and communities all over the world had a vested interest in the continued existence of pirates, who paid well in bribes for protection from arrest, were free spenders and produced an attractive inflow of cheap pirated goods for the delectation of consumers. Such support for pirates was reduced but never eradicated in the two and a half centuries considered in this book and it was a major factor in delaying for so long the eventual victory of the forces of law and order.

If attitudes towards pirates were ambiguous in their heyday, it is no surprise that they should be even more so today, now that piracy of the sort considered here is no longer a threat. Pirates are remembered with affection and even admiration today rather than as thieves and murderers, while the navies of the great age of sail which were once automatically respected and admired as the safeguard of empire are often denigrated as a result of their less admirable institutions, such as excessive flogging and the press gang, or simply because they were the agents of an empire which has now become politically incorrect. And so, despite the boost to naval popularity resulting from the enormous success of historical novels such as those by Patrick O'Brian, the author of a book such as this one cannot be certain that all his readers will necessarily be on the side of law and order. There will no doubt be many who feel tempted to support the pirates rather than the navies who chased them, for pirates have been celebrated since their eclipse as individualist and even proto-radical folk heroes, as lovable rogues and as role models for adventurous boys (and girls) and not as the 'enemies of mankind', vermin to be driven from the sea and annihilated, as most of their contemporaries saw them.

This creation of a pirate fable is discussed in the first chapter and it has to be admitted that even I am susceptible to pirate charm and romance, as will be apparent on occasion in the six chapters describing the customs and activities of pirates across the centuries. Nevertheless, I was brought up to admire the navy and my instincts are on the side of law and order, so that the navy rather than the pirates has my support, as will be clear during the five chapters on pirate hunting where it is such things as naval and Admiralty venality and incompetence rather than naval successes which I regret. Those who wish the pirates well may, however, be pleased to know that the navy was very slow to learn how to win this contest and so ensured that their individualist and daring opponents had a very long innings indeed.

My thanks are due to the libraries and record offices where I have done my research and particularly to the Public Record Office and the British Library whose fast, efficient and cheerful service makes them a joy to work in. Many thanks also to my family and friends who have kept me up to the mark when lethargy threatened the completion of the book. And, finally, my especial thanks to my friend and colleague Dr David Hebb who not only provided me with innumerable ideas and references while I was working on the book, but also read the completed work in typescript and made many invaluable suggestions for its improvement.

# CHAPTER ONE

# Pirates of Fable

# CHAPTER ONE

## *Pirates of Fable*

'All that is told of the sea has a fabulous sound to an inhabitant of the land and all its products have a certain fabulous quality, as if they belonged to another planet.' So wrote Henry David Thoreau, and pirates, those products of the sea who are the subject of this book, certainly reflect this quality.[1] Pirates were already a source of wonder to their contemporaries who, even though they feared them, might marvel that these bold seafaring men could challenge the norms of their age in quite such an insolent, exotic and exciting way. But their fabulous nature has grown almost beyond belief in the years since 1830 when piracy was at last eliminated as a serious problem in the Atlantic and Mediterranean world. Indeed, fable has nearly obliterated fact so that the image of the pirate held today is an unlikely amalgam of Blackbeard and Captain Kidd, grotesquely distorted representations of real people, Long John Silver and Captain Hook, somewhat sinister joke figures of fiction, and Errol Flynn and Burt Lancaster, superbly athletic swash-bucklers of the silver screen, swinging through the rigging sword in hand.

Modern fantasies about pirates are not entirely the fault of historians, who are quite capable of writing serious, realistic and well-researched books about pirates, although this does not inhibit them from demonstrating admiration for the individualism and radicalism of their villainous subjects. Nor indeed does it prevent them from introducing an element of fantasy as a serious comment on the lifestyle of pirates, particularly those of the late seventeenth and early eighteenth centuries. One historian records their 'taste for the bizarre, for the spectacular' and another refers to the 'carnivalesque quality' of pirate life, while the French historian Hubert Deschamps used an even more fantastical adjective when he discussed '*cette histoire grand-guignolesque des pirates . . . Ces êtres valeureux et demoniaques, hors du commun monde.*'[2] Valour, devilry and showmanship, whether in the grotesque and sensational form of the Grand Guignol or in the world-turned-upside-down form of carnival, certainly did play an important part in the make-up and lifestyle of pirates and they really were '*hors du commun monde*', not just as 'the enemies of mankind' as they had been known since Roman times, but as the paradigm of an alternative form of existence.

It is almost as if pirates believed it their business to entertain their terrified and quivering victims in the most grotesque way, as well of course as robbing, torturing and occasionally murdering them, entertainment which no doubt seems more amusing from an armchair today than it did from the decks of a captured and helpless merchant ship three hundred years ago. A pirate ship makes a bold stage where exotically apparelled desperadoes can strut their stuff, drink and swear to excess, and invert the hierarchical and behavioural norms of their age. Such behaviour has made pirates fabulous as well as fantastic and has ensured that even today, nearly two centuries after the last real pirate of the Atlantic world was executed, they still make up an important part of the modern entertainment business.

Many historians consider the pirate ship as more than just a stage on which an entertaining or enlightening show can be played out. For pirate historians have now discovered social history,[3] the branch of history which in the last two decades or so has been the most dynamic and inventive, in both senses of the word. For centuries, pirates have been characterised as white, male and heterosexual, bold masculine heroes (or villains) embodying a European myth of white physical supremacy. But this will no longer do in our politically correct, post-imperial world. Two writers have asserted that all or at least most pirates were homosexuals, thus giving 'a whole new meaning to the phrase

"Jolly Roger"'.[4] The argument rests on fanciful deduction from the undoubted fact that most pirate ships were all-male institutions, and no real evidence is given to support the assertion. Nevertheless, a marker has been put down and textual critics will no doubt consider with interest the occasional use by writers of a more innocent age of the adjectives 'gay' or even 'queer' as epithets for pirates. Other writers have challenged the whiteness of the pirate crews, an argument with rather more substance since blacks certainly formed a large minority of crews in the Atlantic and Caribbean during the early eighteenth century and were often a definite majority in the last great pirate epidemic which followed the Napoleonic Wars. But how much this amounts to an intriguing form of black empowerment in a white-dominated world, as has been claimed, is not an easy question to answer since the records are silent and no more revealing of the status of black pirates than of the sexuality of pirates as a whole.[5]

So if pirates, far from being straight and white were all gay and often black, it is hardly surprising that the make-up of a pirate crew should also have interested another powerful lobby in the new social history: the feminists. Such interest begins (and almost ends) with the undoubted fact that two women, Mary Read and Ann Bonny, were captured off Jamaica in 1720 in a pirate sloop commanded by one Calico Jack Rackam. The main witness at their trial was another woman, Dorothy Thomas, who was herself a female seafarer, and she made it clear that they were not just passengers but active, fighting members of the crew, dressed in 'mens jackets, and long trouzers, and handkerchiefs about their heads' and only identifiable as the women they were 'by the largeness of their breasts'. Four years later, these two female pirates were given immortality in a largely fictional account of their lives by Captain Charles Johnson, who some say is a pseudonym for Daniel Defoe, a major source for the history of piracy in the period around 1720 and for many of the fables which have become attached to it.[6]

Johnson's book has been reprinted many times and these two female pirates have ever since been a source of fascination to men and women alike, so much so that in recent years researchers have made strenuous attempts to add to their number.[7] Such attempts have been largely unsuccessful, since there were in fact very few women pirates in the Atlantic and Caribbean world with which we are mainly concerned, a fact which has not prevented many writers exaggerating their numbers and glorying in this female presence in a male world. And why not? Piracy offerred equal opportunity, if the story of Mary Read and Ann Bonny can be believed, and it provided, too, a wonderful alternative to the humdrum norms of female existence in the early modern world. 'Piracy offered everything to a woman that was denied her on land,' writes Sara Lorimer. 'At sea she had freedom and autonomy. She kept her own hours and spent them playing cards, drinking, gambling, sailing, eating, killing, and plundering. No household to run, no family to support, no chamber pots to empty.'[8] It sounds such a desirable life that it seems a shame that there were not more women to enjoy it and so join the blacks and gays who challenged the myth of the white, male, heterosexual terror of the seas.

If even those serious creatures, historians, cannot prevent themselves from lapsing into fantasy when writing about pirates, it is no wonder that those who write fiction should stray even further from reality. And there are many of them, for pirates have been incredibly popular as the subject of fiction, both on the screen and on the page. A search on the website of Amazon.com found over a thousand matches for the subject 'pirates'. These included several serious academic works of the type which have been useful in the preparation of this book, but the genre is dominated by works of fiction.

Some of these are the modern descendants of the classic pirate stories of the nineteenth century, such as Robert Louis Stevenson's *Treasure Island*. These are often well-researched books aimed mainly at an adult market, such as Nicholas Griffin's *The Requiem Shark*, the tale of a musician forced to serve with the real pirate Bartholomew Roberts, or Björn Larsson's entertaining fictional autobiography of Long John Silver, a picaresque ramble through the early eighteenth-century world.[9] But pirate fiction is aimed mainly at children, sometimes in convincing and informative stories such as *Under the Black Flag* by Erik Christian Haugaard, whose heroes are two teenage boys, one black and one white, who meet on a pirate ship and after many exciting adventures escape from it, having absorbed useful lessons about life, class and particularly race. The titles of other pirate books for children suggest a didactic mission to tell the 'truth' about pirates, but a huge number are simply fantasy and fun for the playroom with titles such as *Do Pirates Take Baths?*, *The Pirates' Colouring Book* or *Rabbit Pirates: a tale of the Spinach Main*. And there is no question of gender inequality in this vast body of children's literature, as the girls of today demand to be the heiresses of Mary Read and Ann Bonny. For every *Edward and the Pirates* there is a *Lucy and the Pirates* or a *Captain Mary, Buccaneer*. This assertion of feminine rights in the fictional pirate world goes back at least as far as *The Queen of the Pirate Isle* of 1886, though it is doubtful if the girls of today would think much of Queen Polly whose duties 'seemed to be purely maternal, [and] consisted in putting the [boy] pirates to bed after a day of rapine and bloodshed'.[10]

These pirates of fiction dress and behave in a way that has been handed down to the modern age as pirate orthodoxy. They are heavily sunburned and they tend to be bearded and have luxuriant moustaches. Their heads are covered in brightly coloured handkerchiefs or bandannas and their ears droop under the weight of huge gold earrings. They have big, bare, flapping feet which can grip a rope as they climb like monkeys through the rigging, though many do not have two feet or two hands as peglegs and hooks are abundant in the fictional pirate community. They look very fierce indeed and their chests are crossed with bandoliers and their belts bristle with pistols and cutlasses. They sometimes swear terrible oaths, but more often shout 'Shiver my timbers' or 'Yo, ho, ho', usually accompanying such outbursts with copious draughts of rum laced with gunpowder. They sail their beautiful ships through beautiful tropical seas before running down a prize and swinging aboard with astonishing agility and ferocity. Gold coins and silver pieces of eight pile up in their treasure chests which are later buried by moonlight on desert islands. They are very kind to their parrots, but not to their prisoners, whom they blindfold before making them walk the plank. They are, in short, a lovable community of rascals whom any child of spirit would be only too happy to make into a role model.

So pirates, violent men of the sea who were robbers, torturers and often murderers, have become the stuff of childhood fantasy and bedtime stories for both boys and girls, a destiny which would certainly have amazed the real villains who appear in this book. And yet this portrayal of the violent as a source of amusement to the innocent is perhaps not so strange as it might seem, as much of children's literature presents a dangerous, frightening and often violent world, a world of dark forests and lonely mountains as well as tumultuous seas, a world which can be obliterated if necessary by hiding beneath the bedclothes. The life of pirates was indeed adventurous, exciting, free and conducted in exotic locations, so it is no wonder that it might appeal to the imagination of the young of both sexes. It was also criminal, cruel and often very sordid, but this can be conveniently forgotten as pirates, like other bugbears of the past such as dragons, wolves and wicked witches, are sanitised or at least tamed for popular consumption. Pirates of the type discussed in this book no longer exist and so no longer present a threat. Other bugbears have taken their place and it may be some time before terrorists or drug dealers become the lovable heroes of children's literature, even though their lives too are no doubt exciting, adventurous and even glamorous.

Just as children grow up on a diet of pirate books, so are they soon likely to be exposed to pirate films, since pirates are probably only outnumbered by cowboys, spies and gangsters as athletic and individualist heroes or villains of the cinema. James Robert Parish in his compendium of pirates and seafaring swashbucklers on the Hollywood screen provides plot summaries and critiques of no less than 137 pirate films.[11] None of these films has any real connection with historical piracy and, like the children's books, they are romantic exercises in escapism in which a surprising number of aristocrats and gentlemen appear as captains aboard the pirate galleon or schooner, whose visual beauty as it sails across 'the magically enticing high seas' is a major attraction of such films. These pirate ships provide the stage for storms and sea fights, bravery and cowardice, treachery and loyalty, athletic swinging through the rigging and wonderfully choreographed sword fights. But what movie-goer would welcome the reality of dirt, drink, disease, suppurating wounds and plebeian captains?

Movie-goers want technicolor beauty, action, excitement and an unlikely plot and this is what they get, as Parish notes in his book. They want their pirate film to 'deal nostalgically with a bygone, heavily-romanticised era in which derring-do, courage and the right of might rules'. They do not want the hero to be just a grasping, greedy cut-throat. He should instead be acting for patriotic reasons or in pursuit of revenge on those who had stolen his inheritance or killed his comrades. He should be a lovable rogue standing up to the establishment, 'a man fighting for the right in a world that does not understand the right as he sees it'.[12] Movie-goers also want beautiful women on their screens and there are plenty of these in pirate films, just as there are in pirate novels, women like Jean Peters in *Anne of the Indies* (1951) who was described in advance publicity as 'a dreaded pirate queen, as ruthless and daring a female as any buccaneer seen on the screen', or the gentler Joan Fontaine whose pirate lover in *Frenchman's Creek* (1944) offers 'a dream fulfillment for any woman who has ever fantasised of abandoning her stable but predictable existence at home for the love of a dashing, masterly pirate who will draw her into an exciting life of dangerous adventure'. The romantic Frenchman himself explains rather cryptically why he became a pirate. 'There's a certain beauty in the world. Something just beyond our fingers' end, which we all desire, but few of us achieve . . . Mine I have found at last as a pirate!'[13]

Pirate fable is good fun and good box office and in among the nonsense there is certainly some realism, since it would be churlish to deny that there was romance, excitement and adventure in pirate life, sometimes even a certain nobility. Nevertheless, real pirates bore little resemblance to fictional pirates and it will be one of the twin tasks of this book to sift the reality of pirate history from the fable and fantasy and to show how that reality changed over time, from the heroic days of the late Elizabethan age to the last and cruellest epidemic of Western piracy in the 1820s. These changes were considerable, for the customs, lifestyle and provenance of pirates, contrary to popular belief, have evolved over time. The pirates of the 1820s were very different from those who pursued their trade around 1600 and neither group shared many characteristics with the buccaneers and pirates of the golden age, who flourished from the 1650s to the 1720s and are seen by many to be the only 'real' pirates who have ever existed, the paradigm of the pirate type which is so popular today. And none of these mainly Northern European and American pirates have very much in common, except a love of loot, with those pirates of the Mediterranean, the Barbary and Maltese corsairs, who plundered throughout the period for the glory of God as well as their own profit and whose strict rules and organisation provide an intriguing contrast to the more anarchic and individualist pirates of the Caribbean and Atlantic, though even these had more self-imposed discipline and rules than one might at first expect.

The other and more original task will be to show how piracy was in fact eliminated by 1830, after many false starts and humiliating failures, and the seas made safe from the scourge which had afflicted them for thousands of years, from the dawn of the maritime trade which was the pirates' prey. This, too, is an epic story since pirates like terrorists, their modern counterparts as enemies of mankind, were far from easy to eliminate. They demonstrated a protean ability to change their nature and their tactics to meet each new threat to their existence and so attractive was the profession that, to use a favourite contemporary metaphor, 'like weeds or Hidras they spring up as fast as we can cut them down'.[14]

The story of the suppression of piracy is therefore a long one and made even longer by the fact that governments were very slow to commit much of their scarce resources to such a policy. At the sharp end, it is the story of individual naval officers and other pirate hunters chasing individual pirates, usually without success since pirates were to prove very elusive and navies were very slow to learn the most effective ways of catching them. But it is also part of the much bigger story of the rise of imperialism and naval power from the late sixteenth century onwards. The expanding tentacles of European empires gradually eliminated more and more of the bases and havens on which pirates depended until, by the nineteenth century, there was hardly anywhere left on the globe which was safe from imperialist attention. Growth of empire was paralleled and sometimes led by a huge growth in European and, later, American navies, so that the sea too was eventually to be denied to the pirates who themselves were no more numerous in the early nineteenth century than they had been in the early seventeenth century, when in numbers they were a serious threat to the small navies of the day.

This then is the story of two sets of predators, one composed of pirates chasing merchant shipping and the other of men of the navy chasing pirates. Both groups of men were ironically drawn from the same milieu and had many customs and skills in common, for both were what contemporaries called 'bred to the sea', men whose early maritime training had been acquired mainly in merchant shipping. Nearly all pirates had this background, becoming pirates as a result of mutiny or capture or deliberate choice, often after a cruise or two serving aboard a privateer had given them a taste for robbery at sea. And nearly all sailors in the navy, at least until the nineteenth century, had also served in the merchant service, many seeing service in a merchantman or a navy ship as largely a matter of indifference and taking the first berth offerred to them, in peacetime at least when pay in the two services was very similar. 'There was no identifiable class of man-of-warsmen,' the naval historian Nicholas Rodger observes of the mid eighteenth-century navy. 'There were simply seamen working at the moment for one particular employer.'[15] Discipline was often but not always harsher in the naval service, but this possible disadvantage could be counterbalanced by normally better food and less work in the navy, since the large crews on royal ships meant that each man's load was likely to be less than on the lightly manned merchantmen. Less work because of large crews was also one of the attractions of service on a pirate ship, though there were of course many others, such as the chance of booty and the comparative freedom of pirate life.

Piracy and pirate hunting tended to be concentrated in peacetime, since those with a taste for maritime violence and robbery could indulge it legitimately in wartime by serving in a privateer, that is a private ship commissioned by the government to attack and loot the shipping of enemy countries. This meant that those who served in naval vessels during anti-piracy campaigns were almost all volunteers, since it was unusual for the navy to have to resort to the press gang in peacetime. It would, however, be a clever observer who could predict which merchant seafarer would choose to become a pirate and which would opt to serve his king or queen in the navy, since neither occupation had a monopoly of good or evil. The fact is that chance, opportunity, good or bad treatment and a host of other factors would determine these important choices for men of the sea but, once the choice had been made, most men were loyal to the ship they served in, whether it be a pirate vessel or a ship of the navy. Whatever their choice, the men on both sides of this long war between the navy and the pirates remained sailors with the same fighting and seamanlike skills and the same vices, such as a love of excessive drinking. The only important differences were that the pirates had freer access to drink and the navy had discipline on its side and so the naval vessels usually won on those rare occasions when they brought a pirate ship to battle.

There was nearly always some piracy somewhere during the two and a half centuries considered in this book, but there were also periods of pirate epidemics when numbers and the damage done escalated to such an extent that governments and navies were forced to increase their efforts to try and eradicate the threat to merchant shipping. These epidemics were usually in the years following the end of major naval wars when large numbers of men accustomed to maritime violence found themselves unemployed or simply wanted to continue the marauding and mayhem which they had previously enjoyed. The first of these epidemics to be considered occurred in the early seventeenth century, in the years following the end of the great Elizabethan war against Spain. This was a time when England's maritime subjects were habituated to piracy. But it was also in these years of the reign of James I (1603–25) that the English government and navy made the first, very modest, beginnings in those pirate wars which would, some two centuries later, eliminate the problem. For the country which was called a nation of pirates in the years around 1600 would eventually become the pirates' greatest scourge, not just in English waters but throughout the world.

# A Nation of Pirates

CHAPTER TWO

# A Nation of Pirates

Piracy is as old as the maritime trade on which it preys and so its history is a very long history, stretching right back into the ancient world. The economics of shipping in a competitive world meant that most merchant ships were lightly armed and carried a relatively small crew, and this attention to profit naturally made such ships vulnerable to predators. And so for thousands of years, well-armed predatory men (and a few women) in a variety of fast and well-maintained vessels have been dashing out from behind headlands, lurking in narrows, deceiving with false colours, chasing, firing on, boarding and capturing merchant ships, usually with great ease. For thousands of years, such men have mistreated and sometimes murdered the captured crews, stripped sailors of their clothing and valuables and tortured them to find the whereabouts of hidden treasure, ransacked the holds, burned or sunk those vessels for which they had no further use, before rowing or sailing back to well-protected bases where a welcoming local population provided harbour and support and a market for the looted goods.

Some pirates were true wanderers, scouring the seas for months or even years with a very limited association with the land. But for most pirates a base ashore was an essential feature in their continued existence, a home where they could return after their voyages to repair and refit their ships, sell their loot and relax and enjoy themselves on the proceeds. Such pirate havens sometimes survived for centuries, sometimes just for a few years before the pirates were driven out by the forces of order and compelled to find a new place of resort. They could be found at different times all over the world, in the Indian Ocean, the Indonesian archipelago, the seas of China and Japan, in the waters of America and the West Indies and, nearer home, in the Mediterranean. But it is now some three and a half centuries since there have been pirate bases in north and north-west Europe, a seaboard which once rang with cries of triumph as the rascals who used them returned home with their booty.

Nowhere was this truer than in late sixteenth- and early seventeenth-century England, a country whose maritime life was so suffused with piracy that it was known as 'a nation of pirates'. Such a description was somewhat exaggerated and was really just a way of being rude to the English, for piracy was endemic in many other parts of Europe, even if the English should seem to be the worst offenders. Most of this piracy was fairly small-scale, usually short-distance and normally backed, financed and protected by notables ashore. Such pirates could be found from the Baltic and the Hebrides to the Adriatic and the Greek islands, but one major area of concentration was certainly in south-west England, south Wales and south-west Ireland.[1] Pirates, or rovers as they were sometimes euphemistically styled, had been operating from these areas for centuries, setting out to plunder foreign shipping, usually close inshore in the English Channel and its approaches, off Brittany and Ireland and other nearby places. As long as English shipping was left unharmed, local opinion did not condemn this piracy which was regarded in the sixteenth century in much the same way that smuggling was in the eighteenth, an illegal activity but a useful one which provided a stream of cheap goods and employment for local toughs who might otherwise have been engaged in robbing their neighbours.

Although the English government had traditionally done very little to combat such piracy, it was of course illegal, and capture and conviction could and did occasionally lead to death by hanging. As a result, these land-based pirates were entirely dependent on the goodwill and support of local landowners, merchants and officials who provided the rovers with many invaluable services. Most importantly, they were the owners of the havens where pirates could fit out their ships and looted goods could be sold. Studland Bay in Dorset was one such haven where the return of a successful pirate would see the local gentry swarm aboard to bargain for the silks and satins laid out on deck or play dice with the pirate crew for a share of their booty.[2]

Gentry interest in piracy sometimes went further than mere conniving and receiving. Some pirates were independent leaders of their companies, but others were virtually the employees of local notables who fitted out the vessels and manned them with their retainers and other local men, often providing a younger brother or other relative as the captain. An important function of these gentlemen, many of them magistrates or local officers of the Admiralty, was to protect those pirates who were caught, ensuring that they were not brought to trial or, if they were, that they were acquitted or pardoned, though in this they were not always successful. In 1581, for instance, it was reported in the Privy Council that John Piers, 'a verie notorious pirate', had been captured in Studland Bay with fifteen of his men and sentenced to be hanged, despite having not just support from gentlemen but also potential supernatural assistance from his 'olde mother dwelling at Padstowe, noted to be a wytche, to whome by reporte the said Piers hathe conveyed all suche goods and spoiles as he hathe wyckedlie gotten at the seas'. Piers managed to escape from Dorchester Gaol after bribing the keeper, a more or less standard event in this period, but on this occasion it was not sufficient to secure his freedom. He was recaptured and hanged near Studland 'to the terryfying of others, for that the same place hath bene muche frequented and the inhabitants molested with pirates'.[3] But the fate of John Piers was unusual and not many pirate captains were hanged. John Callice or Challis, a gentleman who set out in 1571 'to seeke purchase by way of adventuringe', was more typical. After six years of seeking 'purchase', a euphemism for piratical loot, he was arrested and sentenced to death but, in the end, his bribes and backers and promises of future good behaviour were sufficient to get him pardoned. Challis, like many captured pirates both before and after him, offered to turn gamekeeper in return for his life, 'to clear the coasts of other wicked pirates, as he knows their haunts, roads [harbours] and creeks and maintainers so well he can do more than if she [i.e., Queen Elizabeth] sent ships and spent £20,000'. Needless to say, he did not do this once he was pardoned and he was soon back to his old trade.[4]

Many great men could be found among the backers of pirates, such as Sir George Carey, captain or governor of the Isle of Wight, who employed his own ships on pirate cruises and ran a well-advertised market for other pirates who brought their loot to his island, or Sir John Perrot, the leading figure in government, society and piracy in south-west Wales. However, the most notorious of the local supporters of piracy were the Killigrews, a great Cornish family who were hereditary royal governors of Pendennis Castle. In the late sixteenth century, they were led by Sir John Killigrew, vice admiral of Cornwall, a man of immense local power whose influence spread out to Wales and Ireland. He was also, ironically, head of the commission set up by the Elizabethan government to look into the problem of piracy in Cornwall, a subject on which he was well informed since piracy was one of his major sources of income. Many others of his family were or had been engaged in the same business, such as his father and uncle, his mother who was reputed to have led a boarding party in person, first cousins and more distant cousins, while even his maternal grandfather had been a pirate in Suffolk. But worst of all was his son, another John, who was accused in 1595 of living 'chiefly by oppressing his tenants . . . by robbery . . . by cosening his friends and neighbours . . . by receiving of stolen goods, by consorting with pirates, and abuse of his place of command'.[5] There were many such men and, in a period when power rested largely in the hands of the local gentry and interference by the central government was financially and politically very difficult, such a well-organised system of plunder and protection was extremely hard to disrupt. And even though it was ultimately rooted out in the British Isles and indeed in most of Europe, it was to crop up again in the British and French colonies in America and the West Indies. Piracy has always benefited from the support of unscrupulous great men, only too happy to receive bribes and cheap pirated goods at no risk to themselves.

These home-based pirates of the years around 1600 have few of the characteristics one usually associates with the word 'pirate', except that they attacked and looted merchant shipping. They were not enemies of mankind, not 'at war with the whole world', since they rarely attacked English vessels. They did not spend months at sea following the 'pirate round', since they sailed from permanent bases, their own homes in fact, and were often out and back with their loot in the same day or night, such ephemeral voyages providing little opportunity for the development of pirate *mentalité* and customs. One of their historians even claims that they did their job with 'neither excitement nor cruelty', though this seems hard to believe and the evidence suggests that even if these pirates were not guilty of gratuitous cruelty they already made use of the tortures typical of the buccaneers and other later pirates.[6] But there is not yet much sign of the egalitarian and democratic customs often associated with pirates in the popular mind. Captains were not elected by their men as they were to be later, but were either self-appointed or chosen by their gentleman bosses ashore and many were themselves petty gentry who maintained the social hierarchy of the shore aboard their ships. Nor is there any sign of an equal distribution of the booty, the lion's share going in profits to the gentry backers and receivers. In Cornwall, the pirates themselves shared only one-fifth between them and this fifth was not equally distributed between the men. It was in fact just a job, like fishing, gamekeeping or serving gentlemen, or whatever else these part-time, petty pirates did in that majority of the year when they were not out at sea.

A second and rather more impressive collection of pirates were to emerge from Elizabethan England's efforts to expand maritime commerce into new regions and from the long struggle with Spain which was to culminate in open war in 1585. This is a confused period when piracy, privateering, reprisals and 'aggressive commerce' all existed alongside each other and are difficult to disentangle, a period when even the states of war and peace were generally ill-defined. The leading historian of Elizabethan privateering, K.R. Andrews, distinguishes three kinds of activity:

'the indiscriminate, persistent and criminal pursuit of maritime robbery; officially authorized reprisals by merchants for loss of ships or goods; and government-commissioned but privately promoted action against enemy shipping and goods in time of war.'[7] Or, to put it more simply, piracy, reprisals and privateering, three different forms of private maritime violence of which only the first, piracy, was illegal though all three were very similar in motivation and methods. In fact, all these activities tended to merge into each other in Elizabethan times. Merchant ships on apparently legitimate voyages to expand the range of English commerce south and west were well armed for their own protection, but such arms could be and were used for illegal predatory activity when the occasion arose. A piratical dimension was an integral factor in sixteenth-century commerce, writes Andrews, 'not merely a vicious but essentially alien parasite'.[8] Privateering or reprisal commissions were frequently dubious in their legitimacy and the privateers had few fears of discipline from the commissioning authorities, whether these were the English Admiralty, the Prince of Orange as leader of the Dutch fighting for their freedom against Spain, the French Huguenots or, after 1580, the pretender to the Portuguese throne, Dom Antonio. Given a commission, the privateer had some protection from potential punishment and he might confine his attention to those enemies which it specified, whether they be French or Scottish, or more often Spaniards or Portuguese. But the temptation to exceed the commission, turn pirate and attack and ransack neutral shipping was ever-present. Then there were the pirates pure and simple, with no commission at all though many might pretend to have one, since the pirate masquerading as a privateer was as common as the privateer behaving as pirate. Such men might simply be the small-scale pirates of Cornwall, Devon or Dorset, spreading their wings further to the south and west of their accustomed hunting grounds. Or they might be great men backed by courtiers or the Queen herself like Sir Francis Drake, that 'master thief of the unknown world'[9] who was knighted on his own quarterdeck after his return in 1580 from his enormously successful but indubitably piratical voyage around the world.

This extension of piracy, however defined, far beyond its old haunts in the English Channel and the Western Approaches, begins to escalate from the 1550s when English merchant shipping set out to seek new fields of activity, in Morocco, West Africa and the Canaries, and later in Brazil, the Caribbean and the Mediterranean. The incursion of armed merchant ships into these waters inevitably led to clashes with the Spanish and Portuguese, to reprisals, counter-reprisals, violence, imprisonment of English sailors by the Spanish Inquisition and thus to a belief that anything Spanish or Portuguese was fair game and so ultimately to full-scale war with Spain from 1585 to 1603. The attitude of the English government to this escalation of maritime violence, whether legal, quasi-legal or openly piratical, was ambivalent in the extreme. Lip-service was paid to the undoubted fact that piracy was prejudicial to the operation and development of normal commerce, as well as providing continuous diplomatic embarrassment as states protested against attacks upon their subjects and, when no redress was given, issued commissions of reprisal and so escalated the problem. But very little was actually done to suppress piracy, which was seen not just as profitable and a rather effective way of expanding English commerce and encouraging English shipping, but also as a cheap means of waging war by proxy, a process which enabled the Crown to deny responsibility for the uncontrollable activities of those who happened to be English subjects. Some half-hearted attempts were made to control piracy in home waters, though these were tempered by a belief that piracy was a superb school for producing sailors skilled in seamanship and the fighting arts, a belief which was to be reiterated for many years to come and was well phrased by the Jacobean pirate Sir Henry Mainwaring. 'The State may hereafter want such men, who commonly are the most daring and serviceable in war of all those kind of people.'[10] But virtually no attempt at all was made to police the ocean and control long-distance piracy, hardly surprisingly since ministers of state and even the Queen herself stood to gain from it, while nearly every maritime hero of the reign of Elizabeth – Drake, Hawkins, Grenville, Gilbert, Raleigh, Frobisher and many others – spent some of his days either as a pirate or as a privateer who engaged in piracy on the side or was an aider, abettor or employer of pirates.

Piracy in this period, writes the naval historian Nicholas Rodger, was not 'an activity of marginal outcast communities . . . on the contrary, it was often an activity of the wealthy and well-connected, privately and sometimes publicly backed by the Queen and her ministers'.[11] Such attitudes were to change in the future. We will find piracy condoned by the English government and even employed in the advancement of state policy in the Caribbean in the days of the buccaneers in the mid seventeenth century, but not thereafter. The government might not do very much to drive pirates from the seas, some privateers almost inevitably committed acts of piracy in times of war, but from the 1670s the English government never again used pirates as an instrument of policy or personal profit. They still used maritime violence to promote trade and imperial expansion, but such violence was provided by the Royal Navy and properly commissioned privateers, not pirates.

Given the ambiguity of the various forms of maritime depredation in this period, it would be impossible to determine how much of this activity was piracy strictly defined or how many people were out-and-out pirates engaged in 'the indiscriminate, persistent and criminal pursuit of maritime robbery'. However, even though there were probably more legally commissioned privateers than there were pirates, there were certainly very large numbers of the latter and it is easy to see why England at this time should be dubbed 'a nation of pirates'. Meanwhile, the long-term effects of aggression and war at sea were wide-ranging. Those who financed pirates and privateers made money which could be invested in more piracy or in more trade and ships. Trade itself expanded to distant destinations which had never before known English shipping, to the Mediterranean, West Africa and across the Atlantic, while voyages to the East Indies with a considerable piratical content were just about to begin. The English merchant fleet grew considerably in size and, where it had once consisted almost entirely of small ships, now there were many much larger, well-armed ships of 200 to 400 tons, capable of sailing and fighting their way along these longer sea routes. Piracy both led trade and followed in its wake as larger ships with much bigger crews plundered their way from the Levant to the Caribbean. A whole generation of aggressive mariners, rich in knowledge of navigation and fighting at sea, had been created. Most of them, though not all, would resort to more legitimate activities when England at last made peace with Spain in 1603 after the death of Queen Elizabeth and the succession of the peace-loving King James. Those who did not would have the experience and knowledge of the sea to make the leap from being a piratical employee of the local gentry to a true marauder of the oceans.

Little is known of the day-to-day life, social customs and beliefs of the pirates and near pirates of the reign of Elizabeth I, and in any case generalisation is difficult since there was a world of difference between the gracious manners of Drake in the *Golden Hind* serving his Spanish captives off gilded plates to the music of trumpets and oboes and those lesser men who might remember with pleasure the days of maritime glory when 'we might sing, sweare, drab, and kill men as freely as your cakemakers do flies . . . when the whole sea was our empire where we robbed at will'.[12] It is clear, however, that for the most part these pirate vessels and the men who crewed them shared few of the characteristics of the pirate ships of a hundred years or so later. Most of the ships themselves seem to have been bought and fitted out from home ports, mainly in London and the West Country, in the same way as merchant ships or privateers. And since pirate ships, like other ships, were simply another form of shore-based investment, a large share of profits, two-thirds in many cases, went back to the merchants, courtiers and gentlemen who had financed them. Nor was the third that went to the crews in any way equally divided, since vessels of this period were organised on a strictly hierarchical basis with large shares for the captain and other officers, who were normally selected by the investors, so that little remained to be distributed to men and boys whose main hope of real profit would be the rings or money plundered and pocketed in the heat of boarding and battle.

Although these pirates were 'indiscriminate' in the sense that they very often exceeded such commissions as they might have, they were still not 'enemies of mankind' who would attack not just Spanish and Portuguese, Venetians and Frenchmen, but Englishmen as well. They remained very patriotic Englishmen with

English homes and families and were not yet the men of no country, the men of the sea '*sans foi et sans aveu*', that later pirates were to become. They were motivated by a desire for loot, like pirates of all ages, but also by an intense Protestantism, which manifested itself in religious observance and psalm singing aboard and in a passionate hatred for Catholics and especially Spaniards, which led on occasion to iconoclastic orgies in the churches of the Spanish West Indies and the Atlantic islands.

Elizabethan pirates, then, were the illegal but often much admired fighting extension of militant Protestant English expansion and not yet 'real' pirates, though already pirates enough to form the subject matter of many modern films and novels which tend to prefer swashbuckling gentleman heroes as pirate captains to the more squalid, lower-class men who would replace them in the pirates' golden age.

It might have been thought that matters would improve with the arrival of peace between England and Spain in 1603 and there was indeed a decrease in maritime violence as navies were laid up and privateers called in. But this huge reduction of employment for a generation of men bred to fighting at sea soon led to a resurgence of open piracy no longer bearing the many disguises of Elizabethan times. As one contemporary writer on naval and maritime affairs put it, 'those that were rich rested with what they had; those that were poore and had nothing but from hand to mouth turned pirats.'[13] There were many of these poor mariners with a taste for violence and the ten years or so after the peace saw a new wave of pirates who in some ways foreshadowed the much better known pirates of the golden age around 1700. These pirates were mainly English, though there were men of all nations among them, and they can be split into two groups: those who confined their attention mainly to the Mediterranean and those who made their careers in the Atlantic.

Towards the end of the war with Spain, the Mediterranean had become a very dangerous place to sail, as English armed merchantmen and privateers deprived of legitimate prize increasingly turned to piracy. The English, wrote the Venetian historian Contarini, 'entered these seas in the guise of brigands, although they brought merchandise too; and they treated every ship they met as an enemy, without distinguishing whether it belonged to friend or foe'.[14] Venetian, Tuscan and Levantine ships were their main victims, but anyone might suffer at their hands. Most of these illegal prizes were smuggled back to England where the privateers had powerful protectors such as Sir Robert Cecil, the Secretary of State, and the venal Lord High Admiral, the Earl of Nottingham.[15] Many of these pirates saw no reason to give up their profitable plundering with the coming of peace and, if anything, they stepped up the scale of their depredations, especially against the shipping of the republic of Venice, now in the twilight of her long career as a naval and mercantile power.

Complaints by the Venetian ambassador in England led to a stricter interpretation of the law, some illegal cargoes seized in England, several pirates hanged and a requirement that all ships sailing to the Mediterranean should post bonds for their good behaviour. Such restrictions merely forced the pirates to look for alternative markets and places of resort within the Mediterranean and there were plenty of them. The ports of the Morea, especially Patras and Modon, were too far from Constantinople to be effectively controlled by their Ottoman rulers, despite the presence of Turkish pashas, and these were normally open in their welcome to English pirates, so much so that the Venetian ambassador in Constantinople complained in 1608 that 'if steps were not soon taken the Morea would be worse than Barbary'.[16] Just what that meant will be seen in the next chapter, but that somewhere or other should become a second Barbary or Algiers or Sallee was a common cry, such a dreadful label being attached at different times to the Isle of Wight, the province of Munster in Ireland, Jamaica, Bermuda, the Bahamas and the island of Madagascar in the Indian Ocean. The Morea, however, was no Barbary, just a useful place where pirates could sell prizes, maintain their ships and recruit local sailors as crew, one of many such places in this anarchic world where few could resist the temptation of dabbling in such a profitable business.

Barbary or North Africa itself was quite a different matter. English privateers had long sold their more dubious prizes in such places as Tunis and Algiers; one captain, Edward Glenham, 'very unnaturally' went so far as to leave at Algiers 'divers of his souldyers and marryners in pawne for victualles there taken to furnish his shippe withall' and these pawned men were still languishing as slaves in North Africa when the affair came to the attention of the English Privy Council seven years later.[17] The pirate successors to such men continued to sell their booty in Barbary after the coming of peace. When such men were declared outlaws in England, it is not too surprising that many went a stage further, made Barbary their permanent base and, unlike nearly all previous English pirates, attacked English as well as other Christian shipping. Most of these men shocked Englishmen at home even further by becoming renegades or 'turning Turk', a change of faith which enabled them to enjoy the full benefits of a career of plunder in the Muslim world since Christian renegades were treated virtually as equals by the Muslim authorities and could enter the army or the higher posts in the government. Some, however, were so valuable to the Turks that they rose to high positions while remaining Christians, as did for many years the 'archpirate' Captain Jack Ward, 'beyond a doubt the greatest scoundrel that ever sailed from England'. His was a remarkable career and one to catch the imagination of any potential pirate. He was bred a 'poore fisher's brat' in Faversham and at the end of the Spanish war he was fifty years old and on the beach in Plymouth, 'a fellow, poore, base and of no esteeme'. Here, he was pressed into service aboard a royal ship, only to desert with thirty comrades two weeks later. 'They agreed amongst them . . . they freely, and of their owne accord would elect Ward for their Captaine,' this election being one of the first known instances of what would later become standard pirate practice. They then stole a small ship and henceforth nothing could stop the rise and rise of Captain Ward. He made his way to the Mediterranean, stealing bigger and better ships on his way, and rose to command a corsair fleet manned by Turks and Englishmen whose flagship was a Venetian prize with sixty bronze guns. After many, almost unbelievable adventures he was eventually to retire with his accumulated booty to Tunis where he lived in the style of an oriental potentate 'in a faire palace beautified with rich marble and alabaster stones'. Ward was the most successful of the English pirates of the Mediterranean, but he was not the most beautiful or prepossessing if we can believe the description given by an English sailor who saw him in Tunis in 1608. He was 'very short with little hair, and that quite white, bald in front; swarthy face and beard. Speaks little and almost always swearing. Drunk from morn till night . . . The habits of a thorough salt. A fool and an idiot out of his trade.'[18]

There were also Christian havens in the Mediterranean for English pirates with no desire to apostasise or live among the Turks. Foremost of these was Leghorn (Livorno), whose ruler, the Grand Duke of Tuscany, was intent on building up a fleet of Christian corsairs to sail under his flag and was more than willing to employ English sailors and vessels of dubious background to harass Muslims. 'He receives, shelters and caresses the worst of the English, men who are publicly proclaimed pirates by the King.'[19] Nor was he alone in employing Englishmen to build up a private navy. The Duke of Savoy was also keen to join in the corsair game in this chaotic early seventeenth century and he too was to welcome pirates, making his ports of Nice and Villafranca 'an asylum and refuge for all scoundrels, offering safety to everyone of whatsoever sect, religion, creed, outlawed for whatsoever crime', as the Venetian ambassador in Savoy reported to his masters in 1613.[20]

And so a specifically English type of piracy began to vanish from the Mediterranean. Some were absorbed into the war of the corsairs, on both sides, a war which is discussed in the next chapter. Some went home with as much of their loot as they could smuggle and many were captured by such dangerous opponents as the Turkish, Spanish and Venetian navies and sentenced to the galleys or hanged like those English pirates caught by the Venetian Governor of Zante (Zakinthos) in 1603. 'The sentence was carried out on a high tower of this castle, where their bodies remain in sight of the city and of the port until they are consumed, as a terror to all such evil doers.' A few years later, the island of Zante witnessed the great galleys of Venice returning home through the Adriatic with another thirty-six English pirates hanging from their yards. The Venetian ambassador in London reported that this news was received 'in appearance at least, with much satisfaction by the English; but in reality not without some regret for the large gains that were reaped from the booty . . . [and the belief] that their men were not to be beaten'.[21] Such patriotic admiration of English pirates (while acknowledging their sins) was to inform English public opinion for a very long time into the future. Indeed, it probably still exists today.

These English pirates of the Mediterranean were fairly short-lived in their impact on the shipping of the region, but they had a certain style. A captain might be described as 'a person of some consideration in his way' and many were indeed gentlemen dressed in the height of fashion 'in purple satin' or in 'black velvet trousers and jacket, crimson silk socks', a perfect model for the noble or gentleman corsair of later fiction.[22] With the passage of the years their crews became fairly polyglot as men of the Mediterranean were added to their original English crews, especially Greeks who were the best pilots for the Adriatic and Levant where most of their prizes were taken. Most observers were impressed by the strength and armament of the English ships and by the fighting valour of their crews. They were also amazed by the pirates' destructiveness as they ransacked prizes and by 'the indifference with which they lose their ships', both in wrecks and battles, characteristics which we will find again in the pirates of a century later. The English also had a reputation, shared with the Dutch, for blowing up their ships to avoid capture. In 1611, for instance, the Spanish Admiral Don Pedro de Toledo captured a Turkish pirate ship, but its English consort, 'being wont to seek a voluntary death rather than yield, blew up their ship when they saw resistance useless'.[23] Blowing up their ships or at least threatening to do so would become standard pirate practice.

While Englishmen were gallivanting around the Mediterranean, a more workaday type of piracy was developing in the Atlantic. The first reports suggested that this was little more than a resurgence of the long endemic piracy of the West Country and the west of Ireland. But it was soon apparent that a completely new phenomemon was emerging. Instead of operating as single ships on short cruises, this new breed of pirates was spending months at sea and was organised in fleets of ten or more vessels, some of them powerful enough to challenge the smaller of the King's ships. By 1609, they even had an 'admiral', Richard Bishop, 'by farr the most sufficient man amongst them all', a former privateer captain from Yarmouth who was said to have eleven pirate ships and a thousand men under his command. A couple of years later, the most successful of these English pirate admirals, Peter Easton, had two thousand men in his fleet, as many men as the buccaneers or the pirates of the Golden Age could muster in their heydays. More admirals were to follow, of whom the most famous, or notorious, was Henry Mainwaring, a former student of Brasenose and the Inner Temple who took to piracy 'by mischance' in 1613, as he put it, and was later to write a fascinating book called *Of the Beginnings, Practices, and Suppression of Pirates* which he dedicated to the King. He was said by the Venetian ambassador in London to have no equal 'for nautical skill, for fighting his ship, for his mode of boarding and for resisting the enemy'.[24] His career as a pirate was short but profitable, his greatest triumph being a battle in the summer of 1615 with four ships of the Spanish royal fleet who 'were so beaten by them, that with loss of many of their men and great hurt done in their ships were fain to use all diligence for the recovery of the port of Lisbon'.[25] These powerful pirate fleets, attacking mainly French and Iberian shipping along the coasts of western Europe but also plundering way out into the Atlantic, were so well organised that they have been dubbed by their historian 'the confederation of deep-sea pirates'.[26]

These 'deep-sea pirates' operated from Ireland, 'the nursery and storehouse of pirates, in regard of the general good entertainment they receive there'.[27] Their main rendezvous was that modern yachtsman's playground called Roaringwater Bay in the far south-west, a deeply indented inlet of the sea with many coves and islands that lies between Cape Clear and Mizen Head, a region far from the justice of Dublin, let alone London, and with the corrupt local officials that the age so readily provided. Here were good ports at Baltimore and Crookhaven, a veritable pirate fortress at Leamcon, a peninsula virtually impregnable from attack by land or sea, plentiful hiding places in case of pursuit and an impoverished local population who welcomed the relative prosperity that piracy on this scale could bring.[28]

The pirates paid well for food, drink and equipment for their vessels and what could not be supplied locally was brought in by Englishmen, some who had settled there 'with the express purpose of commercing with the pirates',[29] others pretending to be fishermen but in reality supplying the pirates and trading with them. 'Such men allso furnish them with voluntary persons from time to time,' wrote the Lord Deputy of Ireland,[30] and there was indeed no shortage of recruits to this pirate fastness. Many of the pirates 'have their wives and children in these parts', it was reported in 1611, but for those who did not there was no shortage of women. 'They have also good store of English, Scottish, and Irish wenches which resort unto them, and these are strong attractors to draw the common sort of men thither.'[31] South-west Ireland was, in short, a paradise for pirates, a place of almost complete safety patrolled by only one King's ship and that so slow that all pirates could outsail her and so small that most could outgun her, a place where ships could be fitted out and maintained and loot spent on drink, women and all the other delights of the shore. It comes as no surprise to find Lord Danvers, the President of Munster, describing the coast of his province as 'like Barbary, common and free for all pirates'.[32]

Munster may have been a delight for pirates, but most of them were only there in the summer for, like other migratory birds, they sailed south to avoid the Irish winter. 'Against the winter [they] do adventure southward towards Spain and Barbary where they become expert and hard to be dealt withall afterwards.'[33] The pirate fleet normally sailed south in August or September, plundering along the coasts of Spain and Portugal and taking their prizes to a second winter base which they had established in the fairly free and safe port of Mamora [Mehdia or Mahadya] on the Atlantic coast of Morocco, where as many as thirty or forty pirate ships and two thousand men might be seen on occasion.[34] Their presence here was condoned by the Emperor of Morocco who welcomed the wealth they brought in as they sold their loot to merchants attracted from all over the Christian and Muslim Mediterranean by the bargains on offer. Meanwhile, the pirates squandered the proceeds of their plunder in the African winter sun.

Come the spring it was time to set sail again, as danger threatened in the form of Spanish galleys and Dutch warships coming out of their winter hibernation. Some sailed back to Ireland 'when the heat of the sun and the gallyes there do threaten to prosecute them',[35] but many sailed out into the ocean, to Madeira, the Canaries and Azores and further afield. One major summer raiding area, as it was to be for the pirates of the Golden Age, was the Newfoundland Banks where huge fleets of fishermen spent the summer catching, splitting, drying and salting cod for the Catholic tables of the Mediterranean. The main attraction for the pirates, however, was not the fish but the fishermen, some of the hardiest seamen in the world who, willingly or not, were added to the pirate crews. Peter Easton raided the Banks in 1612 and came away with five hundred British fishermen. Mainwaring was to follow him there in June 1614 and 'some of the company of many ships did run away unto them', piracy being an attractive alternative to the 'too toilsom' labour of the fishery. In all he sailed away with four hundred mariners and fishermen, 'many volunteers, many compelled'.[36] And so the pirate round continued, Ireland in the summer, Morocco in the winter and much mayhem on the ocean in between.

These deep-sea pirates only prospered for ten years or so, from about 1606 to 1616, but they provide an interesting link in the history of piracy. Many were men who had served as privateers or pirates in Elizabethan times and they shared many of their characteristics, but they also foreshadowed the more democratic and individualistic pirates of the later seventeeth century. Most ships seem to have been hierarchically organised, often with gentlemen or near gentlemen captains and officers, but there are also some instances of captains being elected by the men, as they were to be later. One finds, too, the use of unpleasant tortures which were to remain standard pirate usage, such as placing lighted matches under a captive's fingernails or tightening knotted cords about their heads, a torment which the buccaneers were to call 'woolding'. One hears some of the later pirates' language, the braggadocio and boasting, 'they would not leave the gates of hell unripped in search of gain',[37] the euphemistic description of their occupation as 'going on the account', calling their vessels 'men-of-war' and replying to a hail from another ship with the challenging piratical response 'we are of the sea'. The men themselves seem to have behaved like pirates and indeed sailors always have, eating and drinking to excess when they got the chance, gambling at backgammon and dice, dressing in exotic finery stripped from their captives, 'carlesse and making merry' so much after taking a prize that their prisoners sometimes escaped. Hugh Baker, a sailor from Youghal, was captured by the pirate crew of John Nutt and later deposed that they ravished any woman they captured and spent the rest of their time playing 'continually for Barbary gold' or drinking, the last activity providing the deponent with the opportunity to escape, 'perceiving the pyrate and his company to be drunke'.[38] Gambling in particular seems to have been an obsession among the pirates of this period, as it was for many more respectable Jacobeans. This could make for a poor return to their piratical labours. After the pirate captain John Johnson and his men captured the *Black Buck*, for instance, one member of the crew won 680 out of the total haul of 800 silver dollars playing dice with his shipmates and such a run of luck was more than likely to cause disharmony aboard the ship.[39]

These men made no secret of the fact that they were pirates, prided themselves on it indeed, but there was not yet that sense of brotherhood or of a floating community set against the whole world which later pirates would glory in. And there was not yet the egalitarianism which would come in the future. These Jacobean pirates were still trapped in a hierarchical and entrepreneurial world where deference was due to those of good birth, where a share of prizes went to capitalist confederates ashore and where the distribution of plunder between the men was far from equal. The booty was divided 'after the fashion of privateers, each member of the crew receiving a certain number of shares in accordance with his outlay in the venture and his office in the ship'.[40] Such a division meant that the lowly got very little after the captain and principal officers had taken for themselves as much as a third or a half of the total loot. This was a long way away from the pattern of distribution among the pirates of the Golden Age where even the captain often only got twice the share of an ordinary foremast hand. The captains in the days of 'the confederation of deep-sea pirates' would have viewed such egalitarianism as ludicrous. They wanted to retire from the sea as wealthy men and many did just that.

# CHAPTER THREE

# God's Plunderers

# God's Plunderers

If there are legal and ideological problems in distinguishing pirate from privateer, the bad from the not quite so bad, in Elizabethan times, the same is even more true for another group of 'pirates' active throughout the period of this book, those involved in what was generically known as the *corso*. These were the corsairs of the Mediterranean who engaged in what they themselves saw as a holy war against the enemies of their faith and what their victims regarded as unprincipled piracy. This difference in interpretation is reflected in language, since such words as *corsaro* or *corsaire* merely mean privateer in Mediterranean languages and *corso* means privateering, while a 'corsair' in English is usually a synonym for a pirate. But, whether they were in fact pirates or privateers, these corsairs were the most feared of all maritime predators for they enslaved those they captured and, although ransom was possible for the fortunate or wealthy, the fate of many of these poor men and women was enslavement for life.

Best known of these terrifying scourers of the sea were the Barbary corsairs, or Barbary pirates as they were known to Englishmen, who operated from the three Turkish North African regencies of Algiers, Tunis and Tripoli (roughly equivalent to the modern countries of Algeria, Tunisia and Libya) and from the port of Sallee on the Atlantic coast of Morocco.[1] The regencies had been conquered by Muslim corsairs and political adventurers in the sixteenth century and, although they accepted the suzerainty of the Ottoman Emperor and fought in his wars when occasion demanded, they enjoyed considerable autonomy and carried out an independent diplomatic and military existence. From their beginnings, the regencies were seen as bases from which to attack Christian shipping and to launch raids on the Christian coastline to secure slaves. And this, 'going a Christian-stealing' as it was described by an English consul in Tripoli,[2] they were to do with varying intensity and considerable efficiency right down to the third decade of the nineteenth century.

In the sixteenth century, the armament of the Barbary corsairs was the galley, the traditional naval vessel of the Mediterranean, the larger ones with complements of up to 150 janizaries, Turkish soldiers who provided the main fighting complement, propelled by as many as 250 Christian slave oarsmen, the smaller ones normally employing free Muslims as rowers who would be added to the fighting force when boarding a potential prize. Galleys were fast over short distances, easily manoeuvrable and could operate in calms and shallow water, so they were ideal plundering weapons in the coastal waters of the Mediterranean, rapidly placing their complement of fierce and well-disciplined fighting men on their targets. Galleys were not, however, very effective in the stormy waters of the Atlantic which limited the range of the corsairs' raids. They were also no match for a well-gunned man-of-war of the galleon type, nor indeed for a really powerful sailing merchantman.

These limitations were to be overcome from the first decade of the seventeenth century when the corsairs began to add fighting sailing ships to their fleets, a process accelerated by the defection to Barbary and Morocco of several hundred English and Dutch pirates and privateers thrown out of work by the ending of the Spanish wars, many of whom brought their ships with them. Such men were vital in the transfer of new maritime skills to the corsairs, but they provided a drunken and hooligan element at odds with the normal sober atmosphere of Muslim cities which in order to retain them were compelled to allow 'every kind of debauchery and unchecked licence', as a visitor to Tunis reported.[3] This period of riotous apprenticeship was not to last for long. Gradually, the Turks began to control the English and Dutch incomers and, by the 1620s, the art of navigating and fighting with a ship-of-war had been learned sufficiently thoroughly for the corsairs to be able to dispense with most of these turbulent northerners, although renegades from the Christian Mediterranean continued to play a very important part in the affairs of Barbary.

There were few shipbuilding facilities in Barbary and most of the sailing ships used by the corsairs were converted from prizes, everything being sacrificed for extra speed in much the same way as the pirates fitted out prizes as 'men-of-war' in the late seventeenth and early eighteenth centuries. Superstructure was stripped off, decorations and ornaments confined to the banners alone, 'the stars, crescents, suns, crossed swords and other devices and writings unknown' that so terrified Christian sailors and passengers at sea when they were unfurled.[4] Sails were out of proportion to masts and all but the largest ships had holes cut for oars to give the corsair extra speed in flight or pursuit. These sailing ships made an enormous difference to the potential scope of the corsairs. No longer were they confined to the Mediterranean, though combined fleets of galleys and sailing ships continued to scour the inland sea. But now, in addition, sailing ships, mainly from Morocco and Algiers, the most westerly of the three regencies, were able to extend their activities beyond the Straits of Gibraltar, along the coasts of Spain and Portugal and in the Atlantic islands, and on occasion to France, England, Ireland and even to Iceland and the Caribbean. It was in these early decades of the seventeenth century that the Muslim corsairs reached the peak of their power. In 1624–5, for example, the Venetian Giovanbattista Salvago claimed that Algiers had six galleys and a hundred fighting sailing ships, of which sixty were large with twenty-four to thirty guns each and the rest much smaller. Tunis also had six galleys, ten or twelve brigantines (much smaller versions of the galley) and fourteen large sailing ships, while Tripoli, which was nearly always the weakest of the three regencies, had only a small fleet of two or three sailing ships.[5]

The men who sailed and fought these vessels carried commissions from their rulers and saw themselves as legitimate warriors of Islam. But to the Christians of the Mediterranean and Western Europe they were pirates, the biggest agglomeration of

pirates in history, tens of thousands of men who typically set out
for two cruises of forty or fifty days each a year, whose only
function was to capture Christian shipping and cargoes and enslave
Christian men and women, whether these were found aboard
captured ships or ashore in raids which quite often ended with the
capture and enslavement of several hundred people. The historian
David Hebb has estimated that from 1622 to 1642 over three
hundred English ships and around seven thousand English subjects
were captured by the corsairs, an average of some fifteen ships and
350 men (and occasionally women and children) a year.[6] English
shipping was especially vulnerable, since much of it went to France,
Portugal, Spain and the Mediterranean, the cruising grounds of the
corsairs. Nevertheless, the English are very unlikely to have been
the greatest sufferers. Raids ashore were much commoner in the
Mediterranean than in the Atlantic, while the bread and butter of
the corsairs was the coastal shipping of the western Mediterranean,
so that Italian, Spanish, Portuguese, French and Maltese slaves are
likely to have far outnumbered Englishmen and women in the
*bagnios*, or slave prisons, of the Barbary regencies and Morocco,
noisy, dirty, crowded and usually very uncomfortable places in
which hundreds of slaves ate, slept, plotted, prayed and bribed
their gaolers to get better treatment. One modern writer has
commented that the description of the slave prisons by the
seventeenth-century French traveller the Chevalier d'Arvieux made
them sound like 'a more rascally version of a debtor's prison in the
time of Dickens', while another vivid account of life in the *bagnio*
by the former slave Emanuel d'Aranda emphasised the entertainment value of listening to the yarns spun by his fellow slaves,
almost all of them 'men of the sea' who between them had travelled
throughout the known world.[7]

Most slaves remained in the *bagnios* only at night, going out
early each morning to work, as galley slaves, as labourers, as
domestic servants or craftsmen, all of them hoping against hope
that they might one day be able to raise a ransom or be freed by one
of the numerous redemptionist organisations which existed all over
Christian Europe. Substantial numbers were in fact eventually
ransomed, some of the wealthy after just a few months, most after

several years, while some unfortunates had to wait much longer, such as a seventy-five-year-old man from Ragusa (Dubrovnik) who was ransomed in 1662 after forty-three years of captivity, many of them spent on the rowing benches of the corsair galleys. And many, of course, died in captivity. Fear of capture and slavery made these years a time of terror when travellers were warned not to walk on the seashore, lest they be picked up by a corsair and given 'a slavish breakfast', and when 'not a sailor goes to sea in a merchant ship but he feels some secret tremor that it may one time or other be his lot to be taken by the Turks', as Daniel Defoe wrote in 1725, though in fact by that date the Turks no longer offered much threat to the Englishmen who were his readers.[8]

This huge system of state-sponsored maritime plunder was very well organised and, given the nature of its business, remarkably well disciplined, the corsairs being generally observant of their own set of rules. In the sixteenth century, most of the corsair galleys belonged to the state and functioned similarly to the navies of other states, with the important difference that they were always at war with Christendom and so set out every year on their predatory voyages. State ownership of galleys and sailing ships continued in the seventeenth century, but many of the latter were now privately owned and operated in a similar way to the privateer ships commissioned by Christian states. Ships were acquired and fitted out by individuals, sometimes the captain, or *rais*, himself, but more often a syndicate of local merchants, shipowners, corsairs and officials and sometimes quite humble people such as shopkeepers, artisans or anyone else who had some savings available to invest in a corsair ship, a very attractive investment since it was likely to satisfy a man's desire for piety and profit at one and the same time.

Captains were chosen by the state or by the private owners, subject to examination by a council of existing captains. Crews were a heterogeneous collection of Turks, Moors, renegades and Greeks, but nearly all included some slaves, not just as oarsmen on the galleys but also as mariners in the sailing vessels, such men normally being confined or chained up during battle. In addition to the crew, all corsair vessels carried a complement of janizaries, fighting men attracted from the Levant by recruiting officers who easily seduced them into service in Barbary by their tales 'of the immense profits that the *corso* against Christians will give them'.[9] These turbaned warriors in their flowing robes served under their own aga and played little or no part in the sailing of the ship, sitting patiently smoking opium or tobacco until that moment of glory when the *khodja*, or purser, 'read out verses from the Koran in a loud voice', as they swarmed over the sides of a prize and, great curving scimitars in their hands, swept through the doomed ship.[10]

Barbary corsair ships were fast and heavily manned and normally had little difficulty in running down and capturing the coasters and small merchantmen who formed the bulk of their prizes. The slaves, the booty and sometimes the ships themselves were then taken back to their home ports and there distributed according to strict rules, which seem to have been remarkably well obeyed. A fixed proportion, normally one-seventh or one-eighth, went to the state and there were also some deductions for the upkeep of the port and the support of officials who played a part in the administration of the business. The remainder was split into two halves, one for the owners and one for the crew, a similar system to the distribution of the booty on a Christian privateer ship of the same period, though according to most observers more honestly administered.

Sallee (Salé), the furthest west of the Muslim corsair bases, was rather different from the North African regencies. Now part of the city of Rabat, it is a riverine port on the Atlantic coast of Morocco which sprang into prominence as a corsair city in the first two decades of the seventeenth century. The main impetus came from the Moriscos, the people of Moorish descent who had been progressively forced out of Spain throughout the sixteenth century and were finally expelled in 1609. The majority of these people, many of them very skilled and all with a bitter hatred of Spain, went to North Africa where they swelled the population of all the corsair cities. Some three or four thousand settled in Sallee where they quickly established a corsair business whose early years were dominated by revenge on the Spaniards. This took the form of captures of Spanish coastal shipping and numerous slaving raids ashore guided to their old homes by those who had been expelled.

The success of Sallee quickly attracted restless adventurers from all over Europe, especially English and Dutch renegades, whose numbers were inflated after 1614 by pirates who had been driven out of the Moroccan port of Mamora by the Spaniards. Now the range of Sallee roving expanded right along the western European seaboard, into the English Channel and out into the Atlantic, to Madeira, the Azores, the Canaries and as far as Newfoundland.[11] Sallee was under the nominal suzerainty of the Emperor of Morocco but, in 1627, a revolt established an independent corsair republic, though not a very democratic or egalitarian one. This was a capitalist republic of the corsair captains and the entrepreneurs who owned and fitted out the corsair vessels and the four decades of its existence were the heyday of the Sallee rovers. During this period they could normally put to sea thirty or forty vessels, sometimes as many as sixty. These were mostly fairly small, as large ships were unable to cross the sandbar at the mouth of the Bou Regreg, the river on which Sallee stands. The typical Sallee vessels were developed from Mediterranean merchantmen such as the tartan, a small one-masted vessel with huge lateen (triangular) sails, or the bigger xebec, the favourite corsair ship of the eighteenth century with two or three masts which were again mainly lateen-rigged. These were all very fast sailers and nearly always equipped with oars as well as sails, so fast indeed that the French Admiral Tourville believed that a Sallee rover could only be caught at sea by a former Sallee rover taken as a prize into French service. These vessels were fairly lightly armed but very heavily manned. Most captains, officers and specialists such as carpenters or gunners were European renegades, the sailors were Moriscos or Christian slaves, while the soldiers who provided the fighting force, the equivalent of the Turkish janizaries on the ships of Algiers and the other regencies, were mainly Moriscos or men from the warrior tribes of the Moroccan interior. Sallee rovers normally operated in small flotillas of two or three vessels in a summer season lasting from April to October. They were reputed to spend the winter, like other pirates, in 'cabarets and other places of debauch, since their greatest passion was to waste on revelry the wealth they'd won at sea'.[12] Whether this was true or merely Christian propaganda is impossible to say, but what is certain is that the Sallee rovers were extremely formidable opponents who were much feared along the western European seaboard.

The Barbary corsairs and Sallee rovers are well known to Western Europeans, whose folklore reflects fears of wild-looking men with turbans and long knives who burst forth out of the mist and drag innocent families away to a lifetime of slavery. Few people realise, however, that they had exact Christian counterparts who attacked ships with Muslim passengers or goods aboard and raided the coasts of North Africa and the eastern Mediterranean in a search for Muslim captives to sell into captivity. For Christendom, too, had its holy war which Pope Urban II had launched in November 1095 when he set in motion the First Crusade. This war between the papacy and Islam was to be a very long one, indeed the longest war in history, since it did not finally end until 1798 when Napoleon captured the corsair island of Malta and so effectively brought to a close the seven centuries of Christian crusading against Muslims.

By the late sixteenth century, the days of the real crusaders were long past and even the long war between Spain and her allies and the Ottoman Empire for control of the Mediterranean had drawn to a standstill. The failure of the Turkish siege of Malta in 1565 and the defeat of the Turkish fleet at the battle of Lepanto in 1571 marked the limits of Turkish expansion. But the end of Ottoman advance did not mean the end of the holy war. Christian corsairs had fought against and looted Muslims for centuries and they were to continue to do so for two centuries more. Many of the Christian potentates of the Mediterranean issued commissions for corsair captains to engage in this activity, such as the King of Spain and his viceroy in Sicily and the Grand Duke of Tuscany whose Knights of St Stephen operating from the port of Leghorn were a potent foe of Islam in the early seventeenth century. However, the most regular issuer of licences for Christian corsairs was the Grand Master of the Order of the Knights of St John who, after being ejected from the island of Rhodes by the Turks, had been settled in Malta since 1530. So much did Malta dominate the Christian corsairs that the generic term for these in the Levant, wherever they originated from, was 'the Maltese corsairs', a terrifying menace from the sea which was just as feared in the east as the Barbary corsairs were in the west.[13]

Malta was a strange anachronism in a Europe increasingly dominated by nation states, a republic of aristocrats whose rationale was to fight *la guerra eterna*, the eternal war against Islam. The Knights of Malta were the younger sons and younger brothers of the aristocratic families of Catholic Europe, young men bred up to ideals of chivalry and military glory whose promotion within the Order depended on serving four 'caravans' or terms of six months' service in the galleys of the Order. There were normally around six or eight of these, the strongest and best equipped galleys in the Mediterranean, and they set out on two or three cruises every year searching for Turkish and Barbary shipping and especially Barbary corsairs, making the occasional raids ashore, and providing part of any more general Catholic maritime force against the Turks. Each galley carried a fighting complement of thirty knights and a large contingent of paid soldiers, a crew of sailors and a propelling force of Muslim slaves and Christian convicts whose numbers were leavened by *buonavoglie*, free but normally desperate men who rowed unchained and were regarded as some protection against mutiny by the slaves. The Maltese galleys were thus similar in their organisation and function to the state-owned galleys of Barbary, with the important difference that their prizes were not distributed among the men and they did not make a profit, being continuously subsidised by the income arising from lands bequeathed to the Order by generations of the pious all over Europe.[14] Profits were, however, expected to be made by the large numbers of Christian corsair ships which were licensed by the Grand Masters to provide a second line of assault on the long-suffering Muslim population of the Mediterranean.

Malta, with its wonderful harbours and strategic position at the centre of the Mediterranean, had been a base for corsairs long before the arrival of the knights, but this business was to get a considerable boost under their rule. In order to achieve a measure of control over such unruly people, a tribunal called the Tribunale degli Armamenti was set up in Malta in 1605 to administer the corsairs. An elaborate set of rules was framed, covering the method of licensing corsair captains, the areas where they were allowed to patrol, the rights of the various claimants to a share of the booty and the procedure for bringing suits before the tribunal in the event of litigation. The corsair business inevitably led to large numbers of such lawsuits being heard, involving such matters as wrongful capture, particularly of Greeks and Jews, disputes about the distribution of prizes, lack of enterprise by captains or embezzlement by crews and a host of other matters and there was provision for appeal to the papal courts in Rome, the ultimate arbiters of the behaviour of these Christian marauders. Papers relating to these lawsuits still survive in the archives of Malta and there are plenty of them, but overall one is impressed how effectively such a basically anarchic and violent business was organised, just as it was in Barbary.

The licences issued to Maltese corsairs were of two types: short voyages of a few weeks or months to Barbary (North Africa) and much longer voyages of up to five years to the Levant, both these areas of plunder being strictly defined by the authorities. Ships cruising in the Levant often wintered in the Greek islands, many of which were quite safe from Turkish attack and, like most places patronised by pirates and corsairs, were well supplied with women. In the island of Argentiera, according to the French traveller Dumont, there were about five hundred women who 'live purely on the work of Nature; so that all merchants and corsairs who come to the island choose a female companion, according to each man's particular fancy'.[15] Such dalliance ended with the spring when the corsairs set out to sea again, stopping and searching virtually every vessel they encountered and quite often raiding ashore to pick up unsuspecting Muslim men, women and children going about their business. These and captives from prizes would either be ransomed on the spot or sent back to Malta to be sold in the island's great slave market. Buyers would include the Order itself acquiring slaves for the galleys or to work on the massive fortifications, agents buying for other Mediterranean galley fleets such as those of France and the Papal States, and individuals who invested in captives for the work or profitable ransoms that they could get out of them.

The Maltese corsairs continued to use oared vessels into the seventeenth century, especially for the short Barbary voyages in the coastal waters of North Africa. For their longer voyages to the Levant, they normally employed various types of well-armed sailing vessels, often in conjunction with an oared vessel for work in calms or shallow water or for raids ashore. These vessels were all privately owned and, as in Barbary, the Maltese *corso* was simply seen as a potentially profitable investment by the local business community who might own shares of ships or fit them out on credit at very high rates of interest. These investors received an even higher share of the booty than their counterparts in Barbary, a typical division, after the 10 per cent due to the Grand Master had been deducted, being two-thirds to the monied men ashore with the remaining third being very unevenly divided among the crew.

Many of the captains in the late sixteenth and seventeenth centuries were the younger and more adventurous of the knights, a type of noble or gentleman corsair captain which was quite common in this period and could be found commanding Western European privateering and pirate vessels. Such men were motivated by a desire for profit, like all corsairs, but were also driven by religious zeal and a lust for adventure and glory which might lead them into attacks on much more powerful ships which would have been left well alone by more mercenary pirates. One such was Gabriel de Téméricourt, named by the Turks 'the scourge of the sea', who together with his elder brother Maximilien, terrorised the eastern Mediterranean in the 1660s, on occasion attacking and overcoming huge fleets of Muslim ships or galleys. In 1665, for instance, the two young brothers together with two other adventurous knights attacked a fleet of about fifty Turkish galleys and after a furious four days' battle were victorious. Both brothers were handsome, chivalrous and totally fearless and both died young, Maximilien from wounds sustained in battle and Gabriel martyred by the Sultan 'as he refused to commit apostasy', according to the inscription on the monument to these two Christian heroes in their family's church in the Ile de France.[16] By the eighteenth century, however, such heroics were a thing of the past and the *corso* was just a business whose participants hoped to die old, rich and in their beds. Most corsair captains were now laymen, some with a background in the galleys but most of them just typical sea captains of the central Mediterranean, Frenchmen, Corsicans, Sicilians and of course many from Malta itself. The crews, too, were drawn from this same maritime environment, with the Maltese themselves providing the largest single component. The piratical reputation of the Maltese was still strong in the nineteenth century, long after the corsairs themselves had been disbanded, and many a novel of piracy has Maltese sailors among the crew, such as Captain Marryat's *The Pirate*. Arturo Pérez-Reverte goes one step further in his entertaining treasure-hunting novel *The Nautical Chart* when he describes a piratical character as a 'Gibraltarian, with a Maltese father and an English mother . . . that is, one hundred per cent pirate genes'.[17]

These rivals and indeed complements of the Barbary corsairs were probably at their greatest strength in the 1660s when there were about thirty corsair ships operating from Malta in addition to the galleys. These varied considerably in size and strength, from small vessels of three or four guns and thirty or forty men to powerful men-of-war of thirty or forty guns and up to two hundred men. Altogether, these thirty corsair vessels had crews of about four thousand men and the galleys employed another three thousand, counting slaves, while large numbers of people ashore were engaged in supplying and maintaining the vessels and dealing in their booty. Since the total population of the island was only about 60,000 at this date, including women and children, it can be seen that the local economy was completely dominated by this unpleasant but strictly legal business. Malta, the capital of Christian piracy, could well bear comparison with Algiers, 'that proud city, that retreat of the men who have made God bankrupt,' as the city was described by Le Sieur des Boys, a French traveller and former slave of the Algerian corsairs.[18]

The corsairs of Malta and Barbary were a mirror image of maritime predation, two businesslike fleets of plunderers set against each other and against the enemies of their faith, but united in motivation, organisation and customs, these being known generically as 'the custom of the corsairs'. They both kept their vessels clean and fast by careening at least every two months, an essential measure for all pirates which involved completely unloading the ship, guns and all, hauling it down on one side and then scraping or burning off all the weed, barnacles and other marine accretions before making the hull watertight by sealing the seams between the planks and coating them with pitch. Both used the same deceptions, those used by all pirates and privateers such as flying false flags and luring ships into danger by pretending friendship. Both rewarded the vigilant and brave among their crews – the first man to sight a prize, the first ten men to board it. Both usually captured their prizes without a fight by fear and overwhelming strength, neither having any desire to kill any of the captured crews, since dead men paid no ransoms and could not be sold as slaves. Both knew all the likely hiding places aboard a ship and both used torture to discover what could not be found, though this was mild compared to the practice of many pirates, a beating usually sufficing, on the feet by the Barbary corsairs, on the buttocks bent over a gun by the Maltese. And other factors were almost identical, right down to such detail as the small share of Barbary prizes given to the marabouts who prayed for their success and of Maltese prizes which went to the nuns of the Convent of St Ursula in Valletta 'who pray continuously for victory against the Infidel'.[19]

The *corso*, Muslim and Christian alike, was underpinned, indeed made possible, by a very sophisticated commercial network of merchants, sea captains and ransom brokers whose activities spread through the whole of the Mediterranean world. Such men bought the prize goods at auction and then recycled them into legitimate trade, having first taken the precaution of altering the marks on bales so that they could not be identified by their original owners. They were also in the forefront of the ransom business, raising loans for captives, negotiating with their friends, relatives and business partners, seeking out Muslim slaves to exchange for Christians or vice versa, arranging for the passage home of those who had raised their ransoms. Such men could be found in all the corsair centres and in the great commercial cities of the Mediterranean, such as Alexandria and Marseilles, from where they built up networks of correspondents many of whom were kin. But there was one city which stood out above all others as the financial nexus of this strange world of the corsairs. This was Leghorn in Tuscany, the great commercial entrepôt of the central Mediterranean whose slave market rivalled those of Malta and Algiers and whose merchants were in the forefront of every aspect of corsair and pirate business, whether this derived from Christian or Muslim sources. Much of this business was handled by Jewish merchants and bankers, the nearest thing to neutrals in this holy war between Christendom and Islam, who had close commercial relations with the large Jewish populations in the corsair cities of North Africa and in Malta.[20] Jews had no monopoly of such profitable business, however, and they were joined by Greeks and Armenians, two other groups who were able to span effectively the gulf between Islam and Christendom, as well as by Muslim and Catholic merchants throughout the Mediterranean. Such commercial networks were a necessary feature of piracy wherever it should flourish and they were always to be found.

These corsairs are difficult to fit into a history of piracy, since in a legal though not functional sense they were not pirates. They were sponsored by their governments and their captains carried licences which entitled them to rob and enslave the so-called enemies of their faiths. As a result, a career in the *corso* was perfectly respectable and unlikely to suffer from any shortage of recruits, given the dual motivation of religion and profit. But, legal and respectable or not, the corsairs were a terrible scourge which sowed fear and did an immense amount of damage throughout the Mediterranean and along the western Atlantic seaboard, a scourge which seemed at times as though it would bring the normal rhythms of maritime commerce to a halt. And of course it was a scourge which coincided in the late sixteenth and early seventeenth centuries with the great upsurge of English and other Western European privateering and piracy. It was not a good time to go to sea unless you were a predator.

## CHAPTER FOUR

# Cleansing Home Waters

# Cleansing Home Waters

Jacobean England faced a threat from pirates on a truly frightening scale. People had learned to live with the small-time, mainly coastal piracy which had been a feature of maritime life for centuries, but the Irish-based marauders and even more the Barbary corsairs were a very different matter. No nation could afford to turn a blind eye to their activities and governments all over Europe vowed to do something about the pirate menace. What that something was naturally varied from country to country but, in an ideal world, it was believed that nothing less than the extermination of piracy would suffice.

The extermination of pirates, however, posed a host of problems, many of them similar to those encountered in attempts to exterminate international terrorists today. These were problems of diplomacy, law and public relations, manpower and resources, intelligence, strategy and tactics and, perhaps above all, motivation and will. Until states were absolutely determined to eradicate piracy and were prepared to devote considerably increased numbers of ships and men to such a policy, little would be achieved. And even with such determination, little could be done without the right ships, the right men and the right methods to ensure that at least some pirates would be caught. Men of the sea had to become convinced that piracy was an unwise choice of occupation and that, if they were so foolish as to follow it, they were more than likely to die, and die violently and soon. What was needed was the creation of a state of maritime and legal terror in which pirates knew that they were likely to be tracked down and killed or captured and, if they were captured, they were likely to be tried and found guilty and, if they were found guilty, they were likely to be hanged. In the end, such conditions were achieved and those pirates who had not been killed were forced from the seas. But this was to take a very long time, well over two centuries from the first tentative attempts to counter the problem.

The starting point for this long story was the late sixteenth and early seventeenth centuries when some advances were made by the forces of order. Most important of these was the virtual eradication of piracy in northern European waters. Historians are not agreed on exactly how, when or why this happened, but one extremely important factor was the growth in power of central governments which were able to curb that independence of the local gentry which had previously provided an umbrella for piracy. Such assertion of central control was greatly aided in the long run by a radical change in attitude by both local officials and by the population of maritime areas as a whole. Piracy, which had once been regarded as a condonable offence, similar to smuggling, was by the 1620s and 1630s much more widely condemned and by the late seventeenth century was perceived by most people as an evil which should be eradicated.

Such changes in attitude are difficult to explain. Over the very long term, it is probable that themes dear to the liberal soul, such as the growth of concepts of citizenship, public order and duty and the decline in tolerance of violence, played their part, though such changes if they really did happen were not very apparent in the seventeenth century. More to the point was the increasingly terrifying threat from the Barbary corsairs whose raids on British shipping and the British and Irish coastline brought home the fact that piracy was no joke. It is ironic that the areas to suffer most heavily from the corsairs were exactly those in which endemic English and Irish piracy had been strongest – Devon, Cornwall and other parts of the English West Country and the south-west of Ireland. No one could have been in any doubt that the world had changed when Baltimore, the epicentre of the Irish-based piracy of the first two decades of the seventeenth century, was raided in 1631 by Muslim corsairs who carried away into slavery 109 men, women and children.[1] Such incidents naturally led to pleas and petitions by local people for greater efforts by the government to suppress piracy, whether from Barbary or not, and to a certain extent these were forthcoming. Hardship and fear made people honest.

Changes in attitude by the people as a whole were paralleled by changes in the make-up of the ruling elite of the pirate-infested parts of Britain and Ireland. Some of this was fortuitous and resulted from sheer extravagance on the part of those great families who had formerly been the main promoters of piracy. The most striking example of this was the fall and ruin of the Killigrew family, the worst of all the gentlemen abettors of piracy. Gambling, huge banquets at their great house of Arwennecke and other forms of conspicuous consumption led to the downfall of two generations of Killigrews in the latter years of the reign of Elizabeth, and the piracy which had depended on their personal patronage collapsed in the wake of their financial ruin. The small-time pirates whom they and other landowners had sponsored were unable to continue in existence since, with the undoing of their former protectors, it was necessary to bribe not just one family but the whole countryside, an outlay which would have ensured that there would be no profit.[2]

The ruin of a few families, however powerful, was not of course enough on its own to eradicate something so deep-seated as West Country piracy. This required a complete change in personnel and attitude among the local magistrates and Admiralty officers who had so woefully failed to do their duty. An unsuccessful attempt to investigate such people and purge the guilty had been made in Elizabeth's reign, the failure due in part to the inclusion of people like the Killigrews on the commissions of inquiry. Much greater success was to be achieved in the reign of James I, a king who ever since childhood had a deep-seated hatred of bullies and men who abused their power or physical strength. As an adult, this hatred was focused particularly on the pirates whose depredations and bullying insolence he considered a personal affront to his honour as king and protector of his subjects. Pirates were, for him, the enemies not just of man but of God as well and he was determined to do his utmost to eradicate them. This utmost was limited by the weakness of his navy and the continued existence of great men who benefited from the plunder of pirates and protected them. Nevertheless, King James's achievement was considerable. The laws against piracy were better enforced, more pirates were captured and convicted and, according to his boast, more pirates were hanged in his reign than in the previous hundred years, nineteen being hanged from Wapping Pier on a single day in December 1608.[3] Such judicial retribution might well have made ordinary sailors think twice about joining a profession where previously it had been believed that, even if caught, only a few of the leaders would be put to death.

Even more important was a determined effort to eradicate the 'land pirates', those great men whose blind eyes and ready acceptance of bribes so often kept the lesser men who went to sea in business. Continuing complaints about English piracy from foreign ambassadors led, in May 1608, to the issue of general piracy commissions to ten leading citizens in each of the maritime counties to investigate the problem, arrest offenders and confiscate booty. These commissioners seem to have been more honourable men than their predecessors in the reign of Elizabeth and in the next two years much was done which promised well for the future. Scandals were exposed, several vice admirals and other officials in Devon and Cornwall lost their posts, were fined and disgraced, and large numbers of pirates and their aiders and abettors were arrested. Attitudes did not change overnight, but the disgrace and punishment of many well-known people certainly acted as a real deterrent. The extent of corruption as well as its potential costs and dangers had been exposed for all to see.[4]

Such actions and the change in mentality implied by the comparative success of the commissioners were sufficient to greatly reduce, if not totally eradicate, piracy in the English West Country. Ireland, however, posed a very different problem and one not likely to be solved by similar methods. Here, the problem of corrupt local officials was as great or greater than in Devon and Cornwall and much more difficult to remove, given the fairly primitive nature of the English administration. There were legal problems, too. It was discovered in 1606 that under Irish law pirates were admitted benefit of clergy, an archaic practice by which literate criminals were able to escape the full rigours of the law by reading a few lines from a book, a skill possessed by many of the pirate captains. 'The chiefest of them will escape with life, for they can read well.' A couple of years later, it was noted that the anti-piracy statute of 1536 under which English pirates were tried was not part of Irish law, a fact which allowed many captured pirates to slip through the legal net.[5] This was a problem which was to crop up again in the English colonies in America and, in both cases, it was eventually resolved. In the meantime, many pirates taken in Ireland had to be carried to England for trial, a process which often gave them opportunities to escape in passage or, if they failed to do this, to be acquitted at their trial because witnesses were not prepared to make the journey to give evidence against them.

These were, however, comparatively minor irritations. The real difficulty in Ireland was the alarming scale of the pirate menace, both in terms of the total number of men involved – up to two thousand at times – and in the size and armament of the individual pirate ships. And these ships were not in any real sense tied to the land as those of Cornish and Devon pirates were. They had shown themselves capable of roaming the ocean at will and they also had a second base, in Morocco, where they could withdraw if threatened by attack from ships of the Royal Navy. Not that there was ever any real danger of that. King James's active navy was weak overall and most of the ships in commission were required to guard the Channel, with the result that the force available to threaten the pirates in Munster was very meagre indeed, rarely more than a single ship at a time and this too slow to pursue a pirate with any hope of catching him and, if by chance it did, too weak in arms and men to capture any but the minnows of the pirate fleet.

On one occasion, the lone royal ship *Tramontana* managed to surprise a pirate vessel lying in harbour at Baltimore, but was forced to withdraw by the arrival of two other pirate ships who greatly out-gunned her. Captain Williamson, the naval commander, was criticised for making merry with the pirates, but in truth he had little choice but to humour them since his own royal ship could quite easily have been taken into the pirate fleet. The pirates deserved thanks for their forebearance as the President of Munster noted. Such was the dishonourable position in which King James's naval officers found themselves, quite incapable of offering more than a token resistance to the pirates. The Lord Deputy of Ireland excused himself in 1610 for only being able 'to temporize with the pirates, considering their power to do harm and his own weakness in shipping, the *Lyon's Whelp* being too weak to grapple with them', an observation which was only too true since this royal pinnace, the whole of his naval force, had just sixty men.[6]

These pirates were in fact to be suppressed, despite 'their power to do harm', but the means employed involved the King in more dishonour. Unable to send to sea a naval force strong enough to overawe the pirates, the King accepted in 1611 a Dutch request to search the English and Irish coasts for pirates, a shameful admission of naval weakness for those who remembered the quite recent glory days of Queen Elizabeth. The Dutch had some success, capturing at least three pirate ships in Irish waters and making a major raid on the pirate base at Crookhaven in 1614, but they did not manage to capture or force from the sea any of the really powerful pirates. This could only be done by the granting of pardons, a policy of appeasement which the monarch shrank from as it once again impugned his honour as the protector of the welfare of his subjects. A king was not supposed to negotiate with thieves.

Pardon may have been dishonourable but it was cheap and many believed that pardoned pirates, 'many of them good mariners', could do good service in the navy, wishful thinking that turned out to be true in a few instances. Some dreamed of other uses for pirates seduced from their profession, such as Sir Richard Moryson, commander of the English garrison at Waterford, who suggested in 1609 that they be employed in the new plantation of Virginia where they could do valuable service in defending and supplying the infant colony.[7] This would have had the extra benefit of sending them a good distance away from Ireland, but it is doubtful whether many pirates would have found such unrewarding work attractive. But pardon itself was certainly of interest to them, if the conditions were right, since most pirates saw their profession as a temporary one which would ideally end with their settling down ashore with some or preferably all of their loot.

Pardoning pirates had a long history and once this new batch had demonstrated their strength and the weakness of their opponents, one soon finds attempts on the part of the authorities to lure them from the sea. The first really notable receiver of a pardon was Captain Richard Bishop, the first 'admiral' of the pirates who claimed that he 'would rather die a poor labourer in mine own country than be the richest pirate in the world'. Such penitence was not put to the test and Bishop was able to take his loot with him when he retired from his career of plunder in 1611. His riches were sufficient to set himself up in a mansion in Schull, a village right in the heart of the pirate fastness in Munster, from where he was not surprisingly suspected of 'ever plotting with and receiving of pirates'.[8] There then followed months of negotiation between the authorities and the large number of pirates who had banded together under his successor as admiral, Peter Easton.

These pirates were in a very good position to bargain, not just because of their strength and mobility but also because they were able to alarm the English government by threatening to accept alternative pardons offered them by potentates in the Mediterranean such as the Grand Duke of Tuscany and the Duke of Savoy. And so, although it was felt to be 'more for the King's honour to consume them all than to accept any to mercy',[9] the Privy Council agreed early in 1612 to offer a General Pardon to all pirates who surrendered, on very generous terms which allowed them to keep all their loot, 'the entire fruition of whatsoever they were then possessed off'.[10] Suspicion, bad faith and dirty tricks delayed the implementation of this offer, but in the end at least twelve pirate crews surrendered and came home to enjoy the benefits of their years of plunder. Other pirates, before and after the General Pardon, made individual and usually less favourable bargains so that this cheap alternative to chasing and fighting pirates could be said to be remarkably effective, even if some of the crews soon returned to their old trade. The pardon option will crop up again and again in this history of the suppression of pirates and, even though it never eliminated them, it nearly always significantly reduced their numbers. Dishonour often pays.

One man who did not accept the General Pardon was the admiral Peter Easton, an arrogant man in the best pirate tradition, 'who haughtily refused the pardon offerred by his Majesty, declaring that he would not bow to the orders of one King when he himself was in a way, a King as well'.[11] He decided instead to accept an offer of asylum from the Duke of Savoy and, early in 1613, sailed into the port of Villafranca with four ships and a huge treasure in plunder aboard. His arrival fascinated Vicenzo Gussoni, the Venetian ambassador in Savoy whose dispatches provide a running commentary on the reception of this great corsair, 'a handsome man of about forty'. Gussoni was certain that Easton had sailed into a trap and that sooner or later he would be clapped into prison and his ships and riches seized, 'as the idea of his riches grows day by day, so hour by hour grows the prophecy of an unhappy end for him'.[12] But Gussoni was wrong and the story of Easton was to have instead a fairy-tale ending. He converted his pirate loot into a large landed income, was created a marquis by the Duke and married a lady of Nice 'of considerable wealth'. He must certainly rank as one of the most successful and fortunate pirates in history.

Similar deals were being made by pirates with other Mediterranean rulers. Several settled in Leghorn, while others made a life in Barbary, some very successfully such as Captain Ward. Ward's great rival among the Christian or formerly Christian corsairs in the service of Barbary was Simon Danzer or Danziker, a Fleming, whose depredations as an Algerian corsair were the byword of the Mediterranean. But he too was restless and, in 1609, after negotiating a pardon from King Henry IV of France he sailed with four great ships including a captured Spanish galleon, into Marseilles, where he was welcomed 'with every sign of joy' by the local governor, the Duke of Guise. When the Spanish ambassador to France demanded restitution of their galleon, King Henry refused, saying 'that he had rendered a service to Spain and other nations by clearing the seas of such a famous pirate', a cynical and self-serving reply that was echoed by other potentates who welcomed pirates. Danzer was not, however, to live long enough to enjoy the honourable and comfortable retirement in France that Easton had in Savoy. Some eighteen months later, he sailed under the French flag against the corsairs of Algiers. He had some success but was then tricked ashore under a flag of truce, taken prisoner and put to death, a suitably treacherous end for a man who had betrayed first his own country and faith and then his adopted one.[13]

Pardons and deals with pirates cleared the seas of several very dangerous and powerful men, but could not be a final solution to the problem since new pirates notoriously sailed into the vacuum left by old ones. In Ireland, the void created by the General Pardon of 1612 was filled the next year by Henry Mainwaring whose fleet of pirates soon seemed as strong as they had ever been. But Mainwaring's career as a pirate was so successful that he was soon to be flooded by even more offers of pardon than his predecessors, not just from such avid navy builders as the Dukes of Savoy and Tuscany and the Dey of Tunis but even from the King of Spain whose royal ships he had so severely mauled. Mainwaring, however, was a loyal subject of King James who prided himself on never attacking English shipping, and he had no wish for asylum in any of these places. In June 1616, he was happy to accept an English pardon for himself and those who had served under him on condition that they returned to England and gave up the trade. This gentleman pirate was so fully taken back into the English fold that he was knighted two years later and served with distinction in various public offices and in the Royal Navy, a striking example of just how well piracy could pay in the early seventeenth century. As the naval historian David Hannay remarked of the Jacobean period, 'piracy was not then a trade from which there was no honourable issue.'[14]

The reformation of Sir Henry Mainwaring really marks the end of the Ireland/Morocco/Atlantic axis of English piracy, which had in any case suffered two serious blows with the capture of the southern base of Mamora by a huge Spanish and Portuguese fleet in August 1614 and the successful Dutch attack on Crookhaven in the same year.[15] English and Irish piracy did not vanish overnight, but it now reverted to the more routine type of depredation which had been the norm before the rise of the pirate admirals. Meanwhile, greater efforts were made to patrol the coasts in search of pirates, using a somewhat enlarged navy, private vessels commissioned for the purpose and the occasional captured pirate vessel such as the barque, 'well-shaped and swift of sail', that was seized by stratagem from the pirate Captain Coward in Youghall harbour and taken into royal service in 1607.[16]

The use of private vessels against pirates had long been sanctioned and was indeed necessary, given the dearth of naval protection. Their numbers increased considerably from 1610 when the Lord High Admiral was empowered to commission such ships and the terms were often very generous, sometimes allowing the private pirate hunters 'to keep for their own use the vessels and goods of such pirates as they shall seize'.[17] Such terms naturally inspired cupidity and several pirates were taken. In 1611, for example, a London merchant who had suffered at the hands of pirates received a commission to man a ship to recover his loss. The venture was successful and a captured pirate ship was brought home, as was reported in a contemporary newsletter. 'All that escaped death in the battle were hanged at Wapping last week to the number of twenty-five.'[18] Despite such successes, the policy of commissioning private ships against pirates had serious short-comings both in the Jacobean period and later when it was adopted in the West Indies and the American colonies. Granting the whole value of a pirate prize to the captors encouraged people to join the game, but led inevitably to conflict with those whose ships and goods had been seized by the pirates in the first place and were of the opinion that only salvage was due in the event of recapture. More seriously, once a well-armed, well-manned vessel was at sea it was difficult to control and many a pirate chaser turned to piracy, Captain Kidd being by no means the only example of such misuse of a commission. Private competition also irritated the navy, with the result that after 1618 the commissions were called in. 'It standeth not with his Majestie's interest, nor honor,' wrote the Secretary of State Sir John Coke in 1623, 'that anie other ships should gward his ports or trade but his own.'[19]

By this date, the navy was certainly doing a better job of patrolling the English and Irish coasts and was even protecting the Newfoundland fishermen, but there were still far too few ships for the service. Some pirates were taken, but the evil was by no means wholly eradicated. Success rates of royal ships are difficult to evaluate, since logbooks have not survived for this period, the only long-run tally being a document recording the achievements of Sir Thomas Button who served as admiral on the coast of Ireland from 1614 to 1622. It must certainly have made a pleasant change to have a naval rather than a pirate admiral cruising on the Irish coast, even if Button was 'one of the most shamefully corrupt of all Jacobean admirals', as the historian Nicholas Rodger describes him. His achievement in the twenty-gun *Phoenix* was, on the face of it, fairly modest. Over a period of seven or eight years, he or his lieutenants recaptured two prizes and took five pirate vessels, some of them virtually his equal in strength such as the 250-ton ship of Captain Omalye which was taken in October 1620 with sixty men, 'whereof eight were slaine in the takeinge, and 26 hangd att Corke', a ratio of hanged to crew which demonstrated that the authorities were by now committed to proving that piracy was a poor career option.[20] Less than one pirate ship captured a year may sound fairly feeble, but this needs to be seen in context. Pirates have never been easy to capture and no royal captain ever took anything like so many pirate ships in the period of full-scale war between the navy and the pirates in the years 1715–25. Button did a good job and if there had been more naval commanders like him and more naval vessels committed to such service, the problem of piracy would never have reached the heights that it did in the Jacobean period.

Greater honesty ashore, greater determination by courts to punish pirates and more commitment by a much enlarged navy was to reduce piracy in British, Irish and northern European waters to a trickle in the late seventeenth and early eighteenth centuries. And when there was news of pirates in home waters, the authorities were quick to act on the information. Reports and descriptions of the suspected men would be sent to the governments of France and the countries bordering the North Sea, in case the pirates should seek haven there, while naval units would be dispatched in search of the pirates. In December 1714, for instance, orders were given to the captains of no less than seven Royal Navy ships to look out for one Alexander Dalzel, an Englishman who with seven comrades had seized a French trading vessel in the port of Le Havre, 'murdered the pylot with a dagger, and tooke the master's brother and tyed his hands and legs and cast him off at sea'. A description of Dalzel was attached to the orders, 'above six feet high, well shaped, about forty years of age, red faced', and he was in fact captured in Aberdeen a few months later.[21]

Ten years later, John Smith alias Gow, led a mutiny aboard the *George Galley* off the coast of Barbary. The mutineers murdered the captain, chief mate, surgeon and clerk, renamed the ship *Revenge* and went on the rampage. News of their activities reached England within a couple of weeks of the mutiny and the Admiralty sprang into action. Letters were sent to the courts of Denmark, Sweden and The Hague, 'so they may seize her if she come to their ports and direct their ships to do the same if they meet her at sea'.[22] Orders were sent to ships in America and the West Indies to keep an eye out for Gow and his men, to Lisbon for ships to cruise off Cape St Vincent in search of them, to the three ships stationed in Ireland to intercept them if they came into the Irish Sea and more directly to Captain Solgard of the *Greyhound*, a famous pirate catcher,[23] to proceed to the Orkneys, Gow's home, whither it was rumoured he was headed. The rumour proved correct and Gow was captured ashore in February 1725, brought down to London by the *Greyhound* and hanged with eight of his crew on 11 June at Execution Dock in Wapping.[24]

Such efficiency and the wealth of ships at the Admiralty's disposal make a striking contrast to the situation a hundred years earlier. How King James would have loved to have three powerful ships to guard the coast of Ireland and others all ready to be sent to chase pirates off the coast of Scotland. The growth of navies and their sensible disposition was to be the key to the suppression of piracy and, by the early eighteenth century, there were more than sufficient royal ships to make the seas around Britain and Ireland no longer safe for pirates. There are, in fact, reports of only about half a dozen pirates operating in home waters in the period 1713–25, the 'Golden Age of Piracy', and all of these were quickly captured. But there was, of course, the rest of the world for them to roam.

# CHAPTER FIVE

# Containing the Corsairs

# Containing the Corsairs

While piracy was slowly being eliminated in British home waters, some progress was also made in the much more serious matter of containing the Barbary corsairs who were reaching their peak strength in the 1620s just as Anglo-Irish piracy began to dwindle into insignificance. This containment was, however, to prove much more difficult than one might have predicted given the relative naval superiority of Christendom over Islam. Since the Muslim corsairs considered all Christians their enemies, one might have expected the Christian maritime nations to join together to combat these dangerous enemies of their faith. And, given the combined strength of the four most powerful Christian navies of the day, those of Spain, Holland, France and England, such an alliance should have been able to destroy the fleets of the corsairs without too much difficulty. But this they never did and campaigns against the corsairs were conducted for the most part by Christian nations acting individually and not in consort, seeking their own advantage and not that of Christendom as a whole, such selfishness enabling the corsairs to survive for another two centuries, albeit on a much smaller scale than in their heyday.

In the early years there was some Christian cooperation. A Franco-Spanish fleet attacked Tunis in 1609; a combined Spanish-Dutch fleet defeated twenty-four Algerian pirate ships in 1618; and the years 1617–20 saw intense but ultimately unsuccessful diplomatic activity by the English to get either Spain or Holland or both of them to join in an attack on Algiers. But, from 1620 onwards, we hear little of such attempts at joint naval operations against the corsairs, the only real cooperation being permission given to the Dutch and English to use ports in Spain, Tuscany and later Malta as bases for campaigns against the corsairs. Without such permission it would have been impossible for the northern naval powers to have sustained any more than a very short campaign in the Mediterranean, and so the English navy got its first experience of the facilities available at such places as Minorca, Gibraltar and Malta, all of which were later to come under British rule.

The absence of a concerted joint effort by the Christian maritime powers allowed the corsairs of Barbary and Sallee to survive into the nineteenth century. This shameful failure of international cooperation had three main causes. In the first place, the great maritime nations were always suspicious of each other's intentions and were often reluctant to believe that a proposed attack on the corsairs was not a cover for some other more nefarious activity. Such suspicions were sometimes justified and so 'an expedition against the Barbary corsairs became the stock diplomatic formula for covering some ulterior and sinister design', as the historian Sir Julian Corbett put it in his study of England's early naval adventures in the Mediterranean.[1] It also soon became apparent to the maritime powers that the Barbary regencies could be valuable allies in the numerous European wars of the seventeenth and eighteenth centuries, as long as peace could be negotiated with them. This made collusion in naval expeditions against Barbary almost impossible, since it became naval policy to exploit friendship with Algiers or the other regencies in order to gain an advantage over whichever of the other European powers was currently the enemy.[2] The last reason for this failure was even more cynical and was noted as early as 1611 by the English consul in Syria. 'He remarked there were difficulties in the way of uniting sovereigns for the suppression of piracy; for some are not displeased that pirates exist and are glad to see certain markets harassed.'[3] This observation made at a time when there seemed to be genuine hopes for cooperation became even truer in later years. The maritime powers, especially England and France, realised that if the corsairs could be persuaded by force and diplomacy to leave their shipping alone, these predators would then concentrate their attention on the shipping of weaker nations and so reduce the competition in trade. The French attitude towards Barbary was summed up in a memorandum of 1729. 'We are certain that it is not in our interest that all the Barbary corsairs be destroyed, since then we would be on a par with all the Italians and the peoples of the North Sea.' What France wanted was 'just enough corsairs to eliminate our rivals, but not too many'.[4] Such sentiments were shared by the English, a nation who first condoned the piracy of its own subjects as it helped them force their way into the commerce and carrying trade of the Mediterranean and then exploited the piracy of the corsairs to sustain and increase their dominant position.

This desirable if immoral position was to take a long time to achieve. The Barbary corsairs, especially those of Algiers, were formidable opponents in the 1620s and 1630s whose well-manned ships need feel little fear of the ships in the generally weak Christian navies of the day, since those they could not defeat in battle they could easily evade. 'It is almost incredible to relate in how short a time those ships out-sailed the whole fleet out of sight,' wrote the English Admiral Mansell after his failure to capture some corsair ships off Majorca on Christmas Day 1620.[5] Algiers itself was virtually impregnable, a large, well-fortified city on what was normally a lee shore whose harbour was protected by a mole and a boom which could be drawn across if danger threatened. The other corsair cities were more vulnerable, but still offered a formidable challenge to those who dared to attack them. And so, although many attacks were made on the ships and cities of the corsairs by the English, Dutch, French, Maltese and especially the Spaniards, not much progress was made in the first half of the seventeenth century. The Barbary corsairs, those 'pirates that have reduced themselves into a Government or State' as the jurist Charles Molloy neatly put it,[6] remained a very great danger to the ships and coastlines of Christian Europe.

The situation was to change in the years after 1650 which saw a huge increase in the naval strength of England, Holland and, later, France and a growing commitment to the belief that one key function of such navies was to protect the nation's trade. These years also saw a change in the make-up of the European navies which had previously been dominated by large and very powerful ships. These remained, indeed became even more powerful, but they were now supported by much larger numbers of relatively small, fast vessels of shallow draught which had been originally designed to catch the privateers of the day but were of course also invaluable against the Muslim corsairs. Given such naval power it was only to be expected that the great maritime powers, when not engaged in mutual destruction, should use their navies to try and remove the constant threat to their merchant shipping in the Mediterranean and elsewhere.[7] It would involve much repetition to describe this activity in detail, involving as it did innumerable wars, treaties and truces between one or other of the maritime powers and one or other of the three Barbary regencies or Sallee, and it is sufficient to show how the corsairs were tamed by England, the nation which in the long run was the most successful in protecting her shipping.

England's efforts did not at first augur well for the future. Diplomatic overtures to the Ottoman Emperor soon demonstrated that he had no real authority over his nominal subjects in the Barbary regencies and it was felt to be dishonourable to attempt diplomacy with the regencies themselves. How could a king treat with a parcel of thieves? Such sentiments, like the dishonour of pardoning pirates, would soon give way to expediency but, in the meantime, it was thought that only naval force could bring the corsairs to heel. With great difficulty the money was raised to equip a fleet of naval ships and merchant auxiliaries which sailed against Algiers in 1620 under the command of Admiral Sir Robert Mansell, a brave but not particularly distinguished veteran of the war against Spain. This expedition had no success at all, though its most recent historian contends that it was only the misfortune of a change in the wind that prevented Mansell's fireships from destroying the Algerian fleet at anchor.[8] Such, however, is the fortune of war and the immediate result of England's first naval venture into the sea she was later to dominate was to stir up the corsairs to even greater assaults on English shipping.

Experience was to show that the best way of using naval force against the corsairs was to establish a tight blockade which could fire on ships at anchor and prevent ships coming in or out of harbour and at the same time maintain a cruising squadron to attack those corsairs that were at sea. If these tactics were employed successfully and sufficient corsair ships were captured or destroyed, then sooner or later the corsair city would sue for peace. Mansell did in fact try to adopt these tactics, but consecutively rather than simultaneously and he was unsuccessful on both accounts, unable to catch corsairs at sea or to maintain a strict blockade. The main reason for his failure was that he did not have the right ships for the job. His powerful men-of-war were sufficiently strong to ensure that he would not suffer the humiliation of defeat, but he had no lighter vessels fast enough to catch a corsair. He also had no shallow-draught oared vessels, which were absolutely essential to prevent the smaller corsair ships from creeping in and out of harbour in the shallow water between the blockading men-of-war and the shore. It was to take the navy a very long time to discover exactly what sort of ships were needed if pirates were to be caught and destroyed.

Mansell's failure was followed by some remarkable diplomacy carried out in the years 1622–4 by Sir Thomas Roe, one of the most accomplished diplomats of his day or indeed any day. He was extremely well travelled, not just in Europe but in the West Indies, South America and India where he undertook an embassy to the Mughal Emperor in which he acquired an understanding of oriental and Muslim ways, which was greatly to assist him on this occasion.[9] He began discussions with the Ottoman Sultan and then, despite King James's distaste for dealing with thieves, was able with some difficulty to negotiate peace and friendship with Tunis and Algiers and the release, for a price, of several hundred English captives, though the sources are ambiguous on just what this price was or the exact number of Englishmen released. What is certain, however, is that his embassy showed that it was very much cheaper to free English slaves by diplomacy than it was by war. Roe had no illusions that his treaties would be more than transitory, since 'I know not by what other trade so many idle villains, nourished in theft, can live',[10] and in fact the peace lasted for less than three years. Nevertheless, Roe had demonstrated that it was possible to treat with the corsairs, thieves or not, and his embassy set in motion the alternation of treaties and 'fire and sword', which was the pattern of England's relations with the regencies in the second half of the seventeenth century.

The English had learned a few lessons by 1637 when they sent out their next venture against the Muslim pirates, this time against the Sallee rovers whose depredations had been growing worse and worse since the late 1620s.[11] The expedition was under the command of William Rainsborough, a practical seaman who knew exactly what to do. He kept the size of his fleet to the minimum capable of doing the business, for ease of control, and he included in it two shallow-draught pinnaces designed specially for the job. These were built for speed, long and narrow in the beam and, most importantly, were fitted with fifteen banks of oars a side in addition to their sails. These pinnaces proved ideal in covering the flanks of a close blockade on the harbour, pressure which was increased by Rainsborough's clever exploitation of the endemic faction fighting between the corsairs living on opposite sides of the river that divided the city. He allied himself with one of the parties, brought cannon ashore and with them was able to destroy no less than thirteen pirate ships at anchor in the harbour. Meanwhile, his cruisers were destroying or capturing pirates still at sea. This combined onslaught accounted for over half of the entire Sallee fleet, a loss sufficient to give the town good cause to surrender on 27 July, some four months after Rainsborough's arrival. Over three hundred English slaves were released who were later paraded in London, 'clothed all anew' by the Moroccans, a celebration which was magnificently orchestrated by the government to demonstrate that it was at last doing something really positive about the Sallee rovers.[12] However, this success has to be seen in perspective. The Salleemen were soon at sea again, even if they avoided English shipping for a while, and were indeed to be a menace well into the eighteenth century. And the English slaves were not freed cheaply. Once the expenses of the expedition are taken into account, each one cost about £118 per head, over twice the market rate of redemption. Such, sadly, was the normal result of expeditions against the corsairs, even those which had enjoyed the success of Rainsborough.

Governments were to be prepared and able to pay a much larger price to protect their ships and subjects from the middle of the seventeenth century onwards, a period which saw a naval revolution with the creation of much larger and more powerful navies, true line-of-battle fleets, paid for with some difficulty by much larger taxation. These fleets were designed to fight the naval wars between the great powers which dominated the maritime history of the next two centuries, but they had an important and largely unintended by-product. For these new Christian navies changed for ever the balance of sea power between Islam and Christendom in the Mediterranean. No longer were the fleets of the corsairs anywhere near the equals in strength of the navies of the maritime powers. The corsairs were about to be contained.

Now that the English government had more money and a much bigger navy, it was possible to develop a double-edged and very effective naval policy to minimise the damage done by the corsairs. Basic to this was the provision of naval vessels to escort convoys of merchant shipping and so protect them from attack, a measure introduced by an Act of Parliament of 1650 which provided for an increase in the customs duties to pay for the new service. This was a completely new concept which involved a huge escalation in the navy's responsibility for the protection of English trading ships, since previously the navy had only acknowledged a duty to defend vessels in the immediate vicinity of the English coast.[13] Such protection was at first against Royalist privateers and other enemies of the Cromwellian regime but it later became a regular institution, in wartime against whoever the enemy was and in peacetime against the corsairs. By the 1670s convoys, usually with one or two naval escorts, were provided on all the most vulnerable shipping routes, down the Atlantic seaboard of Europe, throughout the Mediterranean and, for vessels sailing to America and the West Indies, sufficiently far out into the Atlantic to be safe from the corsairs who usually kept close to land. The convoy system, which was also adopted by the Dutch, was a remarkably effective way of protecting shipping from the corsairs who, despite the small numbers of the escorting ships, preferred to seek out easier prey.[14]

Successful though it was, convoy had its costs. It was slow and cumbersome and subject to delays and it meant that markets were inevitably glutted when a fleet of merchantmen carrying similar goods arrived, all factors which determined some merchants to take the risk of sailing alone. Convoy was also subject to the venal instincts of Royal Navy captains, whose love of money often made them forget their duty. The service was supposed to be provided free of charge but in fact, despite strict Admiralty prohibition and the threat of cashiering, the escort captains demanded gratuities from the merchant captains and at least one naval captain went so far as to fire on a ship whose master was slow to put his hand in his pocket. No doubt such dubious practices compensated the naval captains for the boredom of the duty; it also made them 'very rich' according to Lorenzo Magalotti, a Tuscan who visited London in 1668.[15]

The defensive policy of convoy was coupled with aggression in the form of a series of wars with one or other of the corsair cities who had been adjudged to have broken the terms of a new set of treaties which had been negotiated on behalf of Parliament in 1646 by Edmund Cason, a merchant specialising in trade with Barbary. One of the most dramatic incidents of these wars was the attack made in April 1655 by Cromwell's famous puritan admiral, Robert Blake, on Porto Farina, a port under the rule of Tunis. He sailed straight into the fortified harbour, destroyed the forts and nine ships with gunfire and then sailed out again, 'the Lord being pleased to favour us with a gentle gale off the sea, which cast all the smoke upon them and made our work the more easy', as the admiral reported in a letter home to the Secretary of State. Blake's risky action, which was described by one of his officers as 'a piece of service that has not been paralleled in these parts of the world', had no immediate impact on the Dey of Tunis who believed with some justification that it was the English and not his own subjects who had broken the treaty and so flatly refused to negotiate with the English admiral. Algiers and Tripoli, however, who had not been attacked, were sufficiently impressed by this display of

English naval firepower to quickly renew their treaties granting English shipping immunity from capture and, after sufficient pause to satisfy his pride, the Dey of Tunis signed up too.[16]

Just what was 'English' shipping was made clearer from the 1660s by what were known as 'Mediterranean passes', handsome, parchment documents which carried the name, provenance and description of ships so that they could establish their identity when challenged by a corsair. These passes were nearly always honoured by the Muslims and the system proved reasonably effective, despite such abuses as wholesale forgery of these valuable guarantees of safety. This became particularly serious after the English occupation of Gibraltar and Minorca in the early eighteenth century. So many foreigners settled in these places temporarily to gain the benefit of a British pass that, according to a consular report of 1765, one-third of all trade carried under British colours in the Mediterranean was in fact carried by Italians and others in no way connected with Britain.[17]

Both the English and the corsairs were guilty in succeeding years of ignoring or bypassing the conditions of the new set of treaties negotiated during Blake's cruise in 1655, with the result that England fought several more wars against one or other of the regencies, culminating in a long war against Algiers between 1677 and 1683. In the early part of this conflict, the English fleet was neither very successful in protecting its own merchant ships nor in capturing the Algerian predators. The main problem was that the English Mediterranean squadron did not really have enough ships to provide both a convoy service and a force capable of attacking Algerian ships. This was largely resolved in 1679 when Vice Admiral Arthur Herbert took over command. Convoy was now organised from England, leaving Herbert free to concentrate his whole squadron against the Algerians, a change which was to prove very successful with few English merchant losses and a growing number of Algerian ships taken as prize. Altogether, twenty-eight Algerian ships were destroyed or captured, eight of which were taken into the Royal Navy. Such success was in striking contrast to the failure of Admiral Mansell in 1620 and owed much to the introduction into the Royal Navy of faster and nimbler vessels than had been available earlier. Where Mansell had bemoaned the fact that the Algerian ships 'out-sailed the whole fleet out of sight', Herbert could report in January 1682 that 'they find it so hard to escape any of our frigates that once get a fair sight of them'.[18] Finding the right ships for the job was to prove essential in the long war against piracy and in this campaign it was decisive. No regency could continue to sustain losses of this magnitude and Algiers was in the end forced to accept English naval supremacy, signing a peace treaty in 1683 which was to last until the nineteenth century. Tunis and Tripoli also submitted and this new friendship (and the threat of what its absence would mean) was periodically renewed by visiting English warships bearing gifts such as horses and hunting dogs for the rulers of the corsair cities. The Barbary rulers responded by sending in return splendid stallions and so immeasurably improved the breeding stock of the English racehorse.

Despite the occasional breach of the treaties by opportunist individuals, this really marks the end of attacks by the Barbary corsairs on British shipping, a tribute to the consistently applied policy of convoy and periodic aggression. The Barbary regencies in the eighteenth century were friends and allies of Britain, a relationship well illustrated by the mutually beneficial trade between Algiers and the British naval base in Gibraltar which had been captured from the Spaniards in 1704, a trade which maintained the navies of both parties, since it consisted of the exchange of armaments, gunpowder and naval stores from Gibraltar for grain, livestock and other foodstuffs from Algiers.[19] The only danger now for Englishmen sailing south or to the Mediterranean in peacetime was from the Sallee rovers who still remained a threat, although they rarely set out more than eight or nine ships each year compared with the forty or fifty of their prime. Their principal prey were the Portuguese and Spanish but, despite the sending of numerous expeditions against them, they continued to capture the occasional English ship or enslave Englishmen shipwrecked on their shores and there were English slaves in Morocco well into the second half of the eighteenth century.

France, too, had fought a series of wars against the corsairs and had acquired the same immunities as the English by the end of the seventeenth century. Protection from attack and capture naturally led to third parties greatly increasing their use of English and French ships and so posed the corsairs with a serious diminution in the number of potential prizes sailing in the waters they patrolled, as is well illustrated by a study of the corsairs of Tripoli in the period 1754–73. In these twenty years, they set out on 243 separate voyages of plunder, twelve a year, but only fifty-two of these ships, just over one in five, returned to port with any booty. This consisted of a total of forty-two captured ships, many of which were very small, and ten groups of human beings taken in *razzias*, or raids, ashore. Against this relatively modest credit balance must be set thirteen Tripoli ships captured and twenty wrecked. Such figures suggest that, by this date, the corsair business was no longer profitable (little consolation for the six hundred men, women and children sold into slavery) and only really continued because sailing out to capture Christians was either a religious obligation or so much a customary occupation that no one had the will to stop it.[20]

Not all corsair cities did as badly as Tripoli, but they all shared the same problem of trying to cope with the changed circumstances of the eighteenth century. One response was a drastic reduction in the number of ships in the corsair fleets which often only numbered about twenty vessels altogether, though these numbers could quickly be increased if opportunity beckoned, as it usually did during the major wars between the European maritime states. The other response was to ensure that there was always a sufficient number of enemies for this smaller fleet to prey on, a process which meant that from time to time the Deys and Beys who ruled the regencies were 'obliged to lessen the number of their alliances', as an English traveller observed when discussing the way in which treaties were broken from time to time in order to increase the potential loot.[21] This cynical policy was carried out in the most arbitrary way and the history of the Barbary states in the eighteenth century is one of countless small wars against the lesser maritime powers followed by truces or treaties, these normally requiring the Christian nation to pay over the odds to redeem their captive subjects and then, on top of this, to pay tribute in return for peace and immunity from attack.[22] To round the system off nicely, much of this tribute was paid in the naval stores and war matériel which the corsairs needed to carry on their depredations against other Christian nations – timber, pitch, cables, gunpowder, guns and so on. Only the English and the French were exempt from the payment of tribute and even they were expected to give 'presents' to the rulers of Barbary from time to time. It is no wonder that these treaties with the Barbary powers were normally referred to as 'shameful' by those who did not put their signature to them.

The main sufferers from this reduced but still very unpleasant activity of the corsairs remained those traditional enemies of Barbary, the Catholic countries of Mediterranean Europe. But, with their shipping now so reduced by competition, these enemies were not sufficient to satisfy the corsairs' desire for prey. This posed no great problem since other enemies could easily be found among the weaker maritime powers of northern Europe. Holland was a frequent sufferer, peace with all three major trading nations being seen as too much of a good thing. Later in the eighteenth century, new potential enemies became prominent as they expanded their trade in the Mediterranean – Sweden, Denmark, Hamburg, Prussia and, by the end of the century, the newly independent United States who no longer had the protection of British passes and the Royal Navy.

All these nations had to face the question of whether it made more sense to pay the tribute demanded or to fight, knowing that the latter option would be more expensive in the short run and, in the absence of the massive naval strength with which the French and English could threaten the regencies, might well not achieve any more permanent settlement. 'Bribery and corruption answer the purpose better than a noble retaliation,' argued one official of the young American republic.[23] This was probably true, but nobility would sometimes win the day and so we find among many other little wars the Danes bombarding Algiers from a distance in 1770, only to resume their same old tribute payments a couple of years later, while the Spaniards sent out a huge fleet to support a land and sea invasion of Algiers in 1775. But this turned out to be 'just another *espagnolade*', a derisory term used by the corsairs to describe an enterprise whose end failed to correspond with its grandeur, pomp or preparations.[24] In 1801, it was the turn of the United States who, in its first overseas naval expedition, sent a squadron of fifteen ships under the command of Commodore Edward Preble to attack Tripoli, a feat of arms which is remembered in the words of 'The Marine Corps Hymn', 'from the Halls of Montezuma to the shore of Tripoli'. The campaign was to last for four years, peace finally being signed between the two countries in June 1805 after much haggling about the terms. Three hundred American captives were freed in exchange for a hundred or so Tripolitan prisoners and Commodore Barron, who had replaced Preble, agreed to give the pasha 'for the balance in his favor sixty thousand dollars'. This payment disgusted many Americans at home who felt it unjust that they should have to pay after winning the war, but this was the way that one did business with the corsairs, a business recently described in an article in *The Times* as a 'massive, multinational protection racket'.[25] This is not, of course, how the rulers of Barbary would have seen it, but there is no doubt that what had once been a holy war against the Catholic powers of the Mediterranean had now degenerated into something which shared little of the same grandeur.

The Maltese corsairs also ran into difficulties and went into decline in the eighteenth century. No Muslim power was strong enough in this period to bombard Valletta and demand the signature of the Grand Master to a treaty, but there were other powers able to restrict the activity of the Christian corsairs. Before 1700, both England and France had been able to insist that none of their nationals' ships should be subject to the *visitá*, the search made by the corsairs to see if enemies' goods were being carried in friends' ships. Since English and French ships were now conducting much of the carrying trade of North Africa and the eastern Mediterranean, this forced the Maltese to step up their attacks on the other important common carrier in these areas, the Greeks. But the Greeks, though subjects of the Ottoman Emperor, were Christians and their capture and depredation was to cause serious trouble for the corsairs.

The Maltese had long seized Greek goods, knowing that this was illegal but hoping that the Greek merchants and shipowners would be unsuccessful in suing for their recovery, as was usually the case since it was difficult to prove conclusively that what appeared to be Greek were not in fact Muslim goods being shipped under false papers. The corsairs now went a stage further and claimed that Greek Orthodox Christians were not really Christians at all and so were legitimate prey. Many Greeks were captured and much litigation ensued, but in the end this convenient interpretation of the Orthodox religion could not be sustained, since it was obvious even to the Maltese that the Greeks were not really enemies of the Christian faith. And so, in the 1730s after decades of argument and litigation, the Maltese were forced to submit to pressure from the Pope to discontinue their attacks on Greek shipping while, early in the next decade, the Grand Master decreed that no more corsairs should be licensed to cruise in the waters of the Levant where most Greek shipping plied its trade. This reduced the activities of the Christian corsairs to very little indeed since, by this date, few Muslim trading ships dared to venture to sea in the waters of North Africa, the only area where the men from Malta could still legitimately cruise.

This decline in the impact of the Maltese corsairs was paralleled by a decline in the fighting spirit which had characterised the Knights of St John in earlier years. Contemporary observers commented on the lax morals of the younger knights who transgressed their vows of chastity, charity and obedience 'every day', according to Sir William Young, an Englishman who visited the island in 1772.[26] Such men were said to be more interested in enjoying themselves on land than in crusading against the infidel at sea and, whether this was true or not, knights were no longer to be found among the captains of the corsair ships by the second half of the eighteenth century. Even the navy of the knights, which in the eighteenth century consisted of sailing men-of-war, had by the 1740s lost its role as the cutting edge of Christendom and only rarely ventured into the Levant, the scene of much of its former glory. Cruises were now confined mainly to the western Mediterranean and, although the occasional Barbary corsair ship was still captured, much of the navy's activity was confined to such mundane matters as escorting princes and convoying Malta's vital supplies of food. The fact was that by the second half of the eighteenth century, the whole concept of the crusade, with its chivalrous and religious ideals, was an anachronism, indeed almost an embarrassment, in the rational world of the Enlightenment and the early Industrial Revolution. Nevertheless, this Christian parallel to the Barbary corsairs was to continue in existence until 1798 when Napoleon, on his way to Egypt, seized Malta, freed the two thousand Muslims still held as slaves and terminated the commissions of those corsairs still active, most of whom found alternative employment as privateers when the British captured the island a year or two later. So, after seven centuries, ended the Christian side of the holy war.[27]

In the course of the seventeenth century, the English, French and Dutch had begun to take piracy seriously and had worked out a number of different strategies to deal with different types of piracy. Changes in local elites, a reduction in corruption and a greater determination to punish pirates seem to have been sufficient to eliminate the endemic local form of piracy. Pardon turned out to be the most effective method of dealing with the pirates on the Irish–Moroccan axis. These were cheap options and it is surprising that they were so effective in removing the centuries-old problem of piracy in home waters. Such methods had little relevance in Barbary, so new and much more expensive strategies were devised. These were based on the effective deployment of naval power in convoys and in the occasional campaign of aggression, coupled with a much greater understanding of how to conduct the 'oriental diplomacy' needed to treat with the rulers of the regencies. Such strategies were successful and gave the English, French and, to a lesser extent, the Dutch immunity from attack, which not only protected their subjects but also gave them an immense commercial advantage over their competitors. In effect, the cynical exploitation of piracy, first by their own subjects and then by the corsairs, had given these new maritime powers the naval and commercial control of the Mediterranean.

# CHAPTER SIX

# The Buccaneers

# The Buccaneers

The pirates of popular imagination, the rovers who rove in novels and films, are more often to be found in American or West Indian waters than in the Mediterranean or Western Europe. Such fiction does scant justice to the continued existence of the Maltese and Barbary corsairs, whose numbers in the seventeenth and eighteenth centuries were nearly always greater than their more individualistic Atlantic and Caribbean counterparts, but it does reflect a fundamental sea change in the history of piracy, a change not just in cruising grounds but also in the nature and customs of the pirates themselves. The pirates of the Americas, who flourished from the 1650s to the 1720s, were indeed virtually the only pirates in history to exhibit those characteristics which we expect 'real' pirates to have. They and even more those who have written about them created the modern conception of the pirate.

Privateering and piracy in the Indies were almost as old as Spanish colonisation in the area, for it did not take long for news of the fabulous wealth acquired by the Spaniards to attract a swarm of predators to the Caribbean, 'a cauldron where the bad blood of Europe boiled at will', as the historian A.P. Thornton rather luridly described the area.[1] Most of the early rovers in this region were French Huguenots from ports such as Dieppe or La Rochelle, the notorious *flibustiers* or freebooters, words which derive from the Dutch verb *vrijbuiten* meaning to practise piracy, though some of them did in fact carry privateering commissions. These French adventurers were soon to be joined by the English, and their exploits in such places as Panama, Portobello and Nombre de Dios gave these Spanish colonial cities that magic associated with boundless riches, which they have retained almost to this day.

These early privateers and pirates, of whom Drake was only the most famous, operated from Europe but, from the 1620s, the enemies of Spain in the West Indies began to develop bases nearer to their targets. Many of the small islands in the long chain of the Antilles – Barbados, St Kitts, Martinique and Guadeloupe among others – were settled by English, French, Dutch and Irish adventurers and such men, while mainly engaged in planting and illegal trade with the Spanish colonists, were not averse to the occasional raid on Spanish ships or possessions. But there were to be worse enemies much closer to the Spanish heartland. Foreign corsairs and smugglers had long used ports on the sparsely populated north coast of Hispaniola (the island today divided between Haiti and the Dominican Republic) and this area soon became a general haven for lawless men and adventurers from all over the West Indies. Petty raiding on the Spaniards from canoes and other light craft was supplemented by living off the wild herds of cattle that roamed the nearly empty northern half of the island. Such men, most of whom were French, acquired the name *boucanier* from the *boucan*, the place where they dried strips of meat in the Indian fashion.

The word was soon adopted by the English as 'buccaneer', though it was only the cattle hunters from northern Hispaniola, the 'buccaneers or hunting French-men', who were described as such in contemporary documents.[2] The more general use of the word buccaneer, to mean a privateer or pirate based in the West Indies, comes much later and would have been strongly resented by, for instance, the privateers of Jamaica who considered themselves a cut above the evil-smelling men in crudely tanned skins from Hispaniola. Smelly or not, these men were superb shots, supremely hardy and brave, and totally disdainful of death. They also had a deep-seated hatred of the Spaniards who hunted them in the wilds of Hispaniola as remorselessly as the buccaneers hunted the cattle. As such, they made marvellous crews for the corsair ships which were beginning to use the island of Tortuga, a few miles off the north-west coast of Hispaniola, as a base.

Tortuga, sometimes under English but usually under French control, was soon to have an English rival as a thorn in the flesh of the Spaniards. The first such place was the island of Santa Catalina off the coast of Nicaragua, which was settled by men from Bermuda and England in 1630 and renamed Providence Island.[3] This colony, established only a few hundred miles from such centres of Spanish power and wealth as Cartagena de Indias and Portobello, was an exercise in Puritan anti-Spanish imperialism and the settlers were expected to 'annoy the King of Spain in the Indies' by combining planting with raids on Spanish shipping and the Spanish Main. This they did to such effect that they brought down upon themselves the full-scale wrath of Spain and, after two failed invasions, the island was finally recaptured by an overwhelming Spanish force in 1641. England's next attempt to establish a privateering base in the heart of the Spanish Indies was to prove more long-lasting. In 1654, Oliver Cromwell set in motion his 'Western Design' whose object was to carve out for England a Protestant empire in the Indies, and in the following year a massive English expeditionary force attempted to seize Hispaniola from the Spaniards. The expedition failed miserably, defeated by disease, cowardice and incompetence, but as a consolation prize the leaders decided to attack Jamaica, an island practically deserted by the Spaniards. This proved an easier task and Jamaica, once conquered in 1655, was fortified and held and was to prove the very worst enemy of Spain in the Indies. 'People of desperate fortunes' flocked to Jamaica from the other West Indian settlements and from Britain and Ireland, wrote Charles Leslie in his *New History of Jamaica* published in 1740, and then 'went a rambling on the seas in search of what prizes they could find; and indeed they had such surprising success as will perhaps scarce gain belief in succeeding ages'.[4] Such success was to make the fortune of Port Royal which was soon to acquire the reputation of being at once the richest and the wickedest town in America, a veritable pirate port to match the corsair cities of the Mediterranean.

Cromwell's war in the West Indies was part of a general war

against Spain, but even after peace was signed in 1660 there was no real let-up in hostility to Spain in America. Indeed, it was a given fact of the international diplomacy of the day that peace with Spain in Europe did not necessarily mean peace with Spain in the Indies, for 'beyond the line no other rule is recognized but that of force', as the Venetian ambassador in England reported to the Doge in 1668, this 'line' being the line of longitude passing through the Azores.[5] The European nations did not at this date keep naval vessels permanently stationed in the West Indies, so the 'force' was provided by the privateers and *flibustiers* of Jamaica and Tortuga whose governors were usually only too happy to provide them with commissions 'to attaque, fight with or surprise any vessell or vessells whatsoever belonging to the King of Spain or any of his subjects which you shall meet with . . . and also if you finde it prudential to invade any of their lands, colonys, or plantations in America'.[6]

The English and French privateers normally operated separately, but for a big expedition they were quite prepared to serve together. Such joint ventures usually worked satisfactorily, although with a certain amount of chauvinistic niggling. The main problem was religion. Many of the early *flibustiers* had been Huguenots, but later on Catholics were in the majority and such men strongly objected to the English love of iconoclasm, as can be seen in the contemporary journal of Raveneau de Lussan, an educated Frenchman who joined the buccaneers to pay off his debts. 'They had absolutely no scruples, when entering churches, against knocking down crucifixes with their sabers, firing guns and pistols, and breaking and mutilating the images of saints with their arms, scoffing at the veneration in which Frenchmen held them.'[7]

Whether Catholic or Protestant, the privateers themselves were motivated by lust for loot, love of adventure and an abiding hatred of Spaniards. The governors of Jamaica and Tortuga for their part believed that privateering had many advantages, providing as it did employment for some very rough men, profits from fitting out and victualling the privateers' ships, a stream of prizes to be sold cheaply in their markets and an effective and costless naval defence against counter-attack by the Spaniards. As for the governments at home in London and Paris, they were normally happy to condone or even actively encourage the issue of commissions in the West Indies. They believed that this continued pressure was the best method of encouraging Spain to recognise their de facto colonies in the Indies and ideally allow their traders to break into the lucrative Spanish colonial markets which were maintained as a monopoly for Spaniards. They were also aware that the capture of Spanish shipping was an effective means of removing the competition and so providing an encouragement for English and French merchant shipping to break into the trade of the region. Privateering, or buccaneering as it was to be called after the event, was then just another example of that piratical imperialism which we have seen as the motor of the expansion of English trade and settlement in other parts of the world.

The results of such cynical policies were to be devastating for the long-suffering inhabitants of the Spanish colonies in America. The privateers of Tortuga and Jamaica could, on occasion, put as many as two thousand hardened fighters to sea in an area where the Spaniards had virtually no naval defences, except on the increasingly rare occasions when the great fleets of galleons came to collect the silver and other treasure accumulated in the ports of Portobello and Vera Cruz. These galleons were well manned and armed and were safe from the buccaneers, but nothing else was. The privateers quickly destroyed or captured most of the Spanish merchant ships in the region and then, for lack of other prey, turned their attention to raids ashore against Spanish settlements and cities, not just those on the coastline but often several hundreds of miles inland. Hundreds of men, sometimes well over a thousand, would suddenly appear out of nowhere, screaming, shooting, brandishing their cutlasses and generally sowing terror before settling down to a leisurely process of searching for treasure, collecting ransoms, torture and destruction. Such incursions were sometimes bravely fought off, but they normally met with only the weakest of resistance for, in addition to having no naval defences, the Spanish settlements had few soldiers or militia to defend them and those that they did have were usually poorly supplied with arms and ammunition. It was, in short, a paradise for an adventurous robber, though there were so many robbers and so many attacks that the return to effort was often disappointing.

The scale of this activity is almost unbelievable. In the sixteen years following the English conquest of Jamaica in 1655, the privateers and *flibustiers* sacked eighteen cities, four towns and over thirty-five villages, as well, of course, as seizing any Spanish ships that might be around. Some places were raided time and time again, such as Tolú and Rio de la Hacha, two ports in Colombia, which saw the buccaneers arrive from the sea on eight and five occasions respectively, and smaller villages and settlements on the south coasts of Cuba and Hispaniola were ravaged even more often.[8] Such activity threw up many charismatic captains whose military skill, luck or savagery drew men to their command, such as Jean-David Nau, known as L'Ollonais after his birthplace at Les Sables d'Ollonne in western France.[9] However, the most successful of the privateers and the one best known today was Henry Morgan, a Welshman whose early life and career are obscure but who probably came out to the West Indies with the expeditionary force sent by Cromwell in 1654. He burst into prominence in the mid 1660s as one of the most successful of the privateer captains operating from Jamaica and, in 1668, he was made their admiral, being a man who enjoyed the confidence of the men he was to lead as well as of the authorities in Jamaica, among whom he had many influential friends. He was, in his way, a military genius, a truly remarkable leader of irregular troops whose skill in planning attacks, in implementing them with secrecy and dash and in maintaining throughout amazing discipline over his wild men commands admiration, even if one should deplore his profession.

His career as admiral of the privateers lasted less than four years, but in that time he led his men to the capture of the supposedly impregnable city of Portobello, an equally successful campaign into the inland sea of the Laguna de Maracaibo in Venezuela and, his last expedition and masterstroke, the capture and sacking of Panama in January 1671.[10] So great had become his reputation for success that he was able for this last campaign to attract to his flag virtually every English and French privateer in the West Indies, some two thousand men and one woman, a reputed witch, with whom he sailed in a ragbag fleet of thirty-eight ships and boats to capture the fortress of San Lorenzo de Chagres high above the mouth of the River Chagres, and then lead them on a truly terrible march through the dense and very inhospitable jungles of the isthmus to the savannah, from which they could see the roofs and spires of the city of Panama. 'They began to show signs of extreme joy, casting up their hats into the air, leaping for mirth, and shouting, even just as if they had already obtained the victory,' wrote the buccaneer surgeon Alexander Exquemelin who marched with Morgan and later wrote a fairly accurate account of the campaign in his famous book *The Buccaneers of America*.[11] Next day, they marched out in formation and defeated the Governor of Panama in a pitched battle before the city which they then proceeded to sack. The returns in loot were disappointing as the Spaniards had advance notice of Morgan's approach and had wisely taken most of their riches south to Ecuador, but it was still a remarkable achievement. Morgan today is seen as the epitome of the buccaneer, indeed of the pirate, and innumerable bars, pleasure boats and geographical locations are named after him, a notoriety which would have left him with mixed feelings if he had known of it. Most men would like to die famous, but not for the wrong reasons. For this man, hailed as the greatest or worst of the buccaneers, was no cattle-hunting buccaneer and indeed was never a pirate under English law. He was instead a privateer who always made certain that he sailed with a commission signed by the Governor of Jamaica, however dubious that commission might actually be.

His last commission, which set in motion the expedition to Panama, was certainly dubious, since it was signed by Sir Thomas Modyford several months after the signing of the Treaty of Madrid between England and Spain in July 1670. This treaty opened up a new chapter in Anglo-Spanish relations in the Indies and marked the end of England's reliance on 'that raffish instrument of foreign policy, the privateer', as one historian describes the cynical relationship between the government at home and the Jamaican privateers.[12] In return for Spain's recognition of her colonies, England agreed to cease hostilities in the Caribbean and to give up the old policy of 'No Peace beyond the Line'. The Spaniards were determined to keep commerce with their colonies as a Spanish monopoly and so were still not prepared to open their ports to English trade, but the English had great hopes from the concession that their trading ships might enter Spanish ports under stress of weather or to repair and revictual. Once in a Spanish port, it was realistically believed that the Spanish colonists would hasten to purchase cheap English goods. Nevertheless, trading with the Spaniards remained illegal and it was to be the cause of constant trouble for decades to come. Innumerable foreign sailors and traders were to be captured by the Spaniards and these captives were treated as pirates, some to be executed, others imprisoned for long periods or sent to serve on the galleys in Spain. This, naturally, inflamed anti-Spanish feeling still further in the West Indies and provided a ready-made excuse for continued attacks on Spanish shipping.

A new Hispanophile governor, Sir Thomas Lynch, was sent out to Jamaica to implement the policies enshrined in the Treaty of Madrid. He was instructed to arrest Sir Thomas Modyford and Henry Morgan and send them back to England as a sop to the Spaniards before they engaged in some desperate act to revenge the dishonour of losing Panama to a pirate. But neither man was punished and Morgan was instead fêted as a hero in London and later knighted. Both men would soon be back in authority in Jamaica once the Spaniards had quietened down. Lynch was also instructed to encourage the privateer ships to come in by proclaiming a general pardon to all who submitted within a reasonable time, such an offer being sweetened by the offer of thirty-five acres of land each if they should decide to become planters.[13]

Some of the privateers did come in – some even became planters; but such a settled way of life was of little interest to most of the men who had spent so many years sacking Spanish ships and cities, as a later Governor of Jamaica explained in a letter home. 'These Indies are so vast and rich and this rapine so sweet that it is one of the hardest things in the world to draw those from it which have used it so long.'[14] And so, after a lull in which Lynch's policies seemed to be having some effect, there seemed to be almost as many privateers at sea as in the heyday of the 1660s. 'This cursed trade has been so long followed,' wrote Lynch in 1672, 'that like weeds or Hidras they spring up as fast as we can cut them down.'[15] Some privateers operated openly from Jamaica though this became increasingly dangerous as the naval defences of the island were improved. Others used the island as a market, smuggling prize cargoes into remote coves and creeks or even selling them in Port Royal after ostentatiously paying customs on the pretence that they had been acquired in legitimate trade.

Even those former privateers who appeared to have abandoned their trade were likely to be found in places and occupations from which it would be very easy to recruit them if some great venture beckoned. Such were the men who crewed the Jamaican sloops which traded clandestinely with the Spanish colonists, a dangerous trade which required the sloops to be 'well-armed and trebly manned' to protect them against capture by the Spanish coastguards.[16] Or there were those who drifted to the coasts of the Gulf of Campeche and the Gulf of Honduras to cut logwood, a raw material much in demand from the European dyeing industries. Logwood-cutting was another illegal activity, for these coasts, though inhabited only by Indians, were claimed by the Spaniards who descended from time to time to clear away the cutters. It was, however, an ideal trade for those who were happy to work hard for a few months and then be idle for the rest of the year. 'The wood cutters are generally a rude drunken crew, some of which have been pirates, and most of them sailors,' wrote a later observer. 'Their chief delight is in drinking; and when they broach a quarter cask or a hogshead of wine, they seldom stir from it while there is a drop left.'[17] Such a trade was obviously attractive to former or resting privateers, some five or six hundred being engaged in the business in 1673, a pool of men ready to join in any nefarious and potentially profitable activity.

In the absence of commissions from Jamaica, such men were likely to be employed by the *flibustiers* of Tortuga or Petit-Goave in the French colony of Saint-Domingue (modern Haiti), where the governors were continuing the policy of piratical imperialism now abandoned by the English. Jamaican privateers, any privateers, were welcome there, complained the Governor of Jamaica in 1682. 'The French Governor ... never refuses commissions, whether before or after capture of a prize, providing he receives some present, as, for instance, a tenth share.'[18] The years from 1678 to 1683 were the great age of the *flibustiers* and buccaneers under French patronage, just as the late 1660s had been for Jamaica. Attacks on Spanish shipping were supplemented as before by large-scale raids ashore, culminating in the great buccaneer raid on the Mexican port of Vera Cruz in 1683 from which some 1,200 men each gained 800 pieces of eight or about £160 in loot, much more than Morgan's men got from even his most successful campaign, such figures needing to be multiplied by at least a hundred to give some idea of the value in modern money. Vera Cruz was, however, to prove the turning point in French policy, just as Panama had been in English. A furious Spain declared war on France and, when this was concluded, Louis XIV, somewhat alarmed by the growing hostility of nearly all Europe to his policy of territorial expansion, decided to try and win Spain's friendship by agreeing at the Truce of Ratisbon in August 1684 that there should be peace between the two countries, not only in Europe but also in the West Indies. A new governor was appointed with strict instructions to suppress the *flibustiers*. Since they had seventeen ships and nearly two thousand men at his arrival,[19] he was to have some difficulty, but he claimed to have destroyed them by 1689, only to reinstate many as privateers at the outbreak in the same year of the Nine Years War, in which France had to face the combined navies of England, Holland and Spain. It was not, therefore, till the French capture of Cartagena de Indias in 1697, with a fleet composed of both royal ships and *flibustiers*, that the history of the buccaneers may be said finally to come to an end.[20]

Long before then there had been changes in the strategy and behaviour of the privateers who had once used Jamaica as their base of operations. For ten years or so after the Treaty of Madrid in 1670, they had been able in one way or another to preserve a privateering way of life, even if few of their commissions would have borne close scrutiny, and as late as 1678 it was estimated that there were about

1,200 privateers based at the island.[21] But from then on, naval pressure in and around Jamaica, prohibitions on the acceptance of foreign commissions and a growing aversion to privateers even in Jamaica itself, began to have their effect and some of the privateers set out to practise their old trade in new waters.

The most adventurous and best known of these were called by their contemporaries the South Sea Men. These buccaneers sailed to Portobello, which they raided early in 1680, and then set off on foot across the isthmus of Panama to the Pacific, or South Sea (Mar del Sur) as the Spaniards called it, where, first in canoes and then in captured Spanish vessels, they attacked shipping and raided the western American coastline from Chile to California. Foreign vessels had not been seen in these waters since Dutch incursions in the 1620s and the buccaneers, who were soon reinforced by other men coming overland or sailing round Cape Horn, were to cause havoc for most of the 1680s until those who had survived dispersed. Estimates of the numbers of men involved are not very reliable but, at their peak, there were well over a thousand of these marauders in the Pacific who, according to Spanish sources, had by 1686 taken sixty-two ships, nearly two-thirds of the Spanish Pacific merchant fleet, as well as making innumerable raids ashore. Few of these buccaneers returned with large quantities of booty, but they did an enormous amount of damage.[22]

These men still called themselves privateers, but they had no commissions for their depredations in the Pacific except those which one of their number, Captain Sawkins, said were 'in the muzzells of our gunns'.[23] They were, in fact, out-and-out pirates and the same was true of most of the other 'privateers' who in the 1680s began to move out of the Caribbean to seek new hunting grounds and new places of refuge where they could fit out their ships and sell their booty. There was no shortage of these and reports began to come back to England from scores of places where it was said these latter-day buccaneers were selling their prizes.

The Governor of New Providence in the Bahamas was admonished by the Governor of Jamaica in 1682 for making 'your Government a Tortuga, for certainly all the pirates in the Indies are now lying in your latitude'. The Danish island of St Thomas was described as the worst 'receptacle of pirates . . . this side of Sallee and Algiers', while a report from the Governor of Bermuda in 1685 complained that 'it is the intention of the people to make this island a pirates' refuge'. Piracy was no monopoly of small islands and reports also came in from all along the mainland, from Carolina, a 'Puerto Franco' for pirates, Rhode Island and Boston where it was said that the ships that had taken part in the 1683 raid on Vera Cruz were 'very welcome' and pirates had bought up 'most of the choice goods'.[24] This diaspora of the West Indian privateers saw the end of that exclusive focus on Spanish targets which had been characteristic of the buccaneers. Ships of all nations, including those of England and her colonies, were now vulnerable and the geographical range of attacks extended enormously, with pirate attacks being reported not just in the Caribbean but all along the North American coast and across the Atlantic in West Africa and the Atlantic islands. A pirate ship wrecked in Carolina in 1685, for instance, had sailed from Jamaica to Honduras and then through the Florida channel to Virginia and New England before sailing to Gambia in West Africa and so back to Carolina, very much the itinerary which would later be called the 'pirate round'. These pirate ships of the 1680s had very cosmopolitan crews, as can be seen from the crew list of *La Nouvelle Trompeuse* which, after many depredations, was seized by the authorities in Boston in 1684, though not without complaints and threat of lawsuits from the local merchants who were intent on buying up her booty. Among the 198 pirates found aboard were men from all parts of the British Isles, Holland, France, Sweden, Portugal, Spain and New England, as well as many representatives of the non-white population of the Caribbean – Negroes, Indians and mulattoes.[25] Buccaneering had now given way to open piracy and, although there was to be a lull in this activity from 1689 during the major war known variously as the Nine Years War or King William's War, when peace returned in 1697 the new sort of piracy returned with it.

The buccaneers are better documented than the pirates of the early seventeenth century, there being several surviving books and journals written by people who had themselves sailed with them, such as the buccaneer surgeon Alexander Exquemelin and the great navigator and travel writer William Dampier, as well as much comment from their captives and by observers ashore, especially the French who were fascinated by these early denizens of their West Indian colonies. This material shows that there had been several interesting developments in pirate customs and mentality. What has most intrigued the modern observer is the evidence of a degree of democracy and egalitarianism which ran quite counter to the norm anywhere else in the late seventeenth-century world. This is perhaps most striking among the true hunting buccaneers, a community of exiles who scorned the laws of all nations but honoured their own rules, 'the custom of the coast', and were so determined to forget the social hierarchy of the outside world that it was forbidden to speak of a man's origins, and surnames which might have given those origins away were replaced by *noms de guerre* or nicknames.[26]

The privateers did not go so far as this, but they were still remarkably egalitarian by the standards of their day. They respected the governments of Jamaica and Tortuga from which they drew their commissions and were prepared to pay a share of their prizes for the right to operate from these safe ports, just as the corsairs of the Mediterranean did. They were also sufficiently capitalistic in their mentality to recognise the rights of the owners of their vessels, most of which were owned and fitted out by investors ashore. But they did this with reluctance and the Jamaican privateers were notorious for cheating the owners of their ships, refusing to count as spoil to be shared with investors much that would have been shared by a privateer operating from a European port. Significantly, this included the goods, money and slaves seized in raids ashore, their most important source of booty, but they also had a very liberal interpretation of what was known as 'free enterrance and plunder', goods seized from a prize at sea and divided at the mast before the privateer returned to port.[27] And, once they had become out-and-out pirates, as most of them had by the 1680s, they of course no longer recognised owners at all and shared everything among themselves.

This share was 'a very exact and equal dividend', 'man for man', with the exception that boys got half a share and slaves got nothing, for the buccaneers were not so egalitarian that they would forgo the opportunity to retain 'negroes to do our work', as one of them noted in the journal he kept of his voyage.[28] Captains and other senior officers got more than a man, but not very much more, 'five or six portions' for a captain according to one account, 'a double lot' according to another, while the French missionary Jean-Baptiste Labat reported that even this was not a right but 'a gift which is given them by the rest of the crew'.[29] There were also arrangements for compensation for those who had been wounded or maimed, such as 500 pieces of eight (about £100) or five slaves for the loss of an arm or a leg, slightly more if it should be the right arm or leg, and 100 pieces of eight or one slave for an eye or a finger, while one account says that 'if a man has a wooden leg or a hook for his arm and these happen to be destroyed, he receives the same amount as if they were his original limbs'.[30] Extra payments were also made to those who first sighted a ship later taken, the first to board or the first to storm a fortification, rewards for the sharp-eyed and the brave which were very similar to those accorded by the 'Custom of the Corsairs' in the Mediterranean.

The management of a privateer ship was as egalitarian as its division of prizes. Captains were chosen by the vote or acclamation of their men, and articles of association or *chasse parties* were agreed between captains and crew. In Morgan's time the crew elected two representatives to speak for them, but later there evolved an elected officer whose function was to speak on the men's behalf, to see that they were treated correctly and that the division of booty was really equal. This was the quartermaster, described by Dampier as 'the second place in the ship, according to the Law of Privateers', though a minor office on a merchant ship, and this was a position that the quartermaster would retain among the pirates of the early eighteenth century.[31] Consultations in which decisions on the next move would be made by majority vote were frequent, every day according to one account, and there were also meetings to determine collective codes of behaviour, as on the occasion recorded by the French buccaneer Raveneau de Lussan in his journal. 'We then drew up regulations condemning anyone to forfeit his share of our loot if convicted of cowardliness, rape, drunkenness, disobedience, larceny, and failure to obey orders.'[32] Both ships and men were free to opt out if they so wished, a ship by the collective vote of the men and a man by his own choice. 'Privateers are not obliged to any ship,' wrote William Dampier, 'but free to go ashore where they please, or to go into any other ship that will entertain them,' a freedom which would certainly not have been accorded by the rules of later pirates who bound a man to the ship once he had joined, whether willingly or unwillingly.[33]

This astonishingly democratic organisation was called, no doubt ironically, the 'Jamaica discipline' and was adopted not just by the buccaneers but also by regularly commissioned privateers from the West Indies in the wars against France of the late seventeenth and early eighteenth centuries. 'Every seaman on board a privateer having a vote,' complained an official of the Board of Trade in 1708, 'it is not in the captain's power to prevent them committing irregularities when the majority is against him.' There is 'no regular command among them, being all alike', wrote another complainant. 'Their establishment was more like a commonwealth than an absolute monarchy.'[34] But a commonwealth can be effective and the buccaneers were noted for their remarkable discipline in action, being required by their own rules to obey orders from those whom they had elected. And those who broke those rules could be severely punished. Men who attempted to hide booty from their mates might well be marooned on an uninhabited island, while the punishment for theft could be as severe as on a contemporary East Indiaman or Royal Navy ship, as Dampier reports. 'One of our men ... was found guilty of theft, and condemned for the same to have three blows from each man in the ship [one hundred men] with a two-inch and a half rope on his bare back. Captain Swan began first, and struck with a good will; whose example was followed by all of us.'[35]

In their heyday the buccaneers were unusual among pirates in acquiring the bulk of their loot in raids ashore, only the corsairs of the Mediterranean challenging them at all in this respect. This meant that, during the Caribbean phase of their history, they were not particularly interested in the quality of their ships, which they saw primarily as a means of getting them to wherever it was that they had chosen to raid. They were, however, sufficiently good seamen and navigators to arrive on most occasions at the right destination, usually secretly and at night, the final approach sometimes being made in canoes which they carried aboard their ships and had learned to handle skilfully from Central American Indians who were their friends and often allies against the Spaniards.

To help them select and reach targets, the buccaneers were very efficient in the collection of information, a vital skill both for pirates and for those who hunted them. Anyone cruising along the coast or loitering on the seashore was likely to end up on the deck of a privateer, wrote William Dampier in a general description of the customs and methods of the buccaneers. These prisoners would then be examined 'concerning the country, town, or city that they belong to . . . how many families . . . whether rich, and what their riches do consist in? . . . if fortified, how many great guns and what number of small arms? Whether it is possible to come undescried on them? . . . And if they have any former discourse of such places from other prisoners, they compare one with the other; then examine again, and enquire if he or any of them are capable to be guides to conduct a party of men thither.'[36] Many such prisoners did prove capable of being guides, either willingly or with a halter round their neck and a knife at their back to persuade them of the likely result of breaking silence. Most pirates, and the Royal Navy ships which were to hunt them, attempted to acquire information in similar ways, but no one seems to have been so good at it or so persuasive as the buccaneers.

Another military skill in which the buccaneers excelled was the quality of their marksmanship. Some of the Frenchmen seem to have had a bit of the d'Artagnan in them and such a man might boast of being 'the best swordsman in the Americas',[37] a skill which has, of course, been replicated in countless films. However, the typical personal arms of a buccaneer were a musket, two pistols and a cutlass rather than a sword. The best muskets were known as 'boucaniers' and were French, made in Nantes or Bordeaux, four and a half feet long and as a result of continuous practice very accurate by the standards of the day. French commentators said that the buccaneers were able to hit a coin spinning at 120 paces or to sever an orange from a tree by its stalk and, even allowing for some hyperbole, they were certainly effective marksmen. Ships were thrown out of control as helmsman after helmsman was cut down by the sharpshooters and castles, too, might find their defenders picked off one by one. And once the buccaneers closed in, they were equally successful at close range with their pistols and cutlasses, their attacks being so ferocious that it was said that the Spaniards felt 'their courage freeze up' at the sight of these terrible men from the sea.[38]

If the buccaneers of Morgan's day were not particularly celebrated for their seamanship, the same could not be said of the latter-day buccaneers, particularly those who plied their trade in the Pacific. Some of these South Sea men sailed round Cape Horn both ways, others circumnavigated the globe, while between them they increased English knowledge of the west coast of America enormously, a process aided by the capture of Spanish charts which were later presented to the King and can now be seen in the British Library.[39] They were indeed 'such bold and daring navigators, that they not only attempted but performed things almost incredible', as the eighteenth-century editor of one of their journals remarked. This was undoubtedly true and we are fortunate that so many of these ships carried men of literary ability who were able to record these almost incredible feats for posterity.[40]

The South Sea men also had the skills required to convert the Spanish merchantmen they captured into effective pirate ships. The *Trinity*, for instance, which was captured by Bartholomew Sharpe, was changed beyond recognition at the island of Gorgona off the Pacific coast of Colombia, as was reported in the entertaining journal of Basil Ringrose who sailed with him. 'Wee tooke downe our round house and coache and all the high carved works of her sterne . . . wee find our ship sailes much better for her alteration.' And later on they took off one of the decks 'to make our ship saile still better'.[41] The Barbary corsairs were good at doing this sort of thing in a shipyard, but the buccaneers and the pirates that followed them could transform a captured merchant ship into a 'man-of-war' on a remote beach or in a secluded cove with just their hands and the carpenters' tools that they happened to have on board.

The buccaneers may be justly praised for their military skills, their handiness and their seamanship, but they are normally reviled for their cruelty. The degree of this is difficult to assess, as those who wrote and published books on the buccaneers would be tempted to sensationalise cruelty in order to attract readers, as Alexander Exquemelin certainly does in his description of L'Ollonais, a man who was said to pull out his prisoners' tongues and once cut out a living heart and ate it 'like a ravenous wolf'.[42] The thumbscrew, the knotted cord, mutilation, stringing men up by their wrists, their necks or even their private parts were all in use when the buccaneers tried to elicit information from their prisoners. In one incident, well documented by the Spaniards, the leading lady of Portobello was stripped and placed in an empty wine barrel which was then filled with gunpowder. The grinning privateers then held a lighted match to her face and asked her if she could still not remember where she had hidden treasure.[43] Sometimes one is struck by the very casual way in which such matters are referred to in journals as if they were so far part of the buccaneering way of life that they are hardly worth mentioning. 'We questioned him with the usual ceremonies, that is, by torturing him to find out where we were,' notes Raveneau de Lussan in his journal while, on another occasion when some ransom failed to turn up, 'we were forced to apply to our prisoners the customary rigorous measures used to intimidate our enemies – to have them throw dice to see which men would lose their heads'.[44] This is how one might expect pirates to behave and this, it seems, is how they did in fact behave. But one has to remember that it was a cruel world in which not only pirates were barbarous. Jean-Baptiste Labat was quite shocked when he visited Barbados and discovered the punishments meted out by the English to rebellious slaves who were 'condemned to be passed through a cane mill, or be burnt alive, or be put into iron cages that prevent any movement and in which they are hung up to branches of trees and left to die of hunger and despair'. Labat, a missionary, excused this barbarity since it was necessary to make slaves fear and respect their masters. No doubt the buccaneers also felt it necessary to be cruel to obtain information from their prisoners and to make them fear and respect them.[45]

Buccaneers were not only cruel, they were also 'one of the most unusual homosexually oriented groups in history' according to the historian B.R. Burg, although he admits there is no evidence to support this assertion.[46] The argument rests mainly on the fact that the buccaneers were all men, the shortage of women, especially white women, in the West Indies and, perhaps especially, on the existence of the institution of 'matelotage', in which buccaneers sought out 'a comrade or companion, whom we may call partner, in their fortunes'.[47] The assumption that this relationship was homosexual cannot, however, be proved and is somewhat undermined by the observation that such matelots shared everything 'including women'.[48] Comrades-in-arms, muckers or mates are quite common in military history and some of these couples may well have had homosexual relationships. But it is unrealistic to suggest, as Burg does, that such 'were the only form of sexual expression engaged in by members of the buccaneer community',[49] since buccaneers are regularly described as having relationships with women, albeit mainly with whores, whenever they returned from a voyage or otherwise got the chance.

In this, as in many other aspects of their behaviour, buccaneers behaved no differently from any other pirates or indeed most sailors. They took women when they were available just as they took food when it was available, 'as much as he can eat', and were quite prepared to put up with the absence of both, though a prudent commander would ensure that food was not absent for long, since, as Dampier noted, 'nothing emboldens them sooner to mutiny than want'.[50] And, of course, they also took drink when it was available, often to excess, so much so that on occasion they were so drunk as to let their prisoners escape or were unable to bring their ships alongside and board a prize. But, above all, they loved to gamble for money, just as in their profession they gambled for their lives. Indeed, it was by winning at dice rather than from their share of prizes that most buccaneers were able to accumulate, a fact which often caused dissension aboard, especially in the long voyages undertaken by the South Sea men. Those who had won wanted to go home with their winnings; those who had lost wanted to continue the voyage; and it was a wise commander who was able to keep both parties happy.[51] Gambling was so serious a problem that some later pirates were to include a prohibition on gaming in their articles of association. In the days of the buccaneers, however, the most that anyone did was to ban dice-playing on Sundays, the pious Captain Sawkins going so far as to 'throw the dice over board, catching them in use on the said day'.[52]

Whatever their vices, the buccaneers were a remarkable breed of men. 'The privateers of these parts,' wrote Richard Browne, a surgeon who sailed with Morgan, 'theire bodys are habituated to this country, they knowe each place and creeke, know the mode of the Spanish fighting, townes being never so well fortyfied, the numbers being never so unequall, if money or good plunder be in the case, they will either win it manfully or dye coradgiously.' They were 'men of the sea, a rabble with little social pretension', said a Mexican who had been a prisoner in Jamaica. But their morale was good. 'They are very happy, well paid and they live in amity with each other. The prizes that they make are shared with much brotherhood and friendship.'[53] Most of their qualities, both good and bad, were passed on to the pirates proper, the enemies of mankind, who succeeded them and are considered in later chapters.

# CHAPTER SEVEN

# The Red Sea Men

CHAPTER SEVEN

# *The Red Sea Men*

The piratical imperialism which has been seen as the motor of European commercial expansion in the Mediterranean, the Atlantic and the Caribbean was even more apparent in the Indian Ocean. First, the Portuguese from Vasco da Gama onwards and then, a century later and even more aggressively, the Dutch and the English pursued a violent maritime policy in Asian waters designed to eliminate or overawe their Arab and Indian competitors. This policy was sufficient to enable the Europeans to infiltrate success-fully the existing and very long-established pattern of native shipping in the Indian Ocean. By the later seventeenth century, this stage of aggressive commerce had passed and an era of more settled trade had been established in the region, in which the more valuable long-distance trades had been divided between the ships of the various European East India Companies and those built and based in Asia which were known as 'country ships'. Some of the latter were owned by Europeans, but most belonged to native shipowners, such as Abdul Ghafur, an immensely wealthy Gujurati trader whose fleet of merchantmen based at Surat exceeded in number the fleet of the English East India Company.[1]

These country ships plying in the Indian Ocean were often much larger than the European and American ships which traded in the Atlantic, few of which exceeded 300 tons, while some of the Asian ships were as much as 1,000 tons and 300 to 500 tons was commonplace. These capacious ships were manned with huge crews, usually well over a hundred men, but were weakly armed with only a handful of cannon since they appeared to face no real threat, attacks on native vessels being rare once the European nations had established their naval superiority.[2] It was also thought by Europeans that such ships would offer little resistance if attacked, since the 'Moors' who sailed them 'generally love peace and quietness at sea', as a captain in the Royal Navy remarked.[3] It hardly needs saying that a peace-loving, poorly armed vessel was attractive to a pirate.

Such attractions multiplied when it was realised that ships in the Indian Ocean carried cargoes potentially far more profitable for pirates than those aboard vessels in the Caribbean and Atlantic. There, the only really valuable targets were the Spanish treasure galleons and these were nearly always too well guarded for pirates to attack. Matters were very different in the Indian Ocean. All ships of the European East India Companies carried silver and some-times gold in coin and bars on their outward voyages, often as much as £50,000 on a single ship, about £5 million in modern terms. And some of their home-bound cargoes also contained items of the high-value, low-bulk nature most of interest to pirates, especially the Portuguese ships which frequently brought home jewels and especially huge quantities of diamonds from India. Such ships were well manned and armed, but not totally invulnerable to pirates as will be seen. However, the weakly armed country ships offered the best targets of all and none more so than the fleet of twenty or thirty vessels which sailed each year from Surat, the great trading emporium in north-west India, for Mocha (Al Mukha) at the mouth of the Red Sea, carrying thousands of Muslim pilgrims on the first stage of their journey to Mecca. Many of these travelled free, paid for as an act of charity and piety by the Mughal Emperor, and they were joined aboard by merchants who traded Indian cloth and spices for coffee, gold and jewels in Arabia. Such trading ensured that, when the fleet returned to Surat, it would be carrying an immensely valuable cargo, composed for the most part of those high-value and easily portable items, such as jewels and cash, which pirates of all ages have hoped to find aboard their prizes.

Knowledge of this potential booty travelled along the sea lanes of the world and reached the ears of sailors, buccaneers and pirates in the Americas and no doubt such stories grew in the telling in forecastles and taverns. The Indian Ocean was a long way away, but many sailors in the Atlantic and Caribbean would have known about it, some from having served on East Indiamen in their youth, some from working on the slavers which sailed from New York and Jamaica to East Africa and Madagascar to acquire slaves at much cheaper rates than in West Africa. And then there were of course the South Sea men, some of whom had completed their voyages by crossing the Pacific and returning home through the Indian Ocean. Such news of great riches in the East had its effect and, from the mid 1680s onwards, there were a number of isolated incidents of European piracy in Asian waters, but as yet this did not amount to very much. Matters were to change, indeed threaten to get completely out of hand, in the 1690s as the most outrageously successful series of voyages in pirate history got under way.[4]

Wartime was usually pirate-free, as former pirates flocked to sign up on legally commissioned privateers, but King William's War in the 1690s was to prove different. News that something unprecedented was happening began to reach England in the summer of 1693, when a letter from the Governor of Jamaica reported that privateersmen from his island had 'found their way into the Red Sea, where they have committed unheard of piracies, murders and barbarities. These are now returned with vast wealth to most of the northern plantations in America where they quietly enjoy their ill-gotten gains.' This letter was followed by many others from all over the colonies and from India, and soon the English government had a fat dossier on this 'parcel of pirates, called the Red Sea men . . . who get great booty of Arabian gold'. They also had a dossier on the corrupt colonial officials who accepted their bribes and protected and encouraged them.[5]

The business had begun with the voyage of the *Jacob*, a privateer with a New York commission to hunt down French shipping. But when she set sail in November 1690, she made no attempt to fulfil the terms of her commission and sailed instead via the Cape Verde Islands to Madagascar. She then began to cruise against native Indian Ocean shipping with disappointing results, until she finally hit the jackpot with the seizure of four ships in the Red Sea in June

1692. This coup yielded a very satisfying dividend of £400 or £500 a man, unbelievable riches for the sailors who shared it, and it was a happy crew who sailed away to refresh themselves on the island of St Mary's (Saint-Marie) off the north-east coast of Madagascar. Here, they were pleased to discover that a trading post had been established by a former buccaneer called Adam Baldridge whose activities were financed by Frederick Philipse of New York, the wealthiest merchant in the city, whose primary interest in Madagascar was in buying slaves for the American market. However, both he and his agent quickly saw the potential profit to be had by combining slaving with trade with the pirates, and so Baldridge welcomed the arrival of the *Jacob* with whose men he exchanged food, drink and other supplies for some of their loot and six of the ship's guns, which were mounted on a fort he was building. The pirate crew now split up, some remaining on the island where there was a growing white community of pirates and beachcombers and many delights in the form of drink and native women, while the remainder sailed back to New York where they arrived in July 1693. Here, they found that their possession of Arabian gold made it only too easy to bribe Governor Benjamin Fletcher to allow them to go ashore with their loot, the governor being particularly pleased with the gift of their ship which he sold for £800 profit. And the brothels, bars and merchants of New York were very pleased to relieve the returning pirates of the rest of their booty.[6]

News of the riches to be won in the Red Sea spread fast and at least ten other privateers were to sail in the wake of the *Jacob*, some of them making the voyage twice such as the *Amity* whose captain, Thomas Tew, first sailed to the east in 1692 with the dubious cover of a privateering commission granted by the Lieutenant-Governor of Bermuda. His ship, however, was fitted out and provisioned in his native Rhode Island as were most of the other privateers who engaged in this lucrative but totally illegal business. They never had any trouble in finding crews, as an official in Maryland reported in 1695, for 'their sharing of such large sums tempts the people of these parts to go along with them, and they are a great hindrance to trade, for the seamen run from the merchant-ships to go with them, as do also many of the men from the King's ships'. And, if such men should have a tinge of conscience at attacking peaceful Hindu and Mohammedan shipping, they had no trouble in convincing themselves, as one of their number said at his trial, 'that it was very lawful (as he said he was told) to plunder ships and goods etc., belonging to the enemies of Christianity'. Such sentiments still held sway a quarter of a century later. In 1719, the gunner of the privateer ship *Speedwell* proposed to mutiny and cruise in the Red Sea, 'for, said he, there can be no harm in robbing those Mahometans'.[7]

This disgraceful business was very well organised. American merchants fitted out the ships and financed the voyages and usually received a good return on their investment. Colonial officials collected their bribes and turned a blind eye to the return of the 'Red Sea men', as these enterprising rogues were called. Those American slave traders who were accustomed to seek their human cargo in East Africa and Madagascar took the pirate business in their stride. They loaded their outgoing vessels with rum and beer, European food and clothing, guns and gunpowder and other things likely to be desired by pirates, as well as the trade goods needed for the acquisition of slaves. These were all dispatched to Baldridge who filled his masters' ships with slaves at the same time as he traded with the pirates for some of their loot, being careful not to charge them too much for their rum lest he earn their enmity. And when the slavers returned to America they usually carried, in addition to their shackled cargo, a score or so of pirates who now wanted to return to civilisation after their years of looting and boozing in the Indian Ocean.

Some of these returnees worked their passage, but most travelled home in comfort, having paid their fare, which was typically a hundred pieces of eight, the Spanish silver coin worth about a quarter or a fifth of a pound sterling and which was the nearest thing to a world currency in this period. As the slavers approached their home ports, small coastal vessels sailed out to meet them and smuggle ashore the returning pirates and the illegal cargo of pirate loot, thus leaving the ship to dock with a perfectly legitimate cargo of slaves. This ingenious method of solving a perennial problem for pirates – getting home with their booty – was not completely foolproof as we are told by Edward Barlow, the famous seaman journalist who wrote a fascinating account of his fifty years at sea, many of them in the Indian Ocean. 'And then many of them return home and skulk about and keep out of the way, but some of them now and then are taken and hanged for their pains.'[8] But the skulkers greatly outnumbered the hanged, and the American colonists who welcomed and protected the homecoming pirates were very happy to have their pockets lined and their economy boosted by this influx of Arabian and Turkish gold.

Although most of the Red Sea men sailed with the dubious protection of a privateering commission, this was by no means necessary to join in the game, and the most famous of their number chose a different route to Red Sea riches. In May 1694, two private English warships, the *Charles* and the *James*, were lying in the northern Spanish harbour of La Coruña waiting for other ships to assemble for a raid on the French West Indies. They had been kept waiting nearly a year without wages, first in England and then in Spain, and the men were very discontented, so it was not too difficult for Henry Avery (or Every), second mate of the *Charles*, to incite a mutiny. He allowed the captain and some twenty loyal men to row ashore, welcomed aboard twenty-five disloyal men from the *James*, renamed the forty-six-gun ship the *Fancy* and set sail 'on the account' and into the history books. He sailed south to West Africa, where he increased his crew with volunteers from two captured Danish ships, and so to Madagascar where he took on provisions and more men. Finally, he sailed to the island of Johanna (Anjouan) in the Comoros to complete his preparations for his voyage to the Red Sea, where he intended to cruise off the narrow strait of Bab el Mandeb at its mouth (known as the Babs to the English marauders) in order to intercept the homecoming pilgrim fleet. Here he found company, for waiting in the same place were five of the privateer/pirates from North America intent on the same end.[9]

News of the pirates' presence had reached the twenty-five ships in the pilgrim fleet and they managed to slip through the strait and past the predators in the night, but this smart move was not to do them much good. Soon aware of what had happened, Avery set off in pursuit of the lumbering merchantmen, leaving some of the slower privateers straggling in his wake. First, he caught up and captured a rich ship belonging to Abdul Ghafur, from which he seized some £50,000 or £60,000 in gold and silver. Little time was wasted on this prize, magnificent though it was, for Avery had in his sights a much greater prize whose capture was to earn for him the soubriquet 'the King of Pirates'. This was the *Ganj-i-Sawai* (anglicised as *Gunsway*), a huge ship with forty great guns belonging to the Mughal Emperor Aurangzeb, which had aboard officials and ladies of the imperial court as well as poorer pilgrims travelling on the Emperor's charity. Despite the presence aboard of several hundred soldiers, the *Gunsway* was taken with remarkable ease after a two- or three-hour fight. Most people blamed the disaster on 'the unparalleled cowardice' of her commander Ibrahim Khan who 'made no adequate defence and, after dressing up some Turki slave girls as men and exhorting them to fight, ran down and hid in the hold', as we are informed by a contemporary Muslim historian.[10]

For days the ships drifted together, as the pirates leisurely 'looted and raped their way from deck to deck',[11] until they had piled up sufficient gold and silver and jewels to provide a dividend of £1,000 for each man with a full share. They then left the prize to make its sad way home to Surat and set sail for Réunion where they arrived in November 1695. Here the crew divided, about half deciding to remain in the Indian Ocean until the heat was off while the remainder sailed under Avery's command for the Bahamas, where they were able to bribe the Governor Nicholas Trott to let them ashore with a gift of their ship and twenty pieces of eight from each man. Some of the men stayed in the Bahamas or the Virgin Islands, but most set off in small vessels they had purchased in the islands, some to Carolina, others, including Avery, to Ireland. They had just pulled off one of the most successful pirate voyages in history and one which got the most enormous publicity as a result of the eminence of the shipowners from whom they had stolen their loot. The English government was shocked into action and the hunt for Avery's men was to continue for years. A few were captured, tried and executed, but most were able to make their way ashore to what must have been a somewhat precarious existence, given their vulnerability to treachery and blackmail. Avery himself was traced to London, on the evidence of a captured member of his crew, but what happened to him thereafter is a mystery. Some say he died in poverty, cheated of all his riches, but this may well have been wishful thinking and the truth is that nobody really knows. He was certainly never captured.[12]

Mutiny was a potent source of pirates and Avery and his men were far from being the only mutineers among the Red Sea men. It was reported in 1696, for instance, that 'about three years ago seventy pirates, who ran away with a vessel from Jamaica, came to Charleston with a vast quantity of gold from the Red Sea', and there were other such incidents.[13] Best known was the mutiny on the *Mocha Frigate*, an East Indiaman sailing from Bombay to China in 1696 under the command of Captain Leonard Edgecombe, a notorious bully who was very unpopular with his men. On the night of 16/17 June, off the coast of Sumatra, 'a number of desperate and bloudy minded men', under the leadership of two former pirates who had signed on to the crew in Bombay, secured the gunroom, strangled the captain in his bed and at dawn set eighteen loyal men adrift in one of the ship's boats. The *Mocha Frigate* was a powerful addition to the pirate fleet and she was to pursue a three-year career of plunder all over the Indian Ocean, before being deliberately sunk to protect from attack the entrance to the pirates' harbour at the island of St Mary's.[14]

East Indiamen were rather slow, but they were well gunned and roomy and tended to have stroppy crews, so it is surprising that the *Mocha Frigate* was the only one to mutiny during this period. The long voyages from England, often accompanied with short rations of food and water, were always trying times for captains as they watched with alarm the formation of apparently mutinous cabals among the sailors or heard the ominous rolling of cannon balls across the deck at night, the traditional chilling signal of impending mutiny. The years of King William's War were particularly serious in this respect according to an official in Bombay who, when asked to explain the mutiny of the *Mocha Frigate*, said that 'the seamen were generally so refractory' that there was danger of mutiny on all the East India ships.[15] And yet there was only one mutiny, despite the temptations, though many individual sailors deserted and joined the pirates. Even more suitable as pirate vessels, for which they were often mistaken, were the cruising ships of the Royal Navy but these too did not mutiny, despite much discontent among the men. The only hint of mutiny in these years comes from HMS *Speedwell* stationed in Barbados in 1698 when loyal sailors overheard some of their shipmates plotting to kill the senior officers and sail for Madagascar. 'They seemed to approve it as a place fitt for pleasant living for such as were pirates.'[16] Such it was but, even so, the men of the *Speedwell* did not mutiny.

The most notorious of all the Red Sea men and the man who, together with Henry Morgan, is seen today as the archetypal pirate was not really much of a pirate at all. This was Captain William Kidd, a privateer captain with ambition who managed to persuade a syndicate of powerful Whig lords to back him in a venture to sail to the Indian Ocean to capture the pirates who were creating such havoc there. Kidd received a commission for this purpose, issued by the Lord Keeper of the Great Seal who was conveniently one of the backers of the voyage, and fitted out a suitable vessel, the *Adventure Galley*, which had been purchased by the syndicate. He then sailed from London to New York to complete his crew, this proving no problem as 'many flocked to him from all parts, men of desperate fortunes and necessities, in expectance of getting vast treasure'.[17]

Kidd sailed from New York for the Indian Ocean in September 1696 with a crew of 150 men. Almost from the start it was suspected that the intended voyage was one of piracy, not pirate hunting, but Kidd did not show his hand for a long time and only then because he really had no control over his prize-hungry crew. The one thing he never did was actually try to catch any pirates. As his voyage around the Indian Ocean progressed, he acted in an increasingly piratical way until he finally became an out-and-out pirate, most seriously when he captured the *Quedah Merchant* off the coast of India at the end of January 1698. Much of the cargo of this ship, on her way from Surat to the Spice Islands, belonged to Muklis Khan, a great man at the court of the Emperor Aurangzeb, and this inevitably meant that serious trouble was to ensue. Kidd divided the booty with his men at sea, calling 'every man by the list, and they came with their hats in their hands, and he gave them their money, and they swept it up, and went away'.[18] He then sailed with the prize to Saint Mary's, where he ditched the leaking *Adventure Galley*, and fraternised and drank toasts with the pirates he had been commissioned to catch.

It would have been better for him had he stayed there, as most of his crew did, but Kidd's decisions seem to have been always unwise and he set off in the *Quedah Merchant* with the remaining twenty or so of his crew for America, making his landfall in Anguilla early in April 1699. He then abandoned the suspiciously oriental-looking ship at the island of Mona, purchased a sloop and sailed to Boston where he hoped the governor, who was one of his original backers, would overlook his misuse of his commission. This was a serious misjudgement as government attitudes towards piracy had hardened in his absence, not least because of his own exploits, and Kidd was to be a convenient scapegoat who would receive no favours. He was arrested and sent to London where he was eventually tried in May 1701 on the double charge of piracy and the murder of his gunner William Moore whom he had smashed over the head with a wooden bucket in a fit of rage. Kidd tried his best to defend himself, but the result was inevitable, for the trial was not just a showpiece in the government's new anti-piracy policy, but a means of shaming the great men who had originally backed Kidd and had now fallen from power. He was hanged at Wapping on 23 May 1701, the victim of his own stupidity and puffed-up ambition and not one of the greatest of pirates.[19]

The depredations of first Avery and then Kidd had serious implications for the East India Company who, since the mid 1680s, had suffered from the assumption commonly held in India that all pirates were English and that the company was probably hand in glove with them.[20] So the outrageous pirate attacks on ships belonging to the great and the good of the Mughal imperial court were bound to lead to imperial rage and blame and hardship for the servants of the company. When the shattered *Gunsway* limped back into Surat, the news of the appalling treatment suffered by her pilgrim passengers inflamed the mob, who rose up and attacked the English factory (i.e., trading settlement) where the company's employees lived in great splendour and opulence.[21] Their lives were saved by soldiers under the orders of the governor of the city, but they were confined to their factory as prisoners as the Governor of Bombay reported to the King in November 1695. 'The English President at Surat and all other my masters' servants there are all barbarously and inhumanely chained up in irons, close prisoners.'[22] There they were to remain 'chained together like a company of doggs' until their release was eventually negotiated in return for bribes, payments of compensation and an agreement to send two of their ships each year to convoy the pilgrim fleet. This convoying they were to do efficiently, so making the pilgrim voyages safe and forcing the pirates to seek their prey elsewhere in the Indian Ocean.

Much the same was to happen two years later after Kidd's capture of the *Quedah Merchant*. The English at Surat were locked up again, their trade at a standstill, and more bribes, compensations and promises of convoy had to be made. The whole business was made worse by their Dutch and French competitors who blackened the English name at the imperial court and even more so by the officers of the New East India Company, a rival English company which was established in 1698. Their leader in India, Sir Nicholas Waite, has been described by a historian as 'one of the most unprincipled and vindictive mandarins ever to strut upon the Anglo-Indian scene', and he certainly did everything he could to prolong the suffering of his competitors by branding them as the protectors of pirates. 'One would have thought it almost impossible that an Englishman . . . could prove such a monster,' wrote an official of the Old Company.'[23]

Letters describing the harsh treatment of the English in Surat were sent home to the company's headquarters and to the government in London and were added to the already large files on the Indian Ocean pirate business. English trade and honour were clearly at risk and something had to be done. The debate on policy which ensued was hampered by the grossly exaggerated idea held in

London of the strength of the pirates. Thus, in November 1697, the captain of HMS *Windsor* forwarded information he had received from the master of a vessel which had recently been at St Mary's. 'Here they have built a regular fortification of forty or fifty guns. They have 1500 men, with seventeen sail of vessels, sloops and ships, some of which carry forty guns.' This made the pirates sound formidable indeed, but it was nonsense. Another deponent who had been at the island at about the same time said that there were 'no fortifications at St. Mary's' and only about a hundred English, French and Dutch living there. And a Dutchman who visited the island in the summer of 1699 reported to his masters in Cape Town that 'there is no fort on the island but about 45 or 50 guns lies scattered about on the ground. In this harbour lie various wrecks of pirate ships and of the Moorish prizes captured by them.'[24] Perhaps it is only natural that a government, presented with such conflicting information, should believe the worst, though in fact the problem was not quite so desperate as it appeared. After 1695, the most pirate-infested year, there were seldom more than six pirate ships operating in the Indian Ocean and some six or seven hundred men in their crews or enjoying themselves somewhere ashore, but these men made a great noise in the world.[25]

The government made unprecedented efforts to quell the activities of the Red Sea men. Commissions to capture pirates were given to the captains of East Indiamen and, although they did not take any pirate ships, they did manage to arrest several pirates trying to make their passage home to America, as did Royal Navy ships cruising in American waters. This passage was also made more difficult by the removal of some of the more corrupt officials in the colonies, such as Governor Fletcher of New York and Governor Trott in the Bahamas, and their replacement by men prepared to be hostile to pirates. There were now far fewer doors open for pirates wishing to retire to America and their return was made even more difficult from 1698 onwards as the result of the capture by East Indiamen and the pirates themselves of three of the four slaving ships dispatched from New York to Madagascar in that year, a disaster which naturally discouraged the slavers from sending any more.

Almost inevitably, the government also played the pardon card for all pirates who surrendered, though this option was spoiled, as so often before, by a very legalistic interpretation of the terms which required surrender to just four named commissioners. These officials were not readily accessible to all the pirates and when some, genuinely seeking pardon, surrendered to the Governor of New Jersey who was not named in the commission, they were later arrested and most of them hanged, such a dirty trick understandably resulting in a distrust of pardon by all pirates. The government's final response to the challenge of the Red Sea men was to show the flag in the East, by sending a squadron of four naval vessels under the command of Commodore Thomas Warren, who was replaced, after his death in India, by Commodore James Littleton. This squadron sailed early in 1699 with very specific instructions to destroy the pirate community and its fort in St Mary's and to 'clear the seas of pirates by an utter extirpation of them, unless they immediately surrender . . . when they shall receive pardon'.[26]

But, alas, something seemed to happen to naval commanders in the balmy waters of the Indian Ocean and they did none of these things, as Captain Richard White of HMS *Hastings* reported from Swally Hole near Surat in March 1700. The campaign has been 'soe much unfortunate', he wrote, 'as not to have accomplist any part of the designe sent for, which indeed must be imputed in a great measure to the mispending our time and loytering away in port'. His judgement was confirmed a couple of months later in a letter from Bombay, though this writer believed that, despite the navy's negligence and preference for private trade over duty, the very presence of royal ships in the Indian Ocean had had the desired effect. 'The men of warr sent out to suppress them have not taken one right step to effect what they were designed for, though it's our opinion that the very noise of their being come out hath kept this coast clear ever since last rains.' The devastations of the Red Sea men seemed indeed to be at an end, much to the relief of the beleaguered English officials in Surat. 'We have great hopes ye knott of pyrates is now pretty well broken.'[27]

The knot had not quite been broken, however, and there was

to be European piracy in the Indian Ocean for several more years, fresh blood being introduced in 1706 with the arrival of John Halsey in the *Charles* from Massachusetts, the first American privateer to take the Red Sea route to piracy since the 1690s. But, for most pirates, these early years of the eighteenth century were a time for retirement rather than fresh plunder. For those who had not taken the opportunity of a passage to America or the West Indies, there was the chance of pardon and a welcome refuge in islands such as Réunion and Mauritius which the French were just beginning to develop as colonies. Some remained at St Mary's or other places in Madagascar where many intermarried with the local women, a number founding petty dynasties which would remember for generations to come their white pirate ancestors. For the remainder, old age and tropical disease took their toll and, after a few years, there were hardly enough pirates left to fill a ship at St Mary's and the other settlements on the coast of the main island which had been so busy in the 1690s. When the famous privateer and circum-navigator Woodes Rogers called in at Cape Town in 1711, he was told that the pirates at Madagascar were 'now reduced to sixty or seventy, were very poor, and despised even by the natives from among whom they had taken wives'. And in 1719 there were said to be only seventeen left. The pirate community of Madagascar seemed to be completely moribund when suddenly, in 1720, the whole business sprang into life again.[28]

This revival was a product of the next great boom in piracy which had been ravaging America, the West Indies and Africa since 1715. Four or possibly five of the largest and boldest of the pirate ships with several hundred men in their crews made the passage round the Cape of Good Hope and once again used St Mary's as a base. And once again there were slavers there to trade with them.[29] These pirates, like their predecessors, took some excellent prizes, though most of these were European rather than Moorish ships. Two pirates in consort, Edward England in the *Fancy* and Olivier La Buse ('the buzzard') in the *Victory*, captured the English East Indiaman *Cassandra* after a savage battle at the island of Johanna in August 1720, while, in April of the following year, the *Cassandra*, now converted to a pirate warship under the command of John Taylor, and La Buse in the *Victory* took the *Nostra Senhora de Cabo*, a Portuguese East Indiaman which was lying disabled by a storm at the island of Réunion with her passengers and crew ashore.[30]

This turned out to be one of the richest prizes in pirate history, since she was carrying a fortune in diamonds as well as other very valuable cargo. She was also carrying the Count of Ericeira, returning home after service as the Viceroy of Portuguese India. The story goes that the governor of the island invited La Buse and the viceroy to dine with him. 'How much are you asking for the Viceroy's ransom?' asked the governor. 'A thousand piastres will do,' the pirate replied. 'That's too little for a brave man like you and for a great lord like him. Ask for a lot or for nothing.' 'Hé bien! Let him go free,' said the generous corsair.[31]

News of this fresh incursion into the Indian Ocean reached London from India and once again it was decided to send a naval squadron to cleanse the eastern seas, this time under Commodore Thomas Matthews. This expedition was, if anything, even more incompetently managed than that under Commodores Warren and Littleton in 1699–1701. No pirates were captured as the squadron sailed up 'the wrong side of Madagascar, for the pyratts their being on the east side and we came on the west', as one of the naval captains reported home in a long letter criticising his commodore. Matthews himself was court-martialled for using his ship for private trading, an old fault of the Royal Navy, while HMS *Exeter* was described in an anonymous letter by one of her seamen as 'one of the most noble punch houses in the sea', so continuously drunk was her crew.[32] But incompetence did not seem to matter in the Indian Ocean. On hearing the news of the arrival of the naval squadron, the pirates decided to disperse. Rejecting an astonishing offer by Peter the Great of Russia for asylum at Archangel on payment of two million crowns, they headed for warmer climes. Many of the French pirates took up an offer of amnesty at Réunion, while Taylor in the *Cassandra* sailed for the West Indies where he managed to negotiate a pardon for himself and his men from the Spanish Governor of Porto Bello after threatening to kill every man, woman and child in the town. The price of their pardon was said to have been 121 barrels of gold and silver coins, but the pirates kept the diamonds.[33]

These American and European pirates of the Indian Ocean were similar in organisation and customs to the buccaneers, hardly surprisingly since most of them were either drawn from the buccaneer community or were former privateersmen who gloried in the 'Jamaica discipline'. They generally elected their officers and made collective decisions by majority vote, one ship in South Africa being immediately identified as a pirate in 1697, 'as the men had as much to say as the captain', a state of affairs which would have been unthinkable in a merchantman or a naval vessel.[34] They were clearly fine seamen and navigators to have made the voyages they did and they also knew exactly what to do and where to go when they arrived in the East, being well aware of the wind systems and trading patterns in the Indian Ocean. They were in fact 'a pack of intelligent rogues' as an officer of the East India Company described them.[35] They also shared the ship-altering skills so characteristic of those buccaneers who ventured into the Pacific. In May 1695, some East Indiamen tried to chase Henry Avery's ship the *Fancy* off the island of Johanna, 'but he was too nimble for them by much, having taken down a great deale of his upper work and made her exceeding snug, which advantage being added to her well sailing before causes her to saile so hard that she fears not who follows her'.[36]

Red Sea men employed the customary cruelties to extract information from their prisoners and many an Indian captain and purser suffered at their hands, before inevitably showing them where the treasure was hidden. Such practices are as old as piracy and can perhaps be condoned as a necessary feature of the trade. But, otherwise, these pirates of the Indian Ocean do not seem to have been particularly brutal or indeed racist and it is rare to come across examples of gratuitous violence. They were businesslike pirates, not psychopaths as some of their successors were to be, and they had little fear of being pursued and caught, so that they never seem to have indulged in the mass slaughter that ensured that dead men tell no tales. Their worst excesses seem to have been caused by lust rather than greed or hate, if one can believe the stories about the treatment by Avery's men of the women on the *Gunsway*, noblewomen and slave girls alike. There were unpleasant incidents, too, on some of the islands which they visited in order to careen and clean their ships, a time of extremely hard work and danger in pirate life whose completion was nearly always celebrated with excessive drinking and carousal. Worst hit were the Laccadive Islands, a convenient place to careen, water, provision and party off the south-west coast of India. Here, as was reported by a ship's captain in 1697, Kidd's 'gang had ravisht the women, and murthered men, women and children' and much the same was to happen a quarter of a century later when Taylor's men visited the island.[37] But, back at their base at St Mary's, the pirates treated the native population with friendship, as good policy and their own rules required, and there was no need to ravish the local women who were quite happy to cohabit with such free-spending and generous men.

'Every man should share alike, only he would have two shares' were the words imputed to Henry Avery as he called on the men of the *Charles* to join him in his mutiny.[38] Such egalitarianism was the norm among the buccaneers, as has been seen, and most of the Red Sea men at least paid lip-service to it. But whether equal shares were in fact paid out is less certain. 'What might the shares be?' asked Mr Justice Turton of Philip Middleton at the trial of some of Avery's men. 'Some £1,000, some £600, some £500, and some less, according as the Company thought they deserved' was the reply. Middleton himself claimed to have received £100 which 'was a good share for a boy', though it was later stolen from him by another pirate.[39]

Equal shares or not, these are very large sums of money in a world where, even in wartime when wages were always much higher, an English sailor rarely earned more than two and a half pounds a month, and it was the value of their prizes which most attracted the attention of contemporaries who, in a mixture of jealousy and amazement, described the pirates as 'flush afore and aft with dollars (I mean from cook to captain)'.[40] Figures for share-outs were regularly quoted in colonial and East India Company correspondence and these were nearly always several hundred pounds a head and sometimes in excess of £1,000. One might think that such reports were exaggerated and they probably were, though several pirates were actually captured with this sort of money in their possession. In 1699, for instance, the captain of an East Indiaman arrested twenty-eight pirates who were trying to make their passage home aboard a slaver. Two of these had over £1,000 on them and their average loot was just under £400.[41] Three years earlier, John Dann, one of Avery's men, had the misfortune to be arrested at Rochester, 'a maid having found my gold quilted up in my jacket'. The exotic coins were carefully counted and weighed and were valued at £1,045 in sequins and ten English guineas.[42]

These are huge sums compared with the normal take of pirates in the Caribbean and Atlantic who would be lucky to come away with £10 or £20 after most of their cruises. Even the greatest coups in buccaneer history are hardly in the same league. The four hundred or so men who joined Morgan in looting and ransoming Portobello in 1668, his most profitable venture, shared just over £150 a head, while the men who took part in the great buccaneer raid on Vera Cruz in 1683 got about £160.[43] It is no wonder then that buccaneers and privateersmen rushed to the Red Sea in the 1690s. These marauders in the Indian Ocean were 'the most successful criminals in history', according to their most recent historian who attempts to put a modern value on their booty by first multiplying their reported take by a hundred to convert into modern pounds sterling and then by five to convert into modern American dollars. This calculation produces a dramatic figure of 'more than $400 million' for the ship carrying the Count of Ericeira taken by Taylor and 'at least $200 million' for the two ships taken by Henry Avery from the pilgrim fleet.[44] Such adjustments of historical value are fraught with difficulties, but most historians would be prepared to accept the proposition that sterling values of the 1690s should be multiplied by at least one hundred to give some idea of their value today. Whatever the exact value of their prizes, there seems little doubt that the most successful of the Red Sea men were indeed the most successful pirates in history, though it is possible that some land-based criminals have exceeded even their bonanza.

The other aspect of the Red Sea story which intrigued contemporaries as much as it does the modern student was the strange community, almost a pirate republic, which was established at St Mary's. This had a shifting population, the fairly small numbers of pirates who had settled there permanently, resting between voyages or waiting for a passage home, being increased dramatically when one or more of the pirate ships came in from a cruise. The settlement has acquired a mythological reputation as a model of liberty and democracy, based on a book published in 1726. This was the fourth edition of *The General History of the Pirates* by Captain Charles Johnson (believed by some to be a pseudonym for Daniel Defoe), a collection of descriptions of the careers of pirates. The first and second editions published in 1724 are concerned almost entirely with pirates who flourished in the years immediately before publication and, despite much exaggeration and invention of dialogue, research in Admiralty and colonial correspondence shows that these accounts are remarkably accurate, so much so that it is clear that the author must have had access to official papers, as well as conducting interviews with people who knew the pirates. The fourth edition of 1726 was considerably expanded by the inclusion of accounts of several of the Indian Ocean pirates, but these are much less reliable and have in fact not been used for this chapter.[45]

Some of the accounts are clearly fictional and these include the story of Captain Misson, an anti-clerical and anti-monarchical French pirate who is far too good to be true. He is brave, kind to his prisoners, disgusted by the blasphemy and drinking of other pirates and passionately opposed to slavery. He had not 'asserted his own liberty to enslave others'. He founds a utopian pirate settlement in Madagascar at a place he names Libertalia, the home of the free, and its government is based on equal ownership of treasure and cattle and a perfect form of democracy led by a governor who is elected for only three months at a time. The language and the sentiments are very high-flown and quite different from those in most of Captain Johnson's other accounts, so that it seems probable that it is by another hand. Johnson claimed to have translated the story of Captain Misson from the French and this may well be true, since it seems to belong to a genre of imaginary travel books which were popular in France in the years around 1700. These were distinguished by their geographical realism and were used to make ironic comparisons of an ideal society in some exotic and usually imaginary place with the decadent and priest-ridden society at home. The irony that a society of pirates could be so superior in so many ways to society in the France of the *ancien régime* would have appealed to an author working in this genre.[46]

Historians of piracy are well aware that Captain Misson is fictional and that Libertalia never existed, but many tend to be radically minded or romantic writers who would like their pirates to be as Captain Misson's were.[47] But, alas, there is little or no evidence that this was the case. All that can be said is that the real pirate settlement in Madagascar appears to have been well organised and harmonious and the men free from the restraints of American or European society. When there were fights, they were fights with rules, duels to the death similar to those fought by the logwood-cutters in Central America. Sometimes fights could be on a bigger scale, but still according to rules, as we learn from a deposition made in 1698. The deponent said that, shortly before his arrival in Madagascar, fourteen pirates 'by consent divided themselves into sevens to fight for what they had (thinking they had not made a voyage sufficient for so many), one of the said sevens being all killed and five of the other, so that the two which survived enjoyed the whole booty.'[48] Otherwise, life in this exotic pirate settlement appears to have been pleasant enough with, sad to say, slaves to wait on the freedom-loving pirates, plenty of women, locally produced beef and rice to eat, and drink from the slavers' store or from the natives who fermented honey and sugar to produce a powerful form of mead called *toke*.[49] Endemic malaria probably made it too unhealthy a place to be a perfect earthly paradise, though it must have seemed so to the lawless men who lived there. Its existence certainly scared the authorities, who habitually exaggerated the numbers and power of the men at St Mary's, while fear that somewhere else might become another Madagascar became as potent as the dread of a second Algiers or Sallee.

# CHAPTER EIGHT

# War Against the Pirates

# War Against the Pirates

The squadrons dispatched to the Indian Ocean in the early eighteenth century were by no means the first naval ventures set in motion by the English government to combat piracy in waters far from home, and we will now go back a bit in time to examine the naval response to piracy on the other side of the Atlantic. Ever since the Treaty of Madrid had been signed by England and Spain in 1670, in which it was agreed that peace in Europe should in the future also mean peace in the West Indies, there had been a definitive change in the attitude of the English government towards piracy in American waters. No longer would this be openly (or even covertly) condoned. This change reflected a growing belief in mercantile and shipping circles that piratical imperialism had served its purpose and that it should henceforth be the duty of the government and the navy to eradicate piracy and so make the seas safe for trade and shipping. This belief grew stronger and stronger as the century continued and was held throughout Europe by the 1690s, though not in America where the charms of cheap pirated goods remained potent. Piracy which had once been an 'honourable crime' was now seen as a crime against the human race and pirates themselves were increasingly regarded as pests who should be treated as such. Pirates are 'a vermin in a commonweal and ought to be dangl'd up like polecats or weasels in a warren', wrote the Governor of Virginia in 1699, and this vermin metaphor was to become commonplace.[1] There was, however, to be a serious time lag between the acceptance of the policy that pirates should be eradicated and the actions necessary to carry out that policy effectively.

The problem was, as usual, mainly one of money, though lack of will and ignorance of how to suppress piracy were also contributory factors. It was obvious that the suppression of piracy required naval vessels whose very presence in pirate-infested waters might well have the desired effect. Charles II (1660–85) had a much larger navy than had been available to his predecessors as king, but he did not have enough money to greatly expand its size and most of the suitable vessels available were committed, as has been seen, to the campaigns against the corsairs of Barbary and Sallee. These seemed, quite rightly, to be a much more serious threat than the pirates in the West Indies, who only rarely attacked English shipping, and it was not until the Barbary campaigns were success-fully concluded in the early 1680s that really serious efforts were made against the pirates in American waters.

As a result, the naval force provided in the 1670s for the implementation of the Treaty of Madrid was derisory. Naval ships in this period were rated on a scale from one to six of which the three most powerful need not bother us, as they were usually laid up in peacetime and were never employed against pirates. The largest ships to be used in anti-piracy duty were fourth-rates, ships with at least forty guns and often more in the late seventeenth century, while most of the service was done by fifth-rates (usually thirty to forty guns) and sixth-rates (twenty to thirty guns), the number of guns for each rate tending to rise over time. There were also some smaller unrated vessels employed, such as sloops and ketches. The English government had at its disposal several of all these types of ship, but was not yet prepared to send many of them out to serve in Caribbean and American waters. Jamaica, which had had no naval presence at all for most of the 1660s, usually had just two fifth- or sixth-rate frigates in the 1670s, though the accidents of repairs, late arrival of replacements and penny-pinching on the part of the Admiralty meant that the governor could not always count on these two ships being actually available. Elsewhere, the provision was even less. Barbados had one ship from 1673 and the Leeward Islands a ketch from 1677. The North

American colonies had no naval protection at all, though the Newfoundland fisheries were defended and policed by two men of war.[2] This miniscule naval force could be and was supplemented by taking former privateer ships into royal service or by commissioning prizes or local trading sloops, but even with these auxiliaries there were far too few ships to patrol the thousands of miles of sea and the myriad coves and cays in which pirates might be hidden.

Matters were to improve considerably in the 1680s. Jamaica was now usually provided with four royal ships, supplemented by a number of sloops acquired by the governor and, from 1683, by a purpose-built galley with fifty oars whose very existence was said 'to awe all the rest of the rogues'.[3] The force in the Leeward Islands was increased to two fifth-rates normally based at Antigua and, for the first time, some defence was provided for the mainland colonies, one or two ketches for Virginia from 1684 and a ship in New England from 1685, these ships based in the North American colonies normally being known as 'station ships' since they were tied to a particular station under the overall control of colonial governors and could not roam at will. On the other side of the Atlantic, the ravages of the pirates in the Atlantic islands and West Africa led to the establishment of naval cruisers in that region as well. There were still nowhere near enough ships to do the job properly, but it was certainly an improvement on the position in the early 1670s.

Lack of ships was not the only problem faced by the navy. They had a huge area to patrol which, in the early years at least, they did not know nearly as well as the pirates did, a fact which enabled the latter to evade their naval pursuers with ease on most occasions. There was also the question of who exactly was a pirate or rather who was the sort of pirate the navy could chase without diplomatic repercussions. English traders in the Caribbean suffered repeatedly from the attention of Spanish coastguard vessels, some of which would seize any foreign vessel whether it was trading illegally or not. And some of these coastguards did not behave too kindly to their captives. Don Philip Fitz-Gerald, an Irishman in the service of Spain like many of his fellow countrymen, was a particular bugbear of the English. An English prisoner of the Spaniards was an eye witness when, in 1675, Fitz-Gerald sailed into Havana with a New England ship as prize, whose cargo consisted only of English colonial goods and was therefore not subject to seizure. 'He had five English tied ready to hang, two at the main-yard arms, two at the fore-yard arms, and one at the mizzen peak, and when he came near the More [Moro] Castle he caused them to be turned off, and they hanged till they were dead, and Fitz-Gerald and his company shot at them from the deck of the frigate.' In this case, the English authorities decided, not unreasonably, that Fitz-Gerald was a pirate and a proclamation was issued to that effect, offering a reward to whoever should bring in his head though nobody seems to have claimed it.[4] But the English could not treat all Spanish coastguard vessels as pirates, even if most of them had a piratical streak. Spain was now a friend of England, a country which was just as determined to enforce her own navigation laws, which reserved English and colonial trade mainly for her own subjects, as the Spaniards were to prevent clandestine trade with their colonies.

Even more of a problem was the fact that most of the really powerful 'pirates' were privateers sailing with a French commission. The Governor of Jamaica wrote home in 1682 asking whether he should order the navy to attack such ships, an order he was hesitant to give. 'I do not them so much fear as offending our lords, and bringing the power of France against this island.'[5] The answer to such a question was usually no, since England could not afford to offend Louis XIV, the most powerful monarch of the day, with the result that a complete elimination of the privateers/pirates was simply not possible until the French government changed its policy in 1684 and ordered its governors to cease to issue commissions to privateers.

Such diplomatic problems (and there were others) limited the number of targets available to the English naval forces in the Caribbean. But catching pirates was even harder than identifying those whom it was legitimate to try to catch. English naval officers' knowledge of the navigation of the Caribbean naturally improved over time, but it was never to be as good as that of the pirates. Nor did the navy ever provide the right mix of ships for the job, despite the experience gained in the campaigns against the Barbary corsairs. Naval vessels were nearly always slower than their pirate enemies, 'hee run two foot for my one', as one naval logbook bemoaned, and this lack of speed was aggravated by the naval failure to careen and clean the hulls of their ships as often as the pirates did. He 'rann us out of sight, our ship being growne soe foule [with weed, barnacles, etc.] shee would doe nothing'.[6] The navy's ships also drew too much water to follow pirates into shoal waters or 'into distant and secure creeks and holes'. They were also only rarely equipped with oars, despite their experience in the Mediterranean and against the Sallee rovers. HMS *Guernsey*, for instance, had the good fortune to surprise the notorious pirate ship *La Trompeuse* (Deceiver) at anchor at Isla Vaca, a pirate haunt on the south coast of Hispaniola, 'but, it being calm, could not get near him for want of oars' and later, 'the gale rising, the pirate sailed three feet to his one', as her captain explained in a letter to the Governor of Jamaica.[7] Similar complaints were to come from naval captains into the 1720s, but the navy never did get the right mix of a few powerful ships to overawe the really strong pirates and large numbers of small, fast and light-draft frigates and sloops equipped with oars to catch the rest.

There were also problems of focus and commitment, which undermined the navy's war against the pirates. The governors had many other uses for the naval vessels at their disposal apart from pirate hunting, such as courtesy visits to Spanish ports which might be fun for the captains and crews if they were entertained with 'musicke, dancing and bull baiting' as William Beeston was at Trinidad de Cuba in December 1671. Such visits were also used to try to negotiate the release of the many English prisoners held by the Spaniards, sometimes with success as when Captain Tosier of the *Hunter* managed to free forty-six English captives in Havana in 1679. 'At which newes they sett up a shout and gave his Majesty's ship Hunter ye name of the Blessing of England.' Back in Port Royal, they were welcomed ashore by 'theire friends with great joy and multitudes of people all along ye shore'.[8]

Governors, merchants and naval captains were also more interested in making money out of the Spaniards than in the unrewarding business of catching pirates, many of whom were reputed to have so little loot that it was impossible to get volunteers to man sloops to chase them on a basis of 'No Purchase, No Pay', the well-worn contract by which sailors agreed to serve without wages for a share of the prizes taken. The Spaniards, by contrast, had plenty of money and much naval time was spent relieving them of some of it, by convoying their ships, carrying their bullion, and by delivering cargoes, especially of slaves, to their ports. Such cruises earned good profits, but caught no pirates. Worse still was the situation in the late 1680s, when virtually all the royal ships stationed in Jamaica were engaged in guarding salvage vessels working on a Spanish wreck off the north of Hispaniola, a treasure-hunting expedition in which the recently arrived Governor of Jamaica, the Duke of Albemarle, had a major investment.[9]

The Royal Navy captains as well as the governors had their private agenda. Many feared a West Indian posting, for service in these pestilential waters was rightly seen as a potential death warrant and many of the captains engaged in the war against the pirates did indeed die of disease, as did many of the royal sailors and pirates. It was, however, also seen as a potentially profitable posting with numerous opportunities for illegal convoy fees, freight for carrying bullion for the merchants or outrageous fares for carrying passengers. Such perquisites could almost be condoned, so common were they, but ships of the Royal Navy were also carrying cargoes for their captains and for the merchants, a totally illegal activity which was exposed for all to see when the overloaded HMS *Norwich* ran aground and wrecked near Port Royal in 1682 with a large cargo of merchants' goods, much of it indigo which was only too visible as it stained the sea.[10] Her captain, Peter Heywood, wisely decided to stay in Jamaica rather than go home to face the music, and his loss of one of His Majesty's ships was conveniently forgotten when he became a wealthy planter, so much so that he was later to be appointed governor of the island. The Admiralty naturally strongly objected to these abuses by its captains, whose lust for gain often diverted them from their duty, and in July 1686 general orders were issued on the subject, which incidentally show just what naval captains were supposed to be doing. 'Our service [is] in a most speciall manner exposed from the liberty taken by commanders of our ships (upon all opportunities of private profit) of converting the service of our said ships to their owne use, to the total neglect of the publick ends for which they at our great charge are set forth and maintained, namely, the annoying of our enemies, the protecting the estates of our trading subjects and the support of our honour with forreigne princes.'[11]

Given all the problems and temptations they faced, the Royal Navy captains did quite a good job in this first phase of the war against the pirates, as far as can be told from the few surviving logbooks. They regularly went out on cruises searching for pirates, mainly around Jamaica itself, along the south coasts of Cuba and Hispaniola and in the islands and along the coasts of the Gulfs of Honduras and Campeche, all well known as pirate haunts. Over time, their knowledge of these areas improved and they were able to build up information networks among turtlers, fishermen, trading sloop captains and the few scattered inhabitants of the coasts and islands where the pirates lurked. Such information would include news of the latest known whereabouts of pirates, which could be interpreted by reference to an accumulated knowledge bank of pirate customs and behaviour. In August 1681, for instance, Captain Heywood in the *Norwich* was hunting for a pirate who was reported by a sloop master to be heading for Grand Cayman in order to careen. This was excellent news as pirate vessels were at their most vulnerable when on the careen, since they had all their guns and stores unloaded and were hauled down on one side and so unable to move. By this date Heywood knew all the places in the Caymans where 'pirats usually carine' and he set off in high hope. However, he was to have no luck. 'Finding noe footsteps of them, I by noon gitt on board and ply to windward for Jamaica.'[12] Such failures were the norm in pirate hunting, but for all that the naval commanders had their successes and several pirates and privateers were brought in, usually after following up a tip as to their whereabouts.

In January 1681, Heywood was in Port Royal when he was ordered to man a sloop to go after 'some pirats that are on ye coast'.

The sloop was back the next day with a small pirate sloop as prize and twenty-five prisoners. In the next month, another sloop manned by thirty-six men from the navy and twenty-four soldiers went out after the Dutch pirate Jacob Evertsen who was boarded and captured in Bull Bay. Several of the pirates were killed or wounded in the fight, others jumped overboard and were shot in the sea, while '26 stout men' were brought in. Evertsen's sloop was taken into royal service as a consort for the *Norwich*. Her small draught would enable her to 'sound the dangerous places and [she] is able to pursue pirates where the frigates cannot go'.[13]

One of the most successful cruises was the very first in this long war in which Major William Beeston, 'a gentleman of good estates, parts and conduct', commanded the frigate HMS *Assistance*. Sailing as his consort in the *Lilly* was John Morris, one of Henry Morgan's leading privateer captains, who had been pardoned and taken into royal service, 'a very stout fellow and good pilot, and will not turn pirate'.[14] They set sail from Port Royal in January 1672 for a cruise which was to combine a courtesy visit to Havana with a search for 'stragling privateers'. Beeston's journal betrays his ignorance of waters which would soon become only too familiar to English naval commanders, but he was helped considerably by the presence of Morris who was not only a 'good pilot' but also 'well acquainted with those people and theire customes'.[15]

In his six-week cruise Beeston captured two of these 'stragglers' and, in doing so, showed a determination and resolution which few later pirate chasers would emulate. The pirate sloop *Charity* commanded by Francis Weatherbourn 'being newly cleaned and tallowed, outwent us all', but this did not dismay Beeston. He manned and lowered the pinnace, which 'rowing stoutly (notwithstanding shee rowed allso) caught up', but this success was to end in farce. The officer commanding the pinnace had forgotten to bring the King's colours and so could not order the *Charity* to surrender in the King's name. Nothing daunted, Beeston manned another boat with a fresh crew (and the colours) and these caught up with the *Charity* once again and captured her with twenty-one men aboard. The prisoners betrayed the whereabouts of the *Mary*, another pirate vessel commanded by Captain Du Mangles. She was careening at a cay 'where it was so shoale [shallow] that none but canoes and very small vessells could come at him, he having left his ballast at another cay'. Once again Beeston did not give up. He sent Morris in the shallow-draught *Lilly* and the *Charity* prize after her and they brought the *Mary* in together with twenty-two more prisoners. Back in Port Royal, a council of war was held aboard the *Assistance*, attended by the governor and his officers and the commanders of the ships that were in the harbour. 'They condemned Capt. Francis Weatherbourn and Capt. Du Mangles to be shot to death, for their pyracys in taking Spaniards without commission,' executions which were not in fact carried out for fear of a violent reaction by the local population, many of whom were very much in favour of pirates. These might be small fry, but for all that Beeston should be congratulated. Only one other Royal Navy ship in these years of war against the pirates between the 1670s and the 1720s was to capture two pirate vessels in a single cruise.[16]

Some pirates were far from small fry. The main target in 1683 was the thirty-two-gun *Trompeuse* which was hunted in vain by Captain Tennant of the *Guernsey* among others. She was a former French royal frigate commanded by the French pirate Jean Hamlin, a man who made no pretence to be a privateer and told people bluntly that 'he was a pirate'. After a successful cruise in the Caribbean, he had sailed via the Danish pirate haven of St Thomas for Sierra Leone, from where he rampaged down the West African coast, flying 'the King's Jack and pendant like an English man-of-war', by which stratagem he captured many slavers, some of which had gold as well as men and women slaves in their cargo, as was later deposed by one of his released prisoners. The pirates then landed and shared out the gold taken on the voyage, a process which led to a quarrel and the division of the pirates into two parties, a common occurrence on pirate ships. Those who remained with the *Trompeuse* sailed back to Dominica and then, on 27 July 1683, into the harbour of St Thomas, whose merchants eagerly bought up their prize goods.[17]

This news came to the ears of Captain Carlyle, commander of HMS *Francis* on the Leewards Islands station. On the night of 30 July, with outrageous insolence, he sailed into St Thomas, set fire to *Trompeuse* and another privateer lying alongside her, and then sailed out again. This incident naturally brought about serious diplomatic repercussions, not only from the Danes who ruled the island but also from the French who objected to the burning of a royal ship even if she had turned pirate. The English, however, were jubilant and no one more so than Sir William Stapleton, Governor of the Leeward Islands, who praised Carlyle as 'a brave, discreet young commander', though discretion would seem to have been the least of his qualities. 'This is the ship,' thundered Sir William, 'that took seventeen ships on the coast of Guinea and killed and tortured many English subjects, yet she is protected by the Government of St Thomas, which is worse than the pirates themselves. It harbours them, mans them and victuals them' and, no surprise, is the worst 'receptacle' of pirates 'this side of Sallee and Algiers'.[18] Carlyle's action destroyed the ship, but not the men who escaped ashore and were soon ravaging the seas again in another ship which they called *La Nouvelle Trompeuse*, 'a privateer of the first magnitude, famous in bloodshed and robberies'. She was finally seized in September 1684 with 198 men on board in Boston, a city whose merchants were reputed to have financed her and bought up her booty.[19]

The middle years of the 1680s were dominated for the Jamaica squadron by the saga of Joseph Bannister who in June 1684 ran away with the thirty-gun *Golden Fleece* from Port Royal harbour, picked up a crew 'of the veriest rogues in these Indies' and set off on the piratical account. Little more than a month later he was trapped in the Cayman Islands by Captain Mitchell in the powerful *Ruby*, the best sailer in the Jamaica squadron.[20] The *Ruby*'s guns soon persuaded Bannister to surrender and he and his men were brought back to Jamaica for trial, 'but by corruption of evidence and mismanagement, the Grand Jury threw out the bill'. The Governor of Jamaica would not accept this decision and, determined to try him again with a new jury, had him rearrested. Bannister languished in custody till January 1685 when the resourceful pirate escaped on a dark night through the 'carelessness of the sentries' and set out to sea in his old ship with fifty men, a crew which he was soon able to increase.[21]

The hunt was on again, though this time it was to be a much longer one, and it was nearly eighteen months later that Bannister was cornered by the royal ships *Drake* and *Faulcon* at anchor at Samana in the north-east of Hispaniola. The pirate 'sounded a trumpett' and opened fire and the fight lasted from three in the afternoon of 12 June 1686 till the evening of the following day, by which time the two royal ships had lost twenty-three men killed and wounded and exhausted their powder and 'Bannister's ship was sunke at least two strakes, being as low as the ground would give leave', as the captain of the *Faulcon* recorded in his logbook. With no powder left, the royal ships reluctantly sailed away, leaving the pirate ship a wreck but the pirates themselves fit to fight another day.[22] Six months later, Bannister was finally captured on the Moskito coast by Captain Spragge of HMS *Drake* who, as the Governor of Jamaica related with glee, 'returned to Port Royal . . . with Capt. Bannister and three of his consorts hanging at his yard-arm, a spectacle of great satisfaction to all good people and of terror to the favourers of pirates, the manner of his punishment being that which will most discourage others'.[23]

The story of Bannister provides a good illustration of the determination of the navy once they had really set their minds on something. But it is also an illustration of the most serious problem faced by those whose duty it was to capture and punish pirates. Despite popular fantasy, fuelled by many novels and films, it was extremely unusual for an English naval captain to hang a captured pirate without trial at the yardarm and Spragge had only done so because he had specific orders to that effect, the governor having despaired of ever getting a guilty verdict before a Port Royal jury. Port Royal, indeed English Jamaica as a whole, had grown up and flourished on the profits of privateering and it is no surprise to find that there was a strong body of public opinion and many public officials who were not prepared to condemn to death a captured privateer or pirate. Governors, too, even if they were hostile to pirates which some were not, were fearful of the public consequences of taking matters into their own hands. As a result, very few of those captured by the navy in this period were actually executed.[24] Such attitudes were to change and had indeed already changed considerably by the 1680s. White Jamaicans would be prominent in privateering and piracy for several decades to come but, as trade and planting became the mainstays of the island's economy, opinion was turning against the pirates and later governors would have no scruples and no fears about condemning them to death.

Despite the failure of legal retribution to complete the job, the navy's campaign against the pirates in the 1670s and 1680s could be said to have been fairly successful, the best proof of this being the flight of the pirates from the waters the navy patrolled from 1680 onwards. There was very little naval presence in West African and North American waters and none except the rather ineffective Spanish South Sea squadron (Armada del Sur) in the Pacific, so it was to these regions that pirates went to ply their trade. Some of these were lured from the sea by general pardons offered by the Kings of France and England in the late 1680s, but the real end to this stage in the war against the pirates was signalled by the outbreak of a rather bigger war, the Nine Years or King William's War which embroiled all the great maritime powers from 1689 to 1697. Former pirate now fought former pirate as privateers in the service of England, France, Holland and Spain.

This great war, the most expensive ever fought, and the Glorious Revolution which brought in William III as King of England marked a fundamental change in attitudes of government, a change characterised by a mutual understanding between merchants and bureaucrats that they could make themselves and the nation rich. Henceforth, English governments would be committed to what has been called by one historian mercantile imperialism, 'a grand marine empire', in which trade, shipping and the empire itself would be promoted, protected and controlled for the benefit of merchants and government alike. The state would provide protection for trade and, in return, would receive a flow of revenue from increased wealth and customs duties and a pool of trained sailors to fight in its naval wars. There was to be no place for pirates in this new world, no place for individualist marauders on the periphery of empire. The state would have a monopoly of violence at sea, through its navy at all times and through privateers properly commissioned and policed in times of war. Pirates were to be destroyed, not just as enemies of mankind but as enemies of capitalism and commercial expansion, a nice turnaround from the position only a little earlier in English history when piracy had been condoned as a promoter of the expansion of trade.[25]

Policy is not practice, of course, and the pirates had a long innings ahead of them, but by the late 1720s these policies had been made effective. A very good start was made by the energetic and efficient Board of Trade, which was set up in 1696 to collect information about and propose improvements in colonial administration and the conduct of maritime trade. Among many other things, the Board turned its mind to the problem of the Red Sea men and the more general pirates who were to follow in their wake. There seemed to be three main areas in which improvements were needed and should be made. The most glaring problem was the support given by many colonial governors to the pirates and this was speedily addressed. Several governors, including the notorious Benjamin Fletcher of New York, were dismissed and replaced by governors prepared to act vigorously against the pirates, the most effective being the Earl of Bellomont, who was made Captain-General and Governor of New York, Massachusetts Bay and New Hampshire, and William Nicholson, the Governor of Virginia. The problem of dishonest officials was not solved at a stroke and the Carolinas, in particular, were to remain a haven for pirates for twenty years or so, but there were now far fewer havens in English America where pirates could fit their ships, sell their prizes and surreptitiously or openly slip ashore and become honest men. The colonists would still have liked to buy cheap pirated goods, but their governors increasingly would not let them do so.

A second problem related to the legal process by which captured pirates could be tried, condemned and executed in the colonies. Research by the Board of Trade and the officers of the High Court of Admiralty had shown that existing practices were flawed if not downright illegal. What was needed was a uniform law to be enforced throughout the empire by which specially appointed courts consisting of government officials and naval officers could try pirates, with no fear that clear cases would be dismissed by the favourers or admirers of pirates acting as jurors. Sir Charles Hedges, judge of the High Court of Admiralty, agreed to draft such a law and on 1 April 1700 it came into force.[26] From now on, a seven-person court of officials or naval officers could assemble anywhere to try pirates and hundreds were to experience the rigours of this new and effective law. All it really needed was for two of a pirate crew to be prepared to give King's evidence in return for a promise of pardon, for all the rest of the crew to be found guilty. Some were able to gain acquittal on the grounds that they had been forced to serve on the pirate ship; many were pardoned because of their youth and inexperience or some other whim of the court; but an awful lot of pirates were to be condemned and executed. 'And though it may be thought by some a pretty severe thing, to put an Englishman to death without a jury . . . the wisdom and justice of our nation, for very sufficient and excellent reasons, have so ordered it in the case of piracy.' Most men holding office in the colonies in the early eighteenth century would have agreed with the Attorney-General of Massachusetts that such an apparently severe law was wise and just, though there were still some with nostalgia for the good old days who felt it 'very harsh to hang people that brings in gold to these provinces', as one American official grumbled after the hanging of the first pirate to be convicted under the new law.[27]

The third strand in the policies adopted in the late 1690s was a commitment to a naval presence in colonial waters in peacetime, a policy keenly supported by the navy who naturally wanted to keep as many of their ships and men in pay as possible. Such a policy had been more or less established in the 1680s but, from now on, there was to be no backsliding and ships were to be permanently stationed in both North America and the West Indies whose specific duty was to protect trade from pirates. Lack of government funds and a natural tendency to parsimony in the Admiralty meant that there were never as many ships as colonial governors, merchants or indeed naval officers would have liked, but ships there always were and pirates could no longer hope to roam the seas with complete impunity. It was to be a long time before this naval presence was to make the waters of America as pirate-free as were those around Great Britain, but a start had been made.

It was a good thing that the Board of Trade and the Admiralty had piracy in their sights, for soon after the return of peace in 1697, there was an explosion of piracy on a scale never seen before. The Red Sea men were, of course, still plying their trade, but they were to be joined by a host of pirates of all nations who preyed on shipping throughout the trading world. The reports on this new menace began in June 1698 when letters from Jamaica informed the authorities at home that many former French privateers had turned pirate and were attacking the island's shipping. In August, there was news of pirates in the Cape Verde Islands and the following months saw a crescendo of reports from all over the place: a French pirate who had taken eight or nine ships near Philadelphia; pirates in Newfoundland, Tobago, the Bahamas and the Virgin Islands; 'ten pirate sail on the coast of Africa'; Virginia, Maryland and Carolina infested by pirates who had taken thirty vessels in three months; and, a little further south, a flock of Spanish pirates from Havana who were attacking shipping in the Gulf of Florida.[28] It was a time of suspicion and fear when even such a distinguished man as the astronomer Edmund Halley, in the course of a voyage of exploration, was fired at by merchant ships in the Cape Verde Islands who feared that HMS *Paramour Pink* was a pirate. They 'said they were sorry . . . that they had fired at the King's colours, but that colours were not to be trusted'.[29] And this was sadly only too true.

Most of these marauders were fairly small, with less than a hundred men in the crew, but there were some really dangerous sharks among them with twenty-five or thirty guns and crews of 150 men or more, such as the pirate ship *Alexander* which forced the *Essex Prize*, a royal ship half her size, to flee to safety after a four-hour fight in the waters of Virginia in August 1699. The naval captain described his pirate opponent in a letter to the Admiralty as 'a lusty rawboan'd well set man, very much poxbroken, and a great blemish in one of his eys, he speaks very broad, and a very slovenly fellow'. He was sometimes called John James and sometimes 'Kidd', a name which was attached rather indiscriminately to the pirates of this period.[30]

Faced with this new threat, the Admiralty set out more ships than ever before in peacetime, though naturally not as many as those complaining of the pirates would have liked. The Newfoundland fisheries were still protected by two men-of-war. New England now got one and sometimes two station ships, while New York had one. Virginia and Maryland each had a small vessel for the protection of their trade and these were later reinforced by a fifth-rate frigate. In the West Indies, there were normally two ships each stationed in Jamaica, the Leewards and Barbados, and these six ships were reinforced from late 1699 by a squadron of four vessels under the command of Admiral Benbow. Across the Atlantic, there were two ships cruising in West African waters to protect the slavers from attack and one or sometimes two cruising among the Cape Verde Islands, a colony of Portugal, off the coast of Africa. These islands were a particular haunt of the pirates who not only took prizes from among the ships which called there to pick up provisions, but also traded with sympathisers among the islanders and acquired recruits from discontented sailors in the fleet of ships which went each year to the Isle of May (Maio) to collect sea salt. And, finally, as has been seen, a squadron was operating in the Indian Ocean in the years 1699–1701.[31]

At its maximum, this made up a total of twenty-four royal ships, not counting those in Newfoundland, whose main and in some cases only service was the pursuit of pirates, a far cry from the two ships devoted to this purpose in the early 1670s. Most of the ships were fifth- and sixth-rate frigates, potentially fast ships with twenty to forty guns and from 100 to 150 men, which were roughly equal in strength to the more powerful pirate vessels of the day. There were also some much bigger two-decker fourth-rates with forty-two or more guns and nearly two hundred men, and a few much smaller vessels, such as the *Essex Prize* which was stationed in Maryland and had only ten guns and fifty-five men.[32] Ships of the Royal Navy were only fully manned in wartime and, since this anti-piracy campaign took place in peacetime, these vessels were only permitted their middle complement of men (about one-third less), a fact which outraged Governor Nicholson of Virginia who demanded that the ship on his station have its full complement, 'for that in these parts it is, in a manner, open war, the coasts being daily infested by pirates'.[33] But, even at middle complement, these twenty-four royal ships employed nearly 3,500 men, a huge force which in theory should have overwhelmed what the pirates had available, especially as French, Spanish, Dutch and Portuguese naval ships were also hunting pirates. Pirate numbers are difficult to count in this period, but it seems unlikely that they ever had much more than twenty ships at any one time and less than two thousand men. The Admiralty response to the pirate menace was therefore a massive one and it demonstrated the new determination to crush the pirates before success should swell their numbers even more and allow them to get completely out of hand.

Catching pirates, however, remained a difficult task and most of these naval vessels faced the same problems and had the same lack of success as their predecessors in the 1680s. Jedediah Barker in the *Speedwell* reported 'an abundance of pirates' in the Leeward Islands and the Virgins, 'but I have not had the good fortune to mete with any in my cruse'. Joseph Crowe had no better luck in the *Arundell*, the New England station ship. He cruised after some reported pirates for three weeks, but 'have mett nothing of those whome I went out to seek'. Henry Lumley of the *Ludlow* lay three weeks 'in a small hole' in Tobago to surprise some pirate sloops which were using the island as a base, 'but he did not see any'. Philip Boys in the *Germoon Prize* chased some Spanish pirates, but 'could not come up with none of them, being verey fowle', while the frustration of Peter Pickard of the *Saudadoes Prize* was made plain in his letter reporting his failure to capture two French pirates off Hispaniola. 'Its almost all together impossible to think of catching of them unless had sutch vessells as theirs are, vizt. sloopes and brigeentins, for they keep near shore and run amongst shoulds [shoals] that we darest not follow them without hazarding the shipp.'[34] Such problems and disappointments were inherent in the business of pirate hunting and it is a credit to the captains that they do not seem to have given up. They went out on their cruises, looked into coves and creeks and cays, followed up their inevitably out-of-date information and tried not to lose their ships in the process, not always successfully since seven Royal Navy ships were lost to shipwreck in this fairly brief campaign.[35] And even failure could be a sort of success, for the very fact that naval vessels were cruising in areas where pirates normally congregated was often sufficient to discourage them from doing so. However, the navy, though usually unsuccessful in catching pirates, was not always so.

The greatest triumph of this campaign occurred on 3 May 1700 in Linhaven Bay, Virginia, when Captain William Passenger in HMS *Shoreham* fought the French pirate ship *La Paix* commanded by Louis Guittar, a former privateer from St Malo. The two ships were fairly evenly matched, *La Paix* having twenty guns mounted (and eight more in the hold) and 150 or 160 fighting men and *Shoreham*, a fifth-rate frigate, should have had twenty-eight guns and 115 men, though she was in fact at the time 'very weakly manned, several of her men appearing raw and unskilful, and there being many boys among them'. Ten extra men were, however, to come aboard on the eve of the battle as reinforcements and these included Governor Nicholson, who was determined to see in person the destruction of the pirate who had been raiding his colony's trade.

The fight lasted twelve hours and the pirates fought bravely, but the issue was never in doubt, largely due, according to his admirers, to Governor Nicholson, 'by his example, conduct and plenty of gold which he gave among the men to make them fight bravely'. Nicholson's presence no doubt helped but, in fact, this action demonstrated that even with a numerical inferiority a naval vessel was always likely to defeat a pirate, as a result of its better discipline and rate and accuracy of fire. Captain Passenger was able to keep to windward of the pirate throughout the action, a station which enabled him to dictate the terms of the fight and keep his ship free of gunsmoke. From this position of advantage his men fired away '27 barrells of powder and 1,671 shot' which 'shot all his masts, yards, sailes, rigging all to shatters, unmounted severall guns and [his] hull almost beaten to pieces' before the pirate ship finally struck its colours. *La Paix* had twenty-six men killed and the rest taken prisoner, nearly half of whom were wounded. Those who survived were shipped back to London where, a few months after the battle, the French captain and twenty-three of his men were hanged on the same day, a stark reminder that the government and the navy now meant business in their pursuit of pirates. *Shoreham* had only four men killed and six wounded, two of whom later died. It was a great triumph and a brave fight, but it was really no contest and news of the battle and the legal retribution which followed it struck fear into the other pirates infesting the American coast.[36] One such battle was quite sufficient to drive them away and, a year after the fight, Captain Nevill of the *Lincoln*, the new ship on the Virginia station, was able to report 'no pyrates upon this coast since that the Shoreham took'.[37]

No other royal ship captured a pirate in battle during this campaign, but there were two actions in the Cape Verde Islands which were to have a severely deterrent impact on the pirates who had found a warm welcome in that part of the world. On 26 May 1698, Captain Robert Hollyman of HMS *Bedford Galley*, acting on a tip, sailed into the harbour of the Isle of May (Maio) where two ships with French colours lay at anchor, a fourteen-gun pirate ship, with a polyglot crew of 120 Frenchmen, Irishmen and Greeks, together with their prize. The pirate hid most of his men below and tried to persuade Hollyman that they were merely trading vessels but to no avail and, seeing that the game was up, he cut his cables and headed for sea, retaining on board several members of the naval search party. Hollyman chased the pirate vessel for hours, pouring in broadsides every time he closed with her. 'I fired so many shott into him, as tore him all to peeces, and tis to me a wonder how he swam.' Most of the pirate ship's officers were killed in the action and her decks were littered with corpses, but the survivors still tried to evade their pursuer, throwing everything they could overboard to lighten the ship. Night was to bring some relief for the surviving pirates, but not for long as their shattered ship could swim no more. She sank beneath the waves during the night and on the following days much wreckage and an 'abundance of dead men was drove a shoar'.[38]

This demonstration of naval firepower cleared the islands for a while, but in 1700 the pirates were back again and were to lead Captain John Cranby in HMS *Poole* a merry dance. The greatest excitement came in the early days of July when he chased for several days another French pirate, Emanuel Wynn, who had a crew of 150 men. Day followed day with Wynn, the better sailer, getting out of sight only to be caught up again by Cranby's accurate guesses at his intended route until, on 6 July, Wynn sailed into a cove on the island of Brava. This proved to be an excellent defensive position, as the cove had a very narrow entrance protected by rocks through which Cranby dared not attempt to sail. The water outside was too deep to anchor so he sailed back and forth, firing at and killing several pirates, some of whom had taken up positions on hills above the cove, but there was no way he could sail into the cove and take the ship.

In the end, he decided to sail to the neighbouring island of Fogo to ask the Portuguese governor for help. This was forthcoming and he quickly crossed the straits again and landed a hundred Portuguese soldiers on the other side of the island from where the pirates lay. Cranby then sailed back to protect the entrance to the cove, while he waited for the Portuguese to attack by land. This ingenious plan for a double offensive was, however, spoiled by Cranby's impatience at the failure of the soldiers to appear from the mountains behind the pirate cove. While he sailed round to see what was happening, Wynn took his chance and slipped out to sea at night, leaving about a quarter of his crew ashore to be slaughtered by the Portuguese when they belatedly stormed down from the mountains.[39]

Emanuel Wynn was clearly a resourceful and tenacious pirate, but his chief claim to fame in pirate annals is his flag, which was described by Cranby as 'a sable ensigne with cross bones, a death's head and an hour glass', the very first reference to this classic symbol of piracy. The buccaneers certainly flew flags, many different ones in fact, but none of them reflect the imagery of the imminence of death. They also flew the red flag, but there was nothing particularly piratical about this, the red flag being widely understood to mean that the ship flying it would 'give no quarter' (take no prisoners) in the ensuing battle. The Spaniards 'putt out their bloody flags and wee ours', wrote Basil Ringrose in his description of one of the buccaneer battles.[40]

The actions of Captains Passenger and Cranby in the summer of 1700 really marked the end of this phase in the war against the pirates who now felt that they had had quite enough attention from the Royal Navy. No pirates in the Cape Verde Islands, reported Captain Crowe of the *Mermaid* in April 1702. 'The last that was seen here was she Captain Cranby met with.' 'All things quiet,' wrote Captain Fleetwood Emes from West Africa. 'No account of any pirates on this coast,' came the news from Bombay. No pirates on the coasts of America, reported a letter from Boston, 'but there are several that belonged to pirate's ships who lye skulking up and down the country'.[41] Such men were encouraged to surrender by yet another general pardon issued in March 1701 which, allowing for the time lag needed for the news to reach straggling pirates, covered all offences committed up to 24 June 1701.[42] Some took it up, but most pirates were by now suspicious of pardons and the publicity that surrender would entail, since shipowners were understandably reluctant to employ men known to have been pirates. So most of those still at sea slipped ashore and waited in expectation of the renewal of the long war against France. They did not have long to wait. News of the outbreak of the war which would be known as the War of the Spanish Succession reached the West Indies in the summer of 1702 and the governors immediately began to commission privateers, eight in Jamaica, twelve in Bermuda.[43] The pirates became patriots again.

# CHAPTER NINE

# The Golden Age of Piracy

# The Golden Age of Piracy

'It is the opinion of every one this cursed trade [privateering] will breed so many pirates that, when peace comes, we shall be in more danger from them than we are now from the enemy.'[1] This observation of Edmund Dummer, the man who first developed a mail service to the West Indies, was shared by virtually everyone as the War of the Spanish Succession ground slowly to a halt. But, when peace finally did come in 1713, there was, in fact, no sudden escalation of piracy as there had been at the end of King William's War in 1697. Indeed, only in the waters of the Leeward Islands were there reports of any pirates at all and these were only small fry.[2]

In April 1714, there was a mildly disturbing report on the Bahamas written by the Governor of Bermuda. The islands had been raided repeatedly by the Spaniards and French during the war and Nassau, the main settlement in New Providence Island, had been 'three times plunder'd and lay'd in ashes'.[3] Most of the population had fled, leaving some 'two hundred families scattered up and down . . . who live without any face or form of government, every man doing onely what's right in his own eyes'.[4] And among these masterless men there were 'three setts of pirates' led by one Benjamin Hornigold, soon to be well known but as yet no great threat since these pirates only operated from small open boats with crews of twenty-five in each. The government in London noted the existence of these pirates, but was not very interested in such small-scale villains so far away, little knowing that the Bahamas were destined to become 'another Madagascar' and the 'three setts of pirates' the nucleus of the golden age of piracy. But all this lay in the future as 1714 and most of 1715 passed by with no news of any pirates anywhere but in the Bahamas and not many even there.

It is perhaps appropriate that the greatest boom in piracy in the eighteenth century should have been triggered by its greatest treasure-hunting bonanza. On the last day of July 1715, the treasure fleet returning from Havana to Spain was wrecked in a hurricane on the reefs off the coast of Florida. It was one of the worst shipwreck disasters in Spanish history with ten ships shattered along some forty miles of reefs, a thousand men drowned and a fortune in silver coins and bullion lost in the sea.[5] The survivors sent for help to St Augustine and Havana and, since most of the wrecks lay in fairly shallow water, a salvage expedition was quickly under way. But the Spaniards were not to be the only salvors. News of the disaster soon reached Carolina, Bermuda, the Bahamas and Jamaica, all places with a long tradition of working wrecks, and sloop after sloop was fitted out and headed for the Florida reefs, everyone 'mad to go a wrecking', as one naval captain who had lost some of his men to this pursuit complained. 'It seemed, in fact, as though every seamy character within a thousand-mile range had been attracted, like sharks to blood, by the strong scent of treasure,' writes a modern author who was himself attracted to the same treasure in the 1960s.[6]

Among these sharks were two ships and three sloops fitted out from Jamaica and manned with former privateersmen led by Henry Jennings who had a commission to search for pirates, this being merely the thinnest of covers for a raid on the storehouse on the Florida coast where the Spanish salvors kept their recovered treasure. This raid netted 120,000 pieces of eight and they were soon to add to their success with the seizure of a Spanish ship carrying another 150,000 pieces of eight. However, on their return to Jamaica, they discovered that they had been branded as the pirates they were and were likely to be prosecuted, so they sailed instead to the Bahamas where they linked up with Hornigold and the other pirates whose numbers had grown considerably from the small beginnings reported in 1714. Other sloop captains who had been working the wrecks followed Jennings' example, swelling the pirate community still further with men who were mostly former privateersmen. Still more men were to come as a result of reprisals carried out by the Spaniards in revenge for Jennings' outrageous raid. They fitted out a large expedition to attack the English logwood-cutters who as usual were living illegally in Campeche and Honduras. This was successful, and many English vessels were captured, but the Spaniards foolishly decided to let the six hundred captured Englishmen go in peace, having disarmed them. These men, 'some of which have been pirates, and most of them sailors', as one who had visited their haunts remarked, had little difficulty in deciding where to resettle and soon 'these loose, disorderly people' were also to be found numbered among the crews of the pirate ships operating from the Bahamas.[7]

And so, for a couple of years or so, the Bahamas became 'a receptacle and shelter of pirates and loose fellows', as an Admiralty correspondent from South Carolina put it, a place where the pirates could fit their ships, pick up crews, sell their booty and 'profusely spend what they take from the English, French and mostly from the Spaniards'.[8] In 1716 and particularly 1717, the scale of piracy was at least as great as it had been in 1698–9 and maybe even greater, with the pirates claiming that there were 'thirty company of them'.[9] At first, most of their depredations were in the central Caribbean, around Jamaica, Hispaniola and Cuba, and in the Leeward Islands, but from 1717 reports of attacks were coming in from all along the American coast, from the Carolinas to Newfoundland and throughout the Caribbean. There was a bit of a lull in 1718 and 1719, as the pirates were driven out of their base in the Bahamas and many accepted the pardon discussed in the next chapter. But new bases were found in the Virgin Islands and elsewhere and, from the later months of 1719 into the early 1720s, there was one last surge of piracy on a scale similar to that of 1716–17. In this last period, the more enterprising of the pirates burst out of their American bounds and crossed the Atlantic, leading to reports of attacks in the Cape Verde Islands, the Canaries, West Africa, Brazil and, as has been seen, the Indian Ocean.

Numbers are a little difficult to assess as contemporaries were liable to exaggerate the number of pirate vessels 'lurking', 'hovering', 'swarming around' or 'infesting' their coasts. There was also an understandable nervousness among merchantmen, so that if any ship tried to hail them they would run away 'and it goes for granted they were chac'd by pyrates', whether this was true or not. There could even be a commercial advantage in making false reports of pirates since these were likely to keep competitors away.[10] Nevertheless, there is some consistency in contemporary reports and, using these, the best modern estimate suggests that there were about two thousand pirates at sea in some twenty-five to thirty ships in the peak periods and that overall, during this boom in piracy, some five thousand men went 'on the account' at some time or other. This is a lot of pirates but, somewhat surprisingly, no more than at periods of concentrated pirate activity in the past when the potential booty at sea was much less, as in 1610 when the pirate admiral Peter Easton was also said to be in command of two thousand men.[11]

Among these hordes of pirates it is possible to discern three different types of operation. First, there was the old problem of Spanish coastguard vessels exceeding their commissions and moving into outright piracy. There were always several of these, many with renegade English or Irish officers such as Nicholas Brown and Christopher Winter, two men much hated in Jamaica, who boasted in 1721, while fitting out a vessel in Cuba, that 'they could stretch [their commissions] as farr as they would at the capstan'.[12] Such vessels were normally small but well manned and were often supported by piraguas, forty- or fifty-foot-long canoes, packed with men and with one big chase gun in the bows. The second group, comprising the greatest number of pirates, was based in the Bahamas or in places nearby such as the Virgin Islands. Their vessel of choice was the sloop, fast, handy, shallow-draught and fitted with oars and they normally operated in consorts of two or sometimes three sloops, each with some eight to ten guns and eighty to a hundred men. Their hunting was mainly confined to the Caribbean and the passages leading out of it through the Gulf of Florida or the Bahamas. Ambitious pirates in this group would be looking to capture a large and well-armed vessel which they could fit out as a man-of-war and so join the really powerful pirates in the third group. These operated in ships of two or three hundred tons with twenty or thirty guns, sometimes more, and often as many as two hundred men. They were normally accompanied by a sloop or brigantine as consort, shallow-draught vessels which could chase prey trying to escape into shoal waters. These powerful combines, of which there were rarely more than three or four at any one time, followed what has been called the 'pirate round', sailing out of the West Indies in the early summer and up the American coast as far as Newfoundland from where, like the pirates based in Ireland a century earlier, they sailed south to avoid the northern winter as we are told by Captain Johnson. 'The winters there being a little too cold for them, they follow the sun and go towards the islands at the approach of cold weather.'[13] These 'islands' would normally be the Leeward Islands and Barbados where the pirates lay in wait for the provision ships which arrived around Christmas. And from there, in later years, they would sail to Africa, Brazil and the Indian Ocean, some of them coming back to the West Indies to start the round all over again.

This period of ten years or so from 1715 is often called the golden age of piracy, a soubriquet which may merely reflect the fact that a lot more is known about the pirates of these years than those of any other time. This is principally because they were very thoroughly described in Captain Charles Johnson's book *The General History of the Pyrates* which was first published in 1724 and has been plundered by innumerable historians and novelists ever since. Johnson was well informed and much of the material in his book can be confirmed from other sources, but he also embroidered and invented, so much so that a modern critic has written that 'it is hardly too much to say that [he] created the modern conception of pirates'.[14] However, the historian does not have to rely on Captain Johnson alone. Masses of colonial and naval correspondence and reports have survived, often with detailed depositions by former captives of the pirates. The period is also well served by newspapers, both in London and the colonies, which barely existed at the time of the previous large-scale outbreak of piracy around 1700. These have dramatic accounts of acts of piracy and they also served as a means of warning merchants where pirates might be expected. They also had a useful function for men forced to serve aboard a pirate ship against their will, their unforced shipmates promising to insert a notice of their involuntary service in a newspaper to provide evidence in the event of their later capture and trial. And finally, and perhaps most beneficial for the historian, there exist about half a dozen accounts of life aboard a pirate ship by educated captives, the best of these being by the English slaving captain William Snelgrave and the Dutchman Jacob de Bucquoy.[15] This material will enable us to get some idea of the nature of the pirates of the golden age, beginning with their captains.

As in the days of the buccaneers, captains were elected and their tenure of command was precarious as it depended on maintaining the respect and goodwill of their crew. This they often failed to do and there were frequent changes of command on pirate ships, often with the former captain leaving with those who still supported him to take command of another ship. Captains might be dismissed for any number of reasons, because they took too great risks or too few, because they refused to take English ships, because they were too cruel or too 'gentleman-like'. This led to the wheel of fortune so characteristic of pirate life, as can be seen in the five-year piratical career of Thomas Anstis, who was 'sometimes in the office of captain, sometimes quartermaster and often boatswain and fore-mastman, for the enjoyment of posts aboard them are very precarious, depending wholly upon the will and pleasure of the crew', as we learn from Humphrey Orme, a naval captain who had interrogated several of the pirate's former crew.[16]

Crews might be mercurial in this respect, but their choices were not completely arbitrary and nearly all the captains whose background is known were experienced men of the sea. The typical pirate captain was either an officer from a West Indian privateer or a mate or boatswain from a merchant ship which had mutinied or been captured by the pirates.[17] These would be tough men, used to maintaining order by the force of their personalities and their fists and this they could continue to do on a pirate ship, even though they would now be deprived of the back-up of disciplinary sanctions available to the mate of a merchantman. Quarrels between captain and mate on merchant ships were notoriously frequent, the mate often justifiably thinking himself the better man who was only deprived of command by his lack of enough capital to buy a share in the ship.[18] The chance of commanding a pirate ship, where no respect was paid to gentility, influence or private means, was an obvious if short-sighted way of resolving this frustration.

Observations on the characters of individual pirate captains show a wide spectrum of behaviour and personality, from the basically very nice to the extremely unpleasant. Woodes Rogers, a former privateer himself and the man who drove the pirates out of their Bahamas base in 1718, could admire the pirate Benjamin Hornigold, since 'in the very acts of piracy he committed, most people spoke well of his generosity'.[19] William Snelgrave respected Howel Davis, the Welsh pirate who captured him in Sierra Leone, 'because he kept his ship's company in good order ... a most generous humane person'.[20] The pirate Edward England was even more humane. 'He had a great deal of good-nature and did not want for courage,' writes Captain Johnson. 'He was not avaricious, and always averse to the ill-usage prisoners received; he would have been contented with moderate plunder and less mischievous pranks, could his companions have been brought to the same temper. But he was generally overruled.'[21]

At the other end of the scale were Thomas Cocklyn and his crew who were, according to Snelgrave, 'a set of the basest and most cruel villains that ever were ... They chose him for their commander on account of his brutality and ignorance'.[22] The man with the worst reputation of all among the pirates was Ned Lowe who was described by one of his own officers as 'notorious for his cruelty ... a greater monster never infested the seas'.[23] The best known of these pirates today is probably Edward Teach, or Blackbeard, whose nickname was explained by one of his former prisoners, describing him as 'a tall spare man with a very black beard which he wore very long'. Captain Johnson, as usual, takes this a bit further. 'This beard was black, which he suffered to grow of an extravagant length; as to breadth, it came up to his eyes. He was accustomed to twist it with ribbons, in small tails ... [He] stuck lighted matches under his hat, which, appearing on each side of his face, his eyes naturally looking fierce and wild, made him altogether such a figure that imagination cannot form an idea of a fury from hell to look more frightful.' This grotesque pirate captain was 'a courageous brute' who was probably crueller to his crew than his captives and was said to have sworn 'that if he did not now and then kill one of them, they would forget who he was.'[24]

The most complete description of a pirate captain is that by Jacob de Bucquoy of John Taylor, a former lieutenant in the Royal Navy who was one of the last European pirates to plunder in the Indian Ocean. De Bucquoy had ample opportunity to study Taylor, for he shared his cabin and he tells how the pirate 'often woke suddenly, seized by terror and with horrible oaths reached for his pistols'. Taylor, like many pirate captains, was a man of moods who 'got angry easily and his fury made him out of control'. But he was in full control in times of danger at sea or in battle. 'His calm, his presence of mind, his personal courage in grave circumstances gained him the admiration of his companions.' He could cope with the threat of insurgency among his men by throwing himself fearlessly into their midst and striking out with his fists but, despite his severity, 'he was much loved by his people . . . and often came to chat, gamble, drink and eat from the common pot with them'.[25] Taylor was an exceptionally successful pirate and clearly a fine commander of a ship, but in his alternation of rage and calm, distance and matiness with his crew, he was fairly typical of many of his pirate captain contemporaries.

The make-up of pirate crews changed considerably in the course of the golden age. The first crews were drawn mainly from the men of the West Indian privateering community, well known for their egalitarianism, and they were able to impart these ideas to the many new recruits who joined them from captured merchant ships. As time went on, these former merchant seamen began to predominate in the pirate crews, especially as it was mainly the former privateersmen who accepted the pardon of 1718. Pirate ideology now began to reflect the grievances of the lower deck as well as the ideals of the buccaneers.

Pirate ships recruited men from every sort of vessel which sailed the Atlantic and Caribbean, but there were two trades which stood out as a source of willing men. The first was the Newfoundland fishery which attracted the pirates of the 1710s just as it had those of a century earlier.[26] Here every summer there were some two thousand English and American sailors and fishermen, 'shamefully exploited by the masters of their ships' and doing work of 'extraordinary labour and pains', perfect recruits for the pirate ships who came to Newfoundland 'to get better manned'.[27] The West African slave trade was an even better recruiting ground for pirates, the crews of slavers being 'generally glad of an opportunity of entering with them', as Snelgrave reported.[28] Slavers were notoriously unpleasant ships to work in, with more than their fair share of harsh and brutal captains and with incredibly high mortality among their crews, an average of one in four who shipped at English slaving ports such as London and Bristol not surviving the voyage. Sailors were described by a clergyman eager to redeem them as 'a third sort of persons, to be numbered neither with the living nor the dead: their lives hanging continually in suspense before them'.[29] This was literally true for the crews of slavers, making them very willing to swap their harsh conditions for the easygoing life aboard a pirate ship, even if it was a 'voyage to Hell' in which they would inevitably die sooner or later, as a pirate in Captain Cocklyn's crew described the prospects of the venture on which he had embarked.[30]

In the first three or four years of this period of piracy, few men were forced to join the pirates, except those known as 'artists', skilled men desperately needed aboard the ship such as carpenters, coopers, sailmakers and surgeons or perhaps a tailor, the pirates with their shipworn clothes 'wanting such a person very much', as a tailor forced to serve Bartholomew Roberts against his will declared at his trial.[31] Musicians, such as trumpeters and fiddlers, were also more than likely to be forced on board as music was an essential part of life on a pirate ship. De Bucquoy describes the men on Taylor's ship practising with their weapons on deck, 'while their musicians play divers airs so that the days pass very agreeably', though this might not be so pleasant for the musicians who were ordered 'to play their tune or be beat', as was 'one of the musick' of a slaver captured by pirates in West Africa.[32]

But the general run of sailors, 'being encouraged by the daily and uninterrupted success of the pirates',[33] needed no force to make them enlist, sometimes whole crews at a time, but more often just two or three of the more adventurous or more discontented of the merchant crew. John King, a young passenger on a sloop captured near the Virgin Islands by the famous pirate Black Jack Bellamy, was absolutely determined to join his crew. 'He declared he would kill himself if he was restrained and even threatened his mother who was then on board as a passenger.'[34] But such enthusiasm for the piratical way of life began to wane as time went on and it became increasingly apparent that life as a pirate was likely to be a short one. Now volunteers dried up and more and more men were forced to serve, often with a pistol at their head or with a whip, a change in policy which made pirate crews dangerously divided between forced and willing men and enabled the former to take control of the ship on several occasions.

What motivated sailors to take the dangerous step of volunteering to join a pirate crew? Such a question is of course unanswerable, except in a few individual cases such as that of Simon Jones, the mate of Snelgrave's ship who joined his captors because 'his circumstances were bad at home: moreover he had a wife whom he could not love'.[35] However, there seems little doubt that many who talked of pirate life in the leaking forecastles of merchant ships must have seen it as a veritable sailor heaven. The very first of the articles drawn up by the 'great pirate' Bartholomew Roberts must have made hungry and drink-crazy merchant sailors lick their lips. 'Every man . . . has equal title to the fresh provisions or strong liquors at any time seized, and [may] use them at pleasure unless a scarcity make it necessary for the good of all to vote a retrenchment'.[36] Plentiful food and drink was coupled with an easy life, for there was far less hard labour on a pirate ship with a crew of a hundred or more to sail a vessel which would only employ some ten or twenty men as a merchantman. And then there was the pirate round which ensured that the ship always sailed in pleasant weather, the camaraderie, the freedom from irksome discipline, the informality by which 'every one came and eat and drank with [the captain] at their humour' and, not to be forgotten, the chance of booty. The pirate George Bendall said that 'he wisht he had begun the life sooner for he thought it a very pleasant one, meaning the pyraticall way'.[37] Captain Johnson has Bartholomew Roberts say much the same at rather greater length. 'In an honest service there is thin commons [i.e. food], low wages, and hard labour. In this, plenty and satiety, pleasure and ease, liberty and power; and who would not balance creditor on this side, when all the hazard that is run for it, at worst, is only a sour look or two at choking. No, a merry life and a short one shall be my motto.'[38] Sailors were notoriously short-sighted in choosing a berth and disdainful of death, otherwise how could slavers with their very high mortality ever have been crewed, so perhaps the wonder is why some sailors did not choose to serve on a pirate ship when they had the chance rather than why some did. There must have been a modicum of self-preservation, a basic sense of right and wrong, some loyalty and maybe love of home and country even among the feckless people that sailors were said to be.

There also seems to have been a political and ideological motive for joining a pirate crew in these years which is completely absent in previous periods of piracy. Pirates drawn from merchant crews were often sharply critical of the authoritarianism and harsh discipline aboard some merchantmen and of the dirty tricks of the merchants who sent them to sea. A prisoner of the pirates Bellamy and Lebour said they 'pretended to be Robbin Hoods Men', an observation which Captain Johnson embroidered into a long speech attributed to Bellamy in which he said that he and his men 'plunder the rich under the protection of our own courage', while rich men 'rob the poor under the cover of law'. One of Roberts' gang abused a captured merchant, 'calling him a supercargo son of a b——h, that he starved his men, and that it was such doggs as he as put men on pyrating'. Howel Davis said to Snelgrave that 'their reasons for going a pirating were to revenge themselves on base merchants and cruel commanders of ships', a comment echoed by Captain Francis Willis, commander of a naval vessel on the West African station. He reported to the Admiralty that the men in the slave ships were 'ripe for pyracy. Whether it be occasioned by the masters' ill usage or their own natural inclination I must leave their Lordships to judge.'[39]

Many English pirates had also lost their loyalty to their own country, in strong contrast to the buccaneers and especially the South Sea men who named islands after members of the English royal family or officers of the Admiralty and celebrated loyalist anniversaries such as the Restoration of Charles II and the execution of his father. Pirates of this later age shared no such loyalty, as is nicely illustrated by the report of a Boston sea captain after his capture by the pirate Philip Lyne. When the pirates searched his ship they found Admiralty correspondence aboard, 'which the pyrates wip'd their backsides with, saying that they were the Lords of the Sea'.[40] Pirate hostility to the British establishment is perhaps best exemplified by the strong streak of Jacobitism apparent in many pirate ships of this period. Jacobites were concerned with overthrowing the settlement that had brought in the Hanoverian George I as king in 1714 and two risings with this intent coincided with this phase of piracy, a large-scale and well-known rebellion in 1715–16 and a much smaller affair in 1719 and it is around this later date that expressions of pirate Jacobitism become very common. Many pirate ships were given Jacobite names such as *King James, Royal James* or *Queen Anne's Revenge*. A letter to the widow of James II claimed that the Bahamas pirates 'did with one heart and voice proclaim [her son] James III for their King'. Pirates drank toasts to the Pretender and 'Damnacon to King George' or 'the Turnip Man' as they derisively called their German monarch. The commander of a French slaver captured by pirates in West Africa said they had 'commissions from the Pretender' and that they gave him and his men 'a passport and a medal which they carry as a mark of their fidelity to the Pretender, for whose cause they say they have armed'.[41] Such commissions were almost certainly a fiction and there was never any possibility that the pirates would actually sail to England or Scotland to help the Pretender, but it is significant that they should so defiantly identify with the enemies of the Hanoverian government which, as we will see, was determined to drive them off the face of the earth.

So far we have only considered white pirates, but in fact pirate crews included large numbers of non-whites as well. Since the days of Drake, English pirates and buccaneers had developed friendly relations with many of the native people of Central America, especially the Moskito Indians, and these often formed part of their crews. The Moskitos were famous above all for their skill as 'strikers' who could unerringly spear fish with lance or harpoon and so were much 'coveted by all privateers; for one or two of them in a ship will maintain a hundred', as William Dampier affirmed. They also made fine lookouts, for they 'see farther at sea and better than we', and were good marksmen and fighters. 'They behave themselves very bold in fight and never seem to flinch nor hold back.'[42] No wonder pirates liked to have one or two of these paragons in their crews.

There were also large numbers of blacks aboard pirate ships, these often being distinguished from their white shipmates in depositions, and one modern writer has suggested that as many as 30 per cent of pirate crews were of African descent.[43] This is probably an exaggeration, though not a very great one. The problem is to determine the exact status of these black pirates. Some optimists claim they were treated by their white shipmates as equals and that this early form of black empowerment should be celebrated, an idea rejected by members of the modern black establishment in America who are not at all keen that free black history should 'start with gangsters, which is what pirates were'.[44] Other writers more pessimistically suggest that the blacks were slaves forced by the white pirates to do the pumping and other dirty work of the ship. The truth, as usual, probably lies somewhere in between.

Black sailors were quite common in the merchant shipping of America and especially in the Caribbean, where many sloops and other vessels engaged in coastal waters were crewed almost entirely by blacks.[45] These men were nearly always slaves, most of whose wages went to their shorebound masters, but simply working at sea gave them a taste of freedom denied to their brothers working in plantations ashore. Some of these slave sailors worked aboard privateer or pirate ships on the same conditions. Juan Silvester, a Cuban slave, was ordered by his master to serve on the pirate ship commanded by Augustino Blanco or at least that was what he claimed at his trial in the Bahamas for piracy. 'His master was to have his share except jewells and rings, his master having often sent him out on privateering upon shares.'[46] Such men, with their seafaring and fighting skills, would be welcome aboard any pirate ship which captured them, though whether they would be treated as equals is another matter. 'Black sailors knew full well that race rarely disappeared, even among shipmates,' as a recent historian of black mariners points out.[47]

Pirates also captured large numbers of slavers, but they certainly did not free all the slaves on board and welcome them as brothers. Most were sold as booty, while the female slaves were often abused and raped, a fate shared only rarely by white female captives. Nevertheless, pirates did take many freed slaves aboard as crew. Some of these were exploited simply for their labour, but others were trained up in the seafaring and fighting skills of the pirate. The pirate John Bowen, whose ship the *Speaking Trumpet* was wrecked on Mauritius in 1702, had several black men in his crew, 'very cunning and well trained in the use of arms', useful-sounding men, but he still sold four of them to pay for food and other necessities. 'The entire record of relations between pirates and people of African descent is ambiguous, even contradictory,' writes the historian Marcus Rediker. One can only agree with him.[48]

Pirates of the golden age bound themselves on oath to obey what they called 'Articles of Regulation' and these were taken very seriously, since 'if we once take the liberty of breaking our articles and oath, then there is none of us can be sure of any thing', as one of Lowe's men explained to a prisoner.[49] A few of these articles have survived in full,[50] while references to individual clauses of the articles quite often appear in depositions and other evidence. These are all similar to each other in content and they retain the buccaneers' emphasis on equality, compensation for injuries and rewards for the vigilant, but they are much more comprehensive than any earlier sets of articles. Care was taken for safety, with rules relating to smoking, naked lights and the handling of weapons below deck. Attention was also paid to those things likely to cause disharmony in the crew. Quarrels were to be resolved ashore in a duel to the death supervised by the captain and quartermaster.[51] Theft from shipmates or attempts to defraud them of their booty were extremely harshly treated. Gambling except for trivial stakes was banned in all surviving articles, a reflection perhaps of the problems this had caused among buccaneer crews, though whether this rule was actually observed is unknown.

Cowardice, desertion and, in some articles, drunkenness in battle were serious crimes, as was failure to keep arms in good condition. Good treatment of prisoners was also seen to be important, a sensible policy as well as a humane one, since sailors on merchant ships were unlikely to resist if they believed they would be treated decently as captives. Death was the punishment in Taylor's ship for those who killed anyone who had freely surrendered, while Lowe's men too were 'not to draw blood, or take away the life of any man, after they had given him quarter, unless he was to be punished as a criminal'.[52] Death was also promised on many ships to anyone who forced captured women against their inclination, though in some articles this prohibition was qualified. The articles of Captain John Phillips only protected 'prudent' women, while those of Thomas Anstis specified death only for those who should 'meet with any gentlewoman or lady of honour and should force them against their will to lye with them', a nice distinction between the rapeable and unrapeable members of the opposite sex.[53] Nearly all surviving articles were drawn up in the early 1720s, by which date pirates were increasingly forcing men to serve, so it is not surprising to find severe penalties for anyone who tried to desert or break up the ship's company. The penalty on Ned Lowe's ship was death by shooting for anyone who even spoke about separating or breaking up or attempted to desert, a very different scenario from the easygoing days of the buccaneers.[54]

The man chiefly responsible for discipline was the quartermaster whose powers and responsibilities were now even greater than in the time of the buccaneers. He could even overturn the decisions of the captain and give him instructions on what he should do in the name of the men. He supervised the distribution of both food and booty, called meetings to discuss future policy and acted as judge in the trials of malefactors with a jury of twelve men, half of them chosen by the accused.[55] Such a court could impose four main punishments. For minor offences this was simply left to the offender's shipmates, 'such punishment as the captain and company should think fitt', this normally being some unpleasant extra duty such as pumping. Then there was the form of flogging called 'Moses's Law (that is forty stripes lacking one) on the bare back', severe even by the standards of contemporary Royal Navy ships whose captains rarely ordered more than two dozen lashes as a punishment. There are several surviving reports of pirates being flogged by their shipmates, sometimes with many more than the thirty-nine strokes prescribed. William Watkins, for instance, who tried to run away from Bartholomew Roberts' ship in Sierra Leone 'received two lashes from every man in the company as a punishment' at a time when Roberts had well over a hundred men in his crew.[56] Worst of all were death, normally by shooting, and marooning on a rock or deserted island with 'one bottle of powder, one bottle of water, one small arm and shot', a punishment so much a part of the pirate code that several crews referred to themselves as 'Marooners'.[57] No one knows how well these rules were observed, but drawing them up was as much an integral part of the pirate life of this period as making a black flag and 'declaring war against the whole world'.[58]

The black flag, first noted flying on the ship of Emanuel Wynn in 1700, was now a standard feature of pirate ships. Designs varied from pirate to pirate and some flags were not in fact black, but they all incorporated such symbols of approaching death as skulls, skeletons, crossbones, hourglasses and bleeding hearts. Pirates no longer had any hesitation in proclaiming their identity and it was under the 'Banner of King Death' that they sailed into action. This could be very violent on occasion but was usually a fairly leisurely process, since few merchant ships dared challenge the firepower and manpower of a pirate ship. A hail or a single shot across the bows was normally sufficient to bring about surrender.

There then followed a nerve-racking period of days or often weeks while the prize or prizes lay alongside the pirate ship and were plundered. These were scary times for the captives. Pirates only rarely did any physical harm to captured sailors, but they were unpredictable people and were of course in a situation of absolute power. Nobody could tell what retribution might follow a careless word or gesture of distaste, especially if the pirates were drunk, as they very often were. Captives were warned to be friendly and polite to the pirates, 'like an alehouse-keeper with his customers', as a former prisoner of Lowe advised his readers, not to whisper among themselves lest they arouse the distrust of their captors, not to speak too freely for fear of offending, not to be silent lest they 'be thought contemptuous' and never, never 'to dispute the will of a pirate', as William Snelgrave was cautioned by one of his captors. 'Danger lurked in their very smiles', it was said of Lowe's gang, and while most sailors were eventually discharged unhurt, not all captives were so lucky. Some were beaten, some were killed – occasionally whole crews at a time – and some were cruelly mutilated, such as the crew of a sloop captured by the French pirate Captain Nicolo in 1722. He 'cut off the master's head and the hand of each private man', but just why he should have been so cruel was not explained by the man who provided a Royal Navy captain with this information.[59]

The man most at risk aboard a captured merchant ship was her captain. It was he who was most likely to be tortured to show where the money was or beaten with a 'cutlace for not bringing to at the first shot', as was the captain of a vessel from New York who was captured by the usually humane Edward England.[60] And from about 1718 onwards there were new horrors to be faced by these suddenly powerless men. For the pirates now quite often held a court of enquiry 'into the manner of the commanders' behaviour to their men'. If the captured sailors spoke up for their captain and said, as his crew said of Captain Snelgrave, 'We never were with a better man,' then all was fine, the captain unhurt and often cosseted by the pirates. But if the captain was condemned by his men as harsh, unjust or mean, then things could be very unpleasant indeed. Such erring captains might have their nose and ears cut off, 'for but correcting his own sailors', wrote the Governor of Virginia in a letter begging for a naval vessel to carry him home to England lest he suffer the same fate. Other captains were 'whipped and pickled' or forced to endure 'that piece of discipline used by the merry blades in the West-Indies, call'd blooding and sweating'. This, we are told in a book written by a former privateer, involved running the gauntlet naked through the pirate crew, 'each of them furnished with a sail-needle, pricking him in the buttocks, back and shoulders; thus bleeding they put him in a sugar cask swarming with cock-roaches, cover him with a blanket, and there leave him to glut the vermin with his blood'. And some merchant captains were summarily executed, especially those unfortunate enough to be captured by the pirate Philip Lyne who boasted that he 'had killed 37 masters of vessels', as was reported in the *Boston Gazette* in 1726.[61]

This business of judging and punishing merchant captains is unique in the history of piracy and reflects the radical, 'world-turned-upside-down' nature of the golden age of piracy. How sailors must have loved to see the powerful brought low and the oppressor oppressed. Such vengeance also reflects the make-up of the pirate crews, for never before had these been drawn predominantly from the more disgruntled members of the crews of merchant ships. Few buccaneers had served on long journeys in merchant ships and they could not care less how the Spanish captains of their prizes treated their crews, though they might kill them simply because they were Spaniards. But large numbers of the pirates of the years 1715–25 had served on transatlantic or West African voyages or in the Newfoundland fishery where the effects of harsh captains would have been most severely felt. And for them such cruel revenge must have been very sweet.

While captured sailors cowered and captains were judged, the pirates would be engaged in ransacking the ship. Few of these prizes contained much of the portable, high-value booty which made pirates in the Indian Ocean so quickly rich. For the most part, these were humdrum traders engaged in the carriage of foodstuffs, drink, textiles, furniture and other household goods for colonial markets or, if they were on their way to Europe, the products of America and the West Indies such as sugar, tobacco, dyestuffs and rum. Most ships' masters would carry some money for the incidental expenses of the voyage, but this would not normally amount to much, and it was a lucky Atlantic or Caribbean pirate who found more than £1,000 in cash on a captured ship. The pirates knew all this of course, for they were sailors themselves, and what they chiefly sought aboard a prize were those things which would enable them to maintain their ships and sustain themselves and their way of life, the life itself being as or more important than the dream of returning home rich. And so, while they always looked for money and other valuables, their main focus was on food and drink, clothes, arms and ammunition, cables and sails and whatever else they might need for themselves or for the ship.

This could amount to very little. Benjamin Hornigold captured a sloop off the coast of Honduras, but 'they did us no further injury than the taking most of our hats from us, having got drunk the night before, as they told us, and toss'd theirs overboard', as one of the passengers recorded in his journal with some relief.[62] Some time later, Hornigold took another sloop near Cuba, detained her for fourteen days 'and then permitted her to proceed on her voyage having taken very little from her (to wit) only some rum, a little sugar, powder and shott, cordage and small sayles and four gun carriages with some provisions'.[63] Sometimes what was taken was more substantial if the cargo was of the right nature. In 1720, a captive mariner from Bermuda was an eyewitness when Bartholomew Roberts took a French sloop sailing from Martinique to Guadeloupe, 'laded with claret, white wine and brandy. They emptied her and dismissed her . . . They gott drunk that day and shott at the mast of the French sloop two of their own crew.'[64] Pirates were always unpredictable.

The mood swings evident in their treatment of captives were also apparent in the treatment of cargoes. Quite often the pirates simply asked their captives what was aboard and then ordered them to deliver up whatever it was they wanted. But they could also search a ship in the most berserk way, as Roberts' men did when they captured the Boston ship *Samuel* on the Newfoundland Banks. 'The first thing the pirates did, was to strip both passengers and seamen of all their money and clothes which they had on board, with a loaded pistol held to everyone's breast . . . The next thing they did was, with madness and rage to tear up the hatches, enter the hould like a parcel of furies, where with axes, cutlashes, etc., they cut, tore and broke open trunks, boxes, cases and bales, and when any of the goods came upon deck which they did not like to carry with them . . . they threw them over-board into the sea. The usual method they had to open chests was by shooting a brace of bullets with a pistol into the key-hole to force them open.'[65]

This appalling waste shocked good bourgeois observers such as Captain William Snelgrave. He reported with horror the pirates throwing bale goods overboard, 'money and necessaries being what they chiefly wanted', their spoiling of the cargo that remained 'by pouring buckets of claret over fine linen', their 'knocking off heads of hogsheads of claret and brandy just to dip their cans . . . striking heads off bottles with a cutlace'.[66] And he, like most other observers, was shocked by the pirates' pretensions to equality, their continuous drunkenness, their swearing and blasphemy which was worse even than that of ordinary sailors and their appalling table manners, 'more like a kennel of hounds than like men, snatching and catching the victuals from one another which they said look'd martial-like', according to another former captive.[67]

Ransack and retribution done, the pirates normally discharged the captured ship to continue on its voyage, though if it was a good one they might keep it for themselves and herd their former prisoners into some other prize, a farewell often sugared with an easy generosity with other people's goods as the Governor of Virginia reported in 1720. 'It is a common practice with these rovers upon the pillageing of a ship to make presents of other commoditys to such masters as they take a fancy to in lieu of that they plundered them off.'[68] Alternatively, they might sink or burn the prize, such waste being worst of all in the eyes of Captain Snelgrave. 'Nothing could make them more odious to the world than their destroying, out of mere wantonness, so many ships and cargoes.'[69] Captain Johnson lists the motives for such destruction, 'sometimes to prevent giving intelligence, sometimes because they did not [have] men to navigate them, and at other times out of wantonness or because they were displeased at the master's behaviour'. All these motives were present, as was a desire for revenge on the shipping of places where pirates had been tried and hanged, Blackbeard for instance making a habit of destroying ships from New England for this reason. But perhaps above all, pirates liked to burn ships for the sheer joy of seeing these mercantile symbols of the world they had left behind go up in flames, such entertainment being explained by one captured pirate when asked why he burned ships which 'turn'd to no advantage among 'em. The prisoner laughed and replied 'twas for fun.'[70]

Most individual prizes may have been of little value, but the cumulative effect of the pirates' captures and destruction was immense, for they took a quite incredible number. The surgeon Ezekell David was captured by the pirate Thomas Anstis off the coast of Cuba in November 1721 and forced to serve aboard for ten months, before he and others escaped following the pirate's shipwreck in the Cayman Islands. During this period, Anstis cruised all round the Caribbean and as far north as Newfoundland and 'took at least sixty sail of ships and vessells', an average of roughly one ship every five days.[71] This was good going, but by no means exceptional. Ned Lowe's average was slightly better, 140 ships captured in twenty months, while Bartholomew Roberts is credited with an almost unbelievable four hundred prizes in his three-years career of piracy, a rate of capture nearly twice that of Thomas Anstis.[72] Such productivity is amazing, given the fact that the seas were not packed with merchant shipping and a rover could go for days or weeks without seeing another sail, but it is a sign that these pirates of the golden age took their business seriously even if many might acknowledge, like Joseph Mansfield at his trial in 1722, that drunkenness 'had a great share in drawing him into such company, the love of drink and a lazy life having been stronger motives with him than gold'.[73]

The pirate's life was not just one of hard labour smashing crates in holds and frightening captives. There were the days of easy sailing and good fellowship between prizes. There was the joy of meeting another pirate, saluting him with the great guns and celebrating in days of 'mutual civilities' the solidarity of the pirate community, 'l'ensemble du peuple pirate', in its war against all the world.[74] And above all there were the carousals ashore when the seamen landed to dispose of prizes, divide their booty or clean their ships, a time to party and enjoy themselves, as Captain Johnson records with gusto on several occasions in his book. Roberts' men, for instance, had handsome treatment at the island of St Bartholomew, where the women 'endeavoured to outvie each other in dress and behaviour to attract the good graces of such generous lovers, that paid well for their favours'. Sometimes this sort of thing could get out of hand, as it did when Captain England's men were cleaning their ship in a West African harbour. 'They lived there very wantonly for several weeks, making free with the negro women, and committing such outrageous acts that they came to an open rupture with the natives, several of whom they killed and one of their towns they set on fire.' But such breaches of friendly relations with natives were unusual and most people welcomed the rovers when they came to spend 'some time in a riotous manner, as is the custom of pirates'.[75] Life for these men may have been dangerous, harsh and usually short, but it had its compensations.

# CHAPTER TEN

# Extermination

CHAPTER TEN

# Extermination

'I say, 'tis strange that a few pirates should ravage the seas for years without ever being lit upon by any of our ships of war; when in the meantime they (the pirates) shall take fleets of ships. It looks as if one was much more diligent in their affairs than the other.'[1] Captain Charles Johnson's harsh judgement on the navy's campaign against the pirates of the golden age was written in 1724, by which date it was rather unfair. It was, however, only too accurate a summary of the pitiful efforts of the navy in the first years of the campaign which began in earnest in 1715. No pirate ships at all were captured in 1715 or 1716 and there was just one success in 1717 when, in January, Captain Hume in the *Scarborough* captured a pirate ship and sloop at St Croix in the Virgin Islands.[2] But even this was a hollow victory as the pirates themselves escaped into the woods and later joined the crew of Captain Bellamy in the *Whidaw*. This proved a bad move as the ship was wrecked a few months later near Cape Cod and some 130 or so pirates drowned, a grievous loss – but hardly one that could be attributed to the navy. Meanwhile, some twenty to thirty other pirate vessels roamed the seas with complete impunity and their captives flocked to join the rovers' crews who, according to the Governor of Barbados, had 'little apprehension . . . of the King's ships that are sent into the Indies to suppress them'.[3]

This poor showing of the navy partly reflects the inherent problems in catching pirates which had been only too apparent in previous campaigns. The area to be searched was huge –

throughout the Caribbean, the Bahamas and the American coast, a vast sea area with innumerable coves and cays and other hiding places which were very familiar to the pirates but less so to their naval pursuers, many of whom were young officers in their first command and unfamiliar with American waters. These young men would learn their way around and the habits of the pirates eventually, as had their predecessors in the 1670s and 1680s, but all this took a long time, time in which the pirates could take prizes with little fear of capture. It would take time, too, to develop effective systems of intelligence. Most news of pirates derived from their captives, who, as has been seen, were normally released after having been retained for varying lengths of time. But by the time these released men had got to port, had given information as to the pirates' whereabouts and a naval vessel got ready for sea and set out in pursuit, the pirates were likely to be far away from where they had last been seen. And when information acquired in America was relayed through the government in England to colonial officials and naval officers, as was often done, the time lag was enormous. Government clerks were required to note the date of receipt of incoming letters, and an analysis of these shows that a letter took on average fifty days to reach London from New York and seventy days from Jamaica. And this was just the first leg of the round trip.

These problems were compounded by the sheer competence of the pirates. They used the right sort of vessels for the job, kept them clean and fast, and frequently shifted into swifter or more seaworthy prizes, so that they had few of the ship deterioration problems faced by the Royal Navy. As in the earlier campaigns, they knew the waters where they cruised better than their pursuers and were often able to use that knowledge to their advantage. Naval vessels were left frustrated as shallow-draught pirate sloops sailed or rowed away from them into shoal waters or narrow, twisting channels where pursuit was impossible or unwise. On one occasion HMS *Mermaid* was chasing a sloop commanded by the pirate Lowe and with a good wind was catching up fast. 'But it happened there was one man on board the sloop that knew of a shoal ground thereabouts who directed Lowe to run over it; he did so; and the man-of-war who had so forereached him as to sling a shot over him . . . ran a ground upon the shoal' and was dis-masted.[4] Local knowledge and contacts also provided the pirates with a better information service than that available to the forces of order, which enabled them to know the present whereabouts and future plans of the naval ships. The pirates had spies and sympathisers throughout the West Indies and also collected useful information from the sailors aboard the ships they captured. Jamaicans, both at sea and ashore, were particularly valuable sources of naval intelligence. Commodore Peter Chamberlen excused himself for not telling the Governor of Jamaica where the ships under his command would be cruising, since 'notices of that kind gather so much air as to be very early communicated to the prejudices of the cruises . . . there being (I fear) too many friends to the pirates at Port Royal and other parts of Jamaica'.[5]

The pirates may have made life difficult for their naval pursuers, but they were unwittingly abetted by the Admiralty and the naval captains themselves. The Admiralty, keen to retrench after the huge costs of the War of the Spanish Succession, was at first reluctant to commit many ships to the anti-piracy campaign, especially as there were other pressing commitments nearer home, such as yet another campaign against the Sallee rovers and the need to defend the shores of Britain and Ireland against the Jacobite Rebellion of 1715–16. However, as piracy increased so did the flood of reports and complaints from colonial governors, merchants and others affected and the Admiralty was forced gradually to increase the number of warships in American waters. This reached a peak in the early 1720s when there were nine Royal Navy vessels in the West Indies, five on the American coast and two or three in Newfoundland during the fishing season, roughly the same strength that had been set forth during the previous pirate campaign around the turn of the century. And, as before, this force could be supplemented by the commissioning or pressing of locally owned vessels to chase pirates, either by themselves or in company with the men of war, or by taking a local sloop into government pay as Jamaica did in 1722, to the 'great benefit and advantage' of the island.[6]

These naval vessels all had specific orders to seek out pirates and 'to use your best endeavours to take, burn, sink, or otherwise destroy them'[7] and an attempt was made in June 1717 to arrange for the coordination of the individual ships, stationed as they were in a long line from Barbados to Newfoundland with only those at Jamaica acting as a real squadron. Captains were required to establish a system of correspondence with the captains nearest to them, the New York station ship corresponding with those in New England and Virginia for example, thus being able to exchange information and if necessary request assistance.[8] This was a good idea, but these orders were not sufficient to prevent the naval vessels being seriously hampered in their freedom of manoeuvre by being tied to a particular station. Colonial governors regarded the station ships in their colony as their own and were very reluctant to see naval captains sail too far away in pursuit of pirates and leave them unprotected.

On the face of it, these Admiralty orders and dispositions were sensible enough, but the campaign was simultaneously under-mined by a whole range of petty orders motivated by the government's attempts to keep costs to a minimum. In the early years of the campaign, few ships were manned to their full complement, despite constant complaints. Captains were not allowed to buy provisions in the West Indies because they were more expensive there than in England, with the result that few cruises lasted more than a year. Captains were also forbidden to careen their ships, due to the expense, though this was essential if they were to catch pirates. Crews were crippled by the devastation of malaria, dysentery, yellow fever and other tropical diseases and these sick men needed to be nursed to health ashore, but orders forbade the hire of houses as hospitals, and so on. The list was endless. In some individual cases, such parsimony seems ludicrous or grossly unfair. Captain George Anson, later to become famous as an admiral and circumnavigator, had his expenses for pilots disallowed while serving on the Carolina station, despite the danger of wrecking his ship in these difficult waters. 'I cannot think I am justifiable in going to sea without a pilot,' he protested, 'where there is so much danger and hazard as there is upon this coast and among the Bahama Islands.'[9] Even worse was the experience of

Captain Percy who had twenty-eight men captured by Africans when they went ashore for food and water. He eventually ransomed them for twenty-one barrels of gunpowder, but the Admiralty refused to pay for these and took the cost out of the captain's pay. 'If I had not redeemed these poor people from those savage monsters,' wrote the aggrieved captain, 'all human kind would have judged me deserving of death.'[10]

Parsimony was coupled with a total failure to learn anything from the experience of previous campaigns. Indeed, it seems unlikely that the officers of the Admiralty had in fact studied what had happened in the campaigns of the 1680s and the years around 1700, since no references to them can be found in their correspondence. Anyone who had actually tried knew that you could never catch a pirate with a foul ship and yet careening was forbidden in the West Indies, though ironically not in the simultaneous campaign against the Sallee rovers where the ships involved were required to career every two months.[11] Everyone knew that you needed plenty of fast, shallow-draught vessels equipped with oars to catch pirates and yet, once again, few of these were employed. The Jamaican Commodore Barrow Harris bemoaned this weakness in 1723 when discussing his attempts to catch the Spanish pirate sloops and piraguas (dug-out canoes) operating near the shores of Cuba, 'which makes it only chance if the ships catch any of them'. He begged for 'two or three 6th-rates or sloops of 100 men each (well fitted for rowing)' and said that he would be happy to exchange one of his larger ships for such vessels. This plea was partially heard since he was reinforced later in the year by the *Winchelsea*, a sixth-rate fitted with oars, 'exactly adapted for the service she comes here for'.[12]

This was not the only plea from its captains that the Admiralty eventually reacted favourably to, since it was clear that something had to change if the campaign was going to be a success and the continuous complaints from the captains often made good sense. Ships were usually operating with full complements by the 1720s; orders were given to career twice and then three times a year; better provision was made for repairs and the treatment of the sick. Ships were no longer ordered home once their eight-month supply of

English provisions had been exhausted, as they had been at the beginning of the campaign, an important factor in providing continuity of command and expanding knowledge of local waters. There was still not the right mix of vessels to conduct an anti-pirate campaign, but there were moves in the right direction. The campaign against the pirates, like most campaigns, was a learning process, but it took several years for the Admiralty to learn very much and these were years of almost continuous success for the pirates.

The campaign was also undermined by the greed of the naval captains 'who, by dear experience, we know, love trading better than fighting', as the *New England Courant* put it in 1722. Captains had always been notorious for putting their lust for private gain before their duty, as has been seen, but in this campaign they seem to have surpassed themselves.[13] They traded on the Spanish Main instead of chasing pirates and, even when this had been absolutely banned, they were accused of hiring sloops to trade which they manned out of their own crews and convoyed to market with their own ships. They went out of their way to seek passengers wealthy enough to pay exorbitant fares, hired out their own men as labourers, charged merchant captains illegal convoy money, bought unnecessary equipment and took backhanders from merchants in doing so and had a host of other tricks up their sleeves.[14] The captains on the Jamaican station were the worst offenders, so much so that the governor of the island claimed in 1718 that, as a result of naval trading, the local seafaring men 'have not bread for want of employment which is the chief occasion of so many of them going a pirating'. But captains anywhere had a keen eye for potential profit, sometimes with disastrous consequences as when Captain Waldron of the *Greyhound*, the New York station ship, was murdered by Spaniards while trading on the coast of Cuba.[15] Chasing pirates was likely to be a low priority for such mercenary captains for, as one observer pointed out, 'the taking of pyrates . . . is but a dry business, unless they catch 'em by extraordinary good fortune, with a prize fresh in their mouths'.[16]

While it would be unfair to say that all captains all the time were chasing profits instead of pirates, there does seem to have been a dilatoriness and lack of determination among the Royal Navy captains in the early years of the campaign, which is reflected in their lack of success. However, matters were to improve. Complaints about captains became less common and indeed one later finds considerable praise from colonial authorities for the devotion to duty of particular captains. This improvement in attitude owed something to much stricter directions from the Admiralty, but probably more to the determination of the more active colonial governors, such as Alexander Spotswood of Virginia or General Hamilton in the Leeward Islands, who often sailed in person with the cruising naval vessels, and to the enthusiasm and success of individual captains whose example inspired the rest. Performance naturally varied from captain to captain, but overall they seem to have become more focused on doing their duty in the later years of the campaign and this was to be reflected in an improvement in their success rate from 1718 onwards.

Since naval force alone had been so unsuccessful in combating piracy in the first three years of the campaign, the government decided that it would be necessary to resort to that habitual back-up policy, an offer of general pardon, and by September 1717 copies of the royal proclamation to this effect were ready to be dispatched.[17] The terms were very generous and reflected the official view of the seriousness of the problem and the difficulty of resolving it by any other means. Pardon was offered to all pirates who surrendered before 5 September 1718 for all offences including murder in the course of piracy. The King also agreed that pirates' goods would not be forfeited, though he could do nothing about the legal reality that these were stolen goods which owners might try to recover by actions against the pardoned pirates, a possibility which caused many pirates to think twice about coming in with their loot. 'They doe declare,' wrote the Governor of Bermuda, 'that they will never surrender without the assurance of enjoying that they have gotten, for otherwise say we have ventured our necks for nothing.'[18] The proclamation also promised the full rigour of the law for those who refused to surrender and provided a scale of head-money for captured pirates, from £100 for commanders down to £20 for 'every private man'.

Copies of the proclamation reached Bermuda by December

1717, where Governor Bennett was optimistic about its effect,[19] and in the next few weeks were distributed throughout the colonies and the Royal Navy ships. Captain Vincent Pearce of the *Phoenix* in New York, for instance, received his copies on 25 January 1718, 'some of which I caused to be nailed up in the most public places of this citty', and other captains made similar arrangements for their distribution. Pearce was then sent by the Governor of New York to the Bahamas where he arrived with the proclamation on 23 February. This was a somewhat hazardous venture, since his ship was a small one and he had only a hundred men who could easily have been overwhelmed by the five hundred or so pirates then on Providence, whom he described as 'all subjects of Great Britain and young resolute wicked fellows'. These young fellows were, however, reported as 'all very quiet, respectful to Captain Pearce', and he had received 209 surrenders by the time of his departure on 6 April.[20] Other pirates had surrendered in Bermuda, Jamaica and elsewhere and the policy looked as though it would be effective in dividing the pirates, if not eliminating them.

Pearce's visit to the Bahamas was followed up a couple of months later by a major initiative to prevent the future use of these islands as a 'second Madagascar' by the pirates. On 26 July 1718, a squadron of three men-of-war arrived as escort to the newly appointed royal governor, Captain Woodes Rogers, who commanded a company of foot soldiers and three vessels of his own, including the former East Indiaman *Delicia*. Rogers, a famous former privateer and a bit of a national hero, was well suited for the job. He was commissioned to pardon pirates who surrendered, capture or drive out the rest, fortify Nassau and if possible attract some more peaceful settlers into the islands. His immediate arrival was somewhat spoiled by the insolence and antics of Captain Charles Vane, the only pirate to challenge his authority, who made an unsuccessful attempt to set fire to the royal ships. However, on the next day, when Rogers and his men landed, their reception was very encouraging. 'Governor Rogers made his entry and was received with a great deal of seeming joy by those that stile themselves marooners,' wrote Captain Pomeroy of the *Shark Sloop*, one of the royal escorts, while Captain Johnson embroiders this welcome in a delightful cameo. 'The pirate captains . . . drew up their crews in two lines, reaching from the waterside to the fort, the Governor and other officers marching between them; in the meantime, they being under arms, made a running fire over his head.'[21]

This ecstatic welcome did not blind Rogers to the fact that his was a difficult task in a group of islands said to contain five hundred or a thousand actual or former pirates, but he set to it with determination and was remarkably successful, despite heavy mortality among his men, lack of reinforcement and repeated threats of invasion by Spaniards and by pirates. Although piracy was to thrive in the outer islands for some years, he effectively eradicated 'the nest of robbers' which had terrorised shipping during the three years or so prior to his arrival. And, once his original escorts had left which they did fairly soon after his arrival, he did this with virtually no help from the Royal Navy, despite repeated requests for at least a couple of sloops to assist him.[22] In the summer of 1720, Rowland Hildesley, mate of HMS *Flamborough*, one of the few naval vessels which did go to the Bahamas, was able to report that there were nearly thirty trading sloops in the harbour at Providence, the guardship *Delicia* had thirty-six guns mounted, the fort was in better order than ever with sixty guns, and there were some six or seven hundred well-affected men on the island all in good health.[23] Woodes Rogers had done an amazing job, despite his continuous complaints in his letters home, and maybe the Admiralty was wise to leave him to get on with it without assistance. He was a fine commander and a good organiser and he showed great skill in selecting from among the former pirates those who would remain loyal if he gave them commissions to act as gamekeepers to hunt down their former colleagues.

The Bahamas may have been cleared of pirates, but the rest of the world had not and the favourable reports about the effects of the pardon which had reached England during the first half of 1718 were soon replaced by pessimism. Several pirate crews had ignored or laughed at the pardon, others who surrendered soon 'returned again, like the dog to the vomit', as Johnson elegantly put it,[24] and new gangs emerged, so that by late 1718 there were once again large numbers of pirates menacing the West Indies and the coast of America while some had already found their way to West African waters. 'The greatest part of them who surrendered themselves . . . are roving again', it was reported from New York, and this opinion was echoed throughout the colonies, the commodore in Jamaica writing that most of those who had surrendered there had 'gon off againe, under pretence for want of employ', while Woodes Rogers himself had to admit that the pirates had an 'itching desire to return to their former vile course of life'.[25] The policy of pardon has therefore usually been seen as a failure, though this needs to be qualified. Several competent pirate captains, including Hornigold and nearly all the original Jamaican captains, such as Jennings who led the raid on the Spanish salvage camp, did in fact leave off their trade early in 1718 and so did several hundred of their men. So the cheap option of pardon did have some beneficial effects, even if it resulted in fairly gentle pirates like Hornigold and Jennings, neither of whom attacked English vessels, being replaced by other captains who proved 'more cruel than formerly', as Governor Bennett of Bermuda alleged with some justification.[26]

Although piracy was to reach a new peak in 1719 and the early 1720s, one can see with hindsight that 1718 marked a turning point in the fortunes of the Royal Navy and its auxiliaries. There was certainly no flood of successes, but there were some and the cumulative effect of these was sufficient to demonstrate to a wise pirate that the days of their 'very pleasant' way of life were numbered. In June, Francis Hume in the *Scarborough,* the only naval captain to capture a pirate ship in this campaign before 1718, had his second success when he surprised the French pirate Louis Le Bour at an island off the coast of Venezuela. Le Bour himself 'eat us out of the wind' and escaped in his sloop with fifty men and 'a considerable quantity of gold and silver', but his prize and eighteen of his men were captured and taken for trial at St Kitts, a small enough haul but better than the nothing that had been the norm for naval cruises.[27] In September, a much greater success was achieved with the defeat of Major Stede Bonnet of Barbados and his fifty-man gang in the Cape Fear River of North Carolina.

Bonnet was a rather comical figure among the pirates, a man of no previous maritime experience and the only gentleman among the pirate captains whose piracy, according to Captain Johnson, was 'said to have been occasioned by some discomforts he found in a married state', but for all that he was a pirate and took many prizes. He and his men were captured after a six-hour gun battle with two sloops commissioned by the Governor of South Carolina and led by Colonel William Rhett, an undertaking which the governor believed would 'very much irritate the pirates who infest the coast in great numbers'.[28] Shortly afterwards, the anti-pirate campaign of Governor Woodes Rogers in the Bahamas had its first success. He had gambled on the loyalty of two of the reformed pirates, Captains Hornigold and Cockram, by giving them commissions to go after John Auger, another reformed pirate who had turned rogue. This they did successfully and Auger and ten others were hanged at Providence 'in the sight of all their former companions and fellow-thieves'.[29]

These successes, fairly trivial though they might seem, were important for morale, both for the navy and for the colonial mercantile community as a whole. The names of Le Bour and Bonnet appear regularly in the correspondence of the naval captains as they reported, often inaccurately, their movements and depredations, and the news that they had been discommoded or in Bonnet's case destroyed was received with joy, as had been the news of Bellamy's shipwreck in the previous year. An anti-pirate campaign, like an anti-terrorist campaign, requires the pirates to be picked off crew by crew and man by man until there are none left. Even better was the news of the defeat and death of Captain Teach or Blackbeard, whose insolence and bravado infuriated the many naval captains who had searched for him in vain.

Blackbeard, after terrorising the American coast in 1717, had broken up his company and come into North Carolina, where he surrendered on the pardon with about twenty men. This was the last of the mainland colonies to provide support for pirates and Blackbeard was soon back on the account again, while the governor and other officials turned a blind eye to his activities. Fed up with his depredations and the refusal of the local authorities to do

anything about it, a deputation of local sloop masters appealed for
help to Governor Alexander Spotswood of Virginia, a man well
known for his hostility to pirates who was more than willing to
provide assistance. Two sloops were hired and crewed with sixty
men from the *Pearl* and the *Lyme*, the two royal ships on the
Virginia station, under the command of Lieutenant Robert
Maynard. Guided by local pilots, these sloops made their way to
where Blackbeard and some twenty or so men in the sloop
*Adventure* lay anchored on the inner side of Ocracoke Island, where
they were protected by shoals and sandbanks.

Although the pirates were surprised and most of them drunk,
they fought like furies and the battle on the morning of 22
November 1718 was very nearly a disaster for the navy. Maynard's
sloops first ran aground and then came under heavy fire, so heavy
that Blackbeard assumed he had killed most of the crew of the
leading sloop and boarded with ten of his pirates. Maynard,
however, had hidden most of his men and these now leaped up to
conduct a desperate hand-to-hand fight with the pirates, with
heavy loss on both sides, until Blackbeard was finally dispatched by
a Highlander in Maynard's crew who cut off the pirate's head with
his broadsword, a trophy which Maynard slung below the bowsprit
of his sloop as he sailed away from the bloody battle and into pirate
legend.[30] Eleven of the naval seamen were killed and more than
twenty wounded, a casualty rate of over 50 per cent, while eleven
of the pirates were killed and the remaining men, all badly
wounded, were taken prisoner and later tried in Virginia, all but
two of them being hanged. The Assembly of Virginia gave £300 to
the sailors who had so valiantly fought Blackbeard, but otherwise
the victors received only a modest reward for their bravery as there
was little booty aboard the pirate sloop and they were even cheated
of most of their head money, the Treasury Solicitor being of the
opinion 'that his Majesty's bounty money was only due for those
few that were not killed in the fight'.[31]

Pirate hunting was to give way to the more congenial and more
profitable sport of chasing Spanish shipping in 1719 and the first
few months of 1720. This change in emphasis was the result of the
brief war between the Great Powers and Spain known variously as

the War of the Quadruple Alliance or the War of Alberoni after the cardinal whose invasion of Sardinia had precipitated the conflict.[32] There were no great naval actions in American waters, but threats of invasion and convoy duty kept the royal ships busy while a host of privateers were commissioned by both England and Spain. The pardon for pirates was extended until 1 July 1719 in the hope that they might come in and take commissions against Spain, 'which they have long wisht for', as the Governor of Jamaica affirmed, though in fact most pirates who did take commissions took them from the Spanish, whose privateers were said to be manned mainly by the subjects of Great Britain and France, another instance of the extreme disloyalty of the pirates of this period.[33] Captain Whitney of HMS *Rose* predicted in April 1720 that 'these seas will be fuller of pyrates than ever, if there's a peace, for most of the sloops that have been commissioned by the [Spanish] Governours will never come in when they hear it'.[34] In fact, orders for the suspension of arms were already on their way when he wrote this letter, but Captain Whitney was absolutely right and the West Indies were to be harassed by rogue Spanish privateers for many months and in some cases many years into the future.

Meanwhile, the navy reverted to its anti-piracy campaign and now there was to be a new dimension to it as a result of complaints of very heavy depredations in West Africa and the Atlantic islands. Late in 1719 two forty-gun ships were ordered to convoy outgoing slavers via the Cape Verde Islands to the West African coast and then to search separately for pirates, keeping in correspondence with each other and officials in the slaving stations ashore, and returning home when short of provisions. Another two ships were sent out with similar orders late in 1720, but from 1722 onwards different tactics were employed. Single ships were sent to Africa, staggered by six months or so. After diligent search along increasingly long sections of the coast, they were to convoy the slavers to the West Indies and there join the Jamaican squadron for a month or so before cruising along the North American coast to offer assistance to the station ships. These ambitious orders, linking up the Africa ships with every other ship cruising against the pirates, show the increasing sophistication of Admiralty thinking, though in fact only one of the ships sent out to West Africa in this campaign actually engaged any pirates.[35]

This was the *Swallow* under Captain Challoner Ogle whose defeat of the pirate Bartholomew Roberts and his consort James Skyrme off Cape Lopez in February 1722 was the single greatest success of the whole anti-pirate campaign, a victory which led to a haul of 285 pirates dead or captured, with fifty-two of those captured being hanged at Cape Coast Castle, and a knighthood for the successful captain.[36] This success followed a ten-month game of hide-and-seek along the African coast in which Roberts initially had the advantage. Roberts arrived in Sierra Leone in June 1721 and learned from the English community living there – good friends of the pirates – that Ogle and his consort HMS *Weymouth* had already been and gone two months before. Roberts also discovered that Ogle's orders were to cruise right down the West African coast as far as the Bight of Biafra, where he was to careen, and then sail back with the south-east trade wind to Sierra Leone to repeat the cruise. So much for naval security!

Roberts thus had a clear run down the African coast, several weeks in the wake of the warships, and he made devastating use of it, taking prize after prize, improving his own men-of-war, increasing his crews with willing and forced recruits, and 'sinking, burning and destroying such goods and vessels as then happen'd in his way'. However, Roberts was to be undone by the notorious mortality prevalent in West African waters. There were so many deaths on the two royal ships, especially the *Weymouth*, that after careening Ogle decided to sail back only as far as Cape Coast Castle, in modern Ghana, where he could take on more men and fresh provisions. Here, he learned of Roberts' depredations and the tables were turned, as Roberts was now ahead of him and unaware of his whereabouts and impending approach. Six days later, Ogle left the disease-stricken *Weymouth* behind and set off in pursuit of the pirates. When he arrived in Whydah (Ouidah in modern Benin), he was told that Roberts had departed only thirty-six hours before, after having captured all eleven ships in the harbour. He had demanded a ransom in gold dust for their release which was paid by all but one, the *Porcupine*, which Roberts ordered to be burned, an atrocity which has for ever damned his name since she went up in flames with eighty slaves aboard chained together in pairs. The pirates, like the naval vessels, were unable to keep their future plans a secret and Ogle learned that Roberts and Skyrme planned to go somewhere on the islands or coast of the Bight of Biafra to fit out one of his prizes.

The search took three weeks but at last, on 5 February 1722, Ogle discovered the two pirate ships and their prize anchored at Cape Lopez on the coast of modern Gabon. The wind was such that he was unable to sail directly into the anchorage and, seeing him look in and then sheer off, Roberts assumed that the unknown ship was scared of him and so a potential prize, though it seems incredible that he and his men, all sailors, should fail to recognise the *Swallow* for what she was, a powerful two-decker warship with fifty guns and 280 men. He sent Skyrme in the thirty-two-gun *Ranger* in pursuit and Ogle prolonged the deception by deliberately slowing his ship until the *Ranger* was well out to sea and at close range. He then swung the *Swallow* round and opened fire with his broadside guns. Naval gunnery as usual completely outclassed pirate gunnery and an hour and a half later the pirate ship surrendered with twenty-six men killed or wounded, including her captain who had continued to command the ship after his leg had been shot off.

Ogle repaired his prize and sent her away with the hundred or so men captured, before returning to Cape Lopez to finish the job. He arrived at the anchorage early in the morning of 10 February and once again the pirates, many of whom seem to have been drunk, were not sure what sort of ship she was, despite having in their crew a man who had deserted from the *Swallow* earlier in her cruise. All became clear, however, when the royal ship displayed the King's colours and opened fire on Roberts and his crew of some two hundred men in the forty-gun *Royal Fortune*. Roberts slipped his cable in an attempt to sail past the warship and get clear, but he and his men were doomed as the *Swallow*'s great guns smashed away at his ship. Roberts himself, resplendent in crimson waistcoat and breeches and a hat with a red feather, was killed by a shot in the throat. The loss of their leader took the fight out of the pirates, though it was not till after the mainmast had been shot down that they surrendered and, even then, an attempt to blow up the ship was only narrowly foiled. A total of 262 men were captured from the two pirate ships, of whom seventy-five were black and consigned by Captain Ogle 'to be sold', without any enquiry being made into their status. The remainder were taken to Cape Coast Castle where their trials began on 28 March and were to last for nearly a month.

The complete destruction of Bartholomew Roberts and his gang, much the strongest pirate combine then at sea, was a devastating blow to the pirate community as a whole. It was really rather humiliating that two well-gunned, well-manned pirate ships should surrender so pusillanimously without a single royal sailor being killed in either action. Pirates were supposed to fight to the death, as Blackbeard and his men had done. But the raw courage of an individualist pirate was no match for the discipline of the Royal Navy in a single-ship action, as John Atkins the surgeon of the *Swallow* explained. 'Discipline is an excellent path to victory; and courage, like a trade, is gained by an apprenticeship, when strictly kept up to rules and exercise. The pirates though singly fellows of courage, yet wanting such a tie of order and some director to unite that force, were a contemptible enemy. They neither killed or wounded a man in the taking; which ever must be the fate of such rabble.'[37] The considerable proportion of forced men in the pirate crews – larger than in the ships of the Royal Navy whose men were nearly all volunteers in peacetime – and too much liquor were further problems for pirates when faced with a real battle, as William Snelgrave, among others, pointed out. 'The new-entered men had little courage . . . The far greater part . . . so much in drink, that there could have been no order or conduct amongst them in an engagement.'[38]

The early 1720s were to see many other successful actions by both the naval commanders and the sloop captains commissioned by the colonial governors, though none on quite the scale of Ogle's triumph. Late in 1720, Jonathan Barnet, 'a brisk fellow' in command of a Jamaican sloop, captured with little resistance Jack Rackam, once a pirate of some substance but now operating on a very small scale with only about a dozen men and two female crew members, Mary Read and Ann Bonny, whose presence on the pirate sloop has given rise to innumerable films and novels in which pirate queens play a prominent part. Diligent research has, however, shown that Read and Bonny were virtually the only female pirates, in the Atlantic and Caribbean world at least, but they were certainly participants and not just passengers or concubines.[39] One of Rackam's prisoners, giving evidence against them at their trial, said 'they were very active on board and willing to do any thing . . . when they saw any vessel, gave chase or attacked, they wore men's cloaths; and, at other times, they wore women's cloaths'. Rackam and the men in his crew were hanged, but the two women avoided the noose for the time being by declaring that they were 'quick with child' and no one is sure what finally happened to them.[40]

A few weeks later, the other great joker among the pirates, 'the famous fellow' Charles Vane, who had scorned Woodes Rogers in the Bahamas, was brought in. His career went right back to the beginnings on New Providence but by now he was down on his luck, 'reduced to great straits . . . subsisted chiefly by fishermen'. He shipped on a trading sloop as a sailor, intending 'to pick up a fresh gang' in Jamaica, but he was recognised, clapped in irons and speedily brought to justice. 'He has been tried, condemned and executed, and is now hanging in chains,' wrote Captain Vernon, the commodore in Jamaica. 'These punishments have made a wonderfull reformation here.'[41]

Attention was also focused on the many quasi-pirates who operated under real or pretended Spanish commissions. Early in 1721, Captain Vernon captured the Spanish privateer sloop *Revenge*, with a crew of all nations and colours 'commanded by Simon Mascarino, a Portuguese and noted villain in these parts where he has been privatier and pirate these twenty years'.[42] A year later, Captain Candler in the *Launceston* sent a search party aboard a suspicious-looking sloop which claimed to be a trader from Puerto Rico. They found 'she had most of her men hid in the hold, the whole consisting of 58 men which were all brought aboard'. This turned out to be another 'revenge', the *Vengeance* or *Venganza* which unusually for a pirate sloop was described as 'very old and ill found'. She was commanded by the 'notorious' pirate Matthew Luke (presumably really Matteo Luca since he was said to be Genoese) and her crew consisted mainly of Indians and mulattoes from Puerto Rico, one of whom boasted that he had murdered twenty Englishmen with his own hands. The *Launceston* arrived back in Port Royal on 27 April 1722 and, in less than two weeks, 'the pretended Spanish guarda coasta' had been 'prov'd a pyrate', the men tried and forty-three of the crew hanged, the captain in chains. Such breathless justice naturally appalled the Spanish authorities who had given Luke his commission and their reaction is reflected in the words of a Spanish historian of piracy. 'Such an inconceivable act of barbarism showed clearly how little Jamaica and its governors had changed since the days of Morgan.' Such sentiments had no effect on the authorities in Jamaica who continued to urge the naval captains to hunt down these rogues who attacked their shipping under Spanish colours and, in particular, those most notorious rogues and renegades of all, Nicholas Brown and Christopher Winter.[43]

The following year, 1723, saw the end of two more of the prominent English pirate crews who had flourished in the early 1720s, those of Thomas Anstis and George Lowther. Both these gangs had made unsuccessful attempts to petition for pardon and both had suffered a haemorrhage of their men, as members of their crews took any opportunity they could to escape from what seemed an increasingly dangerous profession. In January 1723, Anstis and his consort John Fenn, 'a one-handed man', sailed to the uninhabited island of Tobago to careen their ship and discuss their future. Dissatisfaction was rife among their men, especially a group led by William Wilks, who had already made one attempt to escape but had been recaptured 'and tried by their jury for desertion for which they were severely whipped'. Now, with Anstis's guns out on the shore and his brigantine heaved over on the careen, they took their chance, seized a prize sloop and sailed for England, 'there to disperse themselves and be conceal'd by running their sloop ashore and pretending themselves cast away seamen'. The remaining pirates argued among themselves and eventually broke up into two groups, one under Anstis, who planned to continue roving, and the other under Fenn, who decided to remain on the island 'untill an opportunity should offer how they might convey themselves amongst some civilised people, conceal'd from the punishment due for their villainy'.[44]

All three paths proved fruitless. Wilks and his men wrecked their sloop near Minehead in Somerset and were then captured by the English authorities ashore. Anstis's men 'mutinied amongst themselves about surrendering and, in the scuffle on board, Anstis was kill'd with one or two more and the brigantine carried into Curaçao'. Here, they were tried and hanged by the Dutch, except 'those concerned in delivering up the vessel' who were acquitted.[45] Meanwhile, news that there were pirates hiding on Tobago had got abroad and Fenn's men were to be hunted by sailors from no less than four royal ships. Captain Charles Brown in the *Feversham* managed to destroy the pirates' boat and capture two of the men, but after a week, on 4 March, he gave up 'finding all my endeavours to persuade the pyrates to come in fruitless, and also seeing it morally impossible to come at them by the thickness of the woods'.[46]

Captain Humphrey Orme of HMS *Winchelsea* was made of sterner stuff and spent over three weeks scouring the island in April. Day after day, he sent out search parties of twenty or thirty men who found huts built by the fugitives and a canoe which they destroyed, bags of clothes, caches of arms, shot and powder, but not one of the pirates who melted away into the thick woods which had baffled Captain Brown. At last, after twelve days' search, Orme saw 'a white handkerchief on a stick', a signal from one of the pirates that he would betray his mates in return for mercy. Even then some pirates defied discovery, but one was killed and nine captured, including Captain Fenn, and all these were hanged in Antigua, except two 'evidences', as those who acted as witnesses against their shipmates were called, 'and one pardoned, Domingo Fort, a lame man whom the Court deem'd an object of pity'.[47] No naval officer in the early years of the campaign would have showed such persistence and devotion to duty, and this was duly recognised by the merchant ships who saluted these famous pirate hunters with their guns when the *Winchelsea* sailed into port, while the

Governor of the Leeward Islands praised 'the indefatigable care' of Orme and his brother captains 'in pursuing the pyrates whenever they hear of them'.[48]

Similar determination was shown six months later by Walter Moore, captain of a sloop in the service of the South Sea Company, the English trading company which had acquired permission to trade in South America. He was sailing from St Kitts to Cumana in Venezuela when, on 5 October 1723, he saw George Lowther's sloop on the careen at the island of Blanquilla. He immediately decided to attack before he should be attacked himself. After a short fight most of the pirates asked for quarter, but Lowther himself 'with about ten or twelve of his crew made their escape out of the cabbin window'. Moore secured his prize and his nineteen prisoners and set off with twenty-five men to search the scrub-covered island for the fugitives. Five days search produced just five of them and he now decided that enough was enough and continued his voyage to Cumana, whose governor sent out another search party which recovered four more men who were condemned to the galleys for life, 'leaveing behind them the captain, three men and a little boy which they could not take.' What happened to the three men and the little boy is unknown, but Captain Lowther appears to have committed suicide 'upon that fatal island where his piracies ended', for he was later found dead 'and a pistol burst by his side', some indication of just how depressing the prospects of pirates had become.[49]

The most celebrated success of 1723, however, did not take place among the woods and scrub of subtropical islands, but in the ocean off Long Island, New York, where for the first and only time in this campaign a man-of-war caught up, fought and captured a pirate vessel in the open sea, a sure sign that the navy was at last beginning to use the right ships.[50] The hero of the hour was Captain Peter Solgard of HMS *Greyhound*, a 'rowing 6th-rate' with twenty guns and 130 men. In the early hours of 10 June 1723, he sighted the two pirate sloops of Edward Lowe and his consort Charles Harris, each with eight or ten guns and some 175 men between them. He tacked and sailed away from the pirates to encourage them to give chase and then, when they had closed, went about and bore down on them. They hoisted their black flags and, when Solgard showed no sign of surrender, their red flags to indicate that they would give no quarter. Fire was exchanged for an hour or so, but the pirates, getting the worst of it, broke off the action and tried to escape with their oars. But, for once, this did not help them, for Solgard left off firing and put over half his crew on to his own oars and came up between the two pirate sloops whom he engaged from both sides of his ship. At four in the afternoon, the mainsail of Charles Harris's sloop was shot away and he soon after called for quarter, but Lowe, the great escaper (some say the great coward who deserted his consort), got away as night began to fall.

Harris and twenty-five of his men were later hanged in Rhode Island and Solgard was much fêted by the Corporation of New York who gave him the freedom of the city. But, as so often before, the monetary rewards for him and his men were disappointing. Solgard was promised by the Admiralty that 'the whole produce of the . . . pirate sloop [would] be bestowed on my self, officers and ship's company when a year and a day shall be expired', in theory quite a generous reward for taking a pirate prize but in fact not much, since Harris's sloop had 'nothing on board but provisions and arms, the company's chest (as they call it) being on board the other'. Later, some released prisoners said that this chest contained 'nearly £150,000 value in gold and silver coin and plate' which sounds rather a lot, but is just possible given the huge number of prizes that Lowe had taken.[51] Nor did the men of the *Greyhound* have much joy of the head money they had earned by their strenuous rowing and accurate gunfire, £100 for a commander and £20 for 'every private man'. Nearly two years after the battle, in March 1725, Captain Solgard reported to the Admiralty that he was having trouble with his crew who were demanding prize money that he could not give, since 'His Majesty's royall bounty' had not yet been received. Such impatience! Delays and dirty tricks by the authorities in the payment of prize money were notorious. Captain Ogle and his men only got the prize money for their victory over Roberts three years after the battle, in May 1725, and even then the head money was paid out of the value of the gold that had been captured and not, as it should have been, in addition to it.[52]

So many successes meant that by the end of 1723 the war against the pirates was virtually won, a remarkable turnround in fortune for the navy after the repeated failures of the early years of the campaign. Getting on for a thousand pirates had been killed or captured on their ships or in attempts to escape ashore. Many hundreds of others had been pardoned or had crept ashore in haunts such as the Virgin Islands, the Bay Islands of Honduras, the Moskito Coast, Madagascar or West Africa where many former pirates were said to be living among the natives. Many hundreds more must have died of the diseases prevalent in West African and West Indian waters, for mortality was likely to have been higher in the densely packed and very unhygienic pirate ships than in those of the Royal Navy who lost well over a thousand men to disease in this campaign. Such destruction and dispersal meant that there were not many pirates left at sea, less than two hundred according to one estimate,[53] most of them in gangs led either by Lowe or by former consorts or subordinates of his, such as Spriggs, Cooper, Lyne and Shipton. These last remaining pirate captains and their men were to be hunted remorselessly by the navy, but they were to prove amazingly elusive.

In September 1723, Captain Wyndham of HMS *Diamond* heard news of Lowe's presence in the Cape Verde Islands. 'I follow'd him by intelligence I met from island to island', but Lowe always kept an island ahead, though the need for hasty departures meant that he leaked men left ashore, eighteen in all, half killed and half captured.[54] In the summer of 1724, Lowe and Farrington Spriggs, his former quartermaster but now captain of his own ship, were being chased about the Virgin Islands with no success, and then, at the end of August, it looked as though Captain Wyndham had Spriggs and his consort Shipton trapped at anchor at Belize in Honduras. But once again the pirates escaped; 'the ship got away through the South Channel, the sloop in the East Channel . . . I judge our misfortune in not taking them is owing to . . . the intricateness and difficulty of the channels for a ship of our draught of water.'[55] A year later, virtually all the remaining pirates were back in the Gulf of Honduras whose coasts and islands had always been a favourite haunt. Most of the gangs were now very small, constantly arguing with each other and breaking up into different groupings, and they were to live a desperate existence as they were hunted from island to island by the *Diamond* and the *Spence Sloop*. The most successful of these naval cruises was the last, conducted in January and February 1726, by Lieutenant Bridge in a Spanish sloop recaptured from the pirates and manned with fifty sailors from the *Diamond*. First, he caught sight of the pirate Cooper at the island of Bannaco in a large Bermuda sloop which he boarded after forcing it aground on a shoal. 'The pyrats were very obstinate and, being beaten from their deck, they retired into the cabbin and blew it up,' the explosion killing one of Bridge's men and wounding eight. 'The pyrates had four killed and the rest exceedingly wounded to a man, being in number aboard twenty-four,' three of the wounded later dying, including Captain Cooper. Bridge then searched the islands of Utila and Roatán where Spriggs was found camped out on a small key with just six men. Two were captured but the rest, including Spriggs, got away in the night. Next call was the Moskito coast where, guided by Indians, Bridge took three more of Spriggs's men and also Captain Shipton who was captured in bed, a shameful end for a pirate captain. He finally returned to Bannaco where he sighted the mighty Lowe under the west end of the island, now fallen to the command of just eight men in a piragua. The royal sailors pursued him in a canoe, but it foundered in a storm and the lieutenant now decided to call it a day and return to the *Diamond*.[56]

No one knows the fate of Spriggs, but the other two remaining pirate captains, Philip Lyne and Ned Lowe, were eventually taken by the Dutch and the French respectively, both of which nations were also active against the pirates though not with the same commitment as the British. The captain of the Barbados station ship reported in March 1726 that Lyne had 'been taken by two Dutch vessels belonging to Curaçao', while Captain Johnson in a postscript to his account of Lowe's piratical career says that 'his barbarity caused a mutiny among his men, who set him adrift in a small boat without any provisions. The next day he was picked up by a French boat.' The great escaper could not escape this time and he was hanged at Martinique.[57]

Lieutenant Bridge's spirited campaign just about marked the

end of piracy, though unfortunately no one informed one William Fry of this fact. His bid for piratical glory was, however, to be extremely brief, lasting just forty-six days from his leadership of a mutiny aboard the *Elizabeth Snow* on 27 May 1726, through his taking a couple of prizes, the retaking of the Snow by some of his prisoners, and so to his hanging in chains at the entrance to Boston harbour on 12 July.[58] After this, it was really just a question of a bit of mopping up, nicely symbolised by the arrival at Jamaica in November 1726 of the sloop master John Drudge with a keg of rum containing the severed head of his former schoolfellow, the long sought-after pirate in Spanish service Nicholas Brown, whose head was sufficient to earn for Drudge the reward of £500 promised by the Jamaican government for his capture, dead or alive.[59]

And so at last the golden age of piracy came to an end. The freedom- and drink-loving pirates had their moment of fame, but in the long run the navy, the law and the self-destructive nature of the pirates themselves ensured that piracy was not an occupation with a very long life expectancy. Of the fifty-five pirate captains of this period whose fate has been determined – about two-thirds of the total number – twelve surrendered and lived out their lives in varying degrees of comfort or destitution, one retired in poverty to Madagascar, six were killed in action, four drowned in shipwrecks, four were shot by their own men, one shot himself and one was set adrift by his men in an open boat and never heard of again. The remaining twenty-six were hanged, often under their own black flags, by the French, Dutch, Portuguese and Spaniards as well as by the British, in Africa and Antigua, Boston, the Bahamas and Brazil, Carolina, Curaçao and Cuba, London, Martinique, Rhode Island and the island of Bourbon in the Indian Ocean where Olivier La Buse, the last pirate captain of the golden age to be captured, was hanged on the beach in July 1730 'before a cheering crowd'.[60]

It was not just captains that were hanged. This was 'an extermination campaign', when pirates were no longer punished by the token hanging of three or four of their number chosen by lot or a throw of the dice, as had been the custom in the past. Pirates in this period were hung in tens and twenties and, in the case of Roberts' men, over fifty at a time. The historian Marcus Rediker has estimated that 'no fewer than 400, and probably 500–600 Anglo-American pirates were executed between 1716 and 1726', a colossal number even in an age notorious for its love of the gallows.[61] The great majority of these unfortunate men were tried in the colonies in the jury-free courts set up by the Act of 1700.[62] These courts were fair by the standards of the day, though hardly by those of ours. They were, after all, trying men deemed to be 'enemies of mankind', men who had for the most part been captured in arms while openly defying the world under their black flags. The courts had no sympathy for such men, but nevertheless took pains to determine who among those captured were deserving of mercy.

Most of the defendants pleaded not guilty, relying on 'the hackney defence made by every pirate upon trial, namely, that he was a forced man'.[63] This defence was, of course, quite often true and the courts did not dismiss it out of hand. Evidence on the defendant's behaviour when a prize was taken might be gained from former captives of the pirate ship, but the most effective means of sorting out the sheep from the goats was to acquit two or three men at an early stage in the proceedings and then use their evidence for and against their shipmates to determine who should be acquitted in their turn. In this way, no less than seventy-seven of Bartholomew Roberts' men were acquitted in their trials at Cape Coast Castle, to be set against the fifty-two who were hanged and the thirty-nine who received lesser but not necessarily less lethal punishments, such as serving in the mines in Africa.[64]

The transcript of these trials enables us to see what evidence was likely to sway the judges. Witnesses for those who were acquitted might say that they were beaten to force them to join the pirates and had a pistol at their head while signing the articles. They were likely to have taken little or no part in battles or the capture of prizes, to have attempted to escape or at least consulted 'together of some manner of escape, though it was death or marooning amongst them to be found or known so doing'. They were described as creeping about the decks or hiding in corners with a long face, 'allways melancholy and discontented, lamenting the condition of life he was in', as one witness averred at the trial of

Robert Lilburn. Lilburn, once acquitted, was himself introduced as a witness on behalf of other prisoners such as Thomas Wills whom he said 'was no pirate in heart, never swearing or drinking but on the contrary commonly reading of good books'. The court commented, as they acquitted Wills, that it was 'a pity so godly a man should have been so long in such ill company'.[65]

The guilty, by contrast, went about with a cheerful air and were well affected to the pirates, quick to board a prize or man a gun in battle. They might be described by hostile witnesses as being 'look'd upon as a trusty hand among them', 'as forward a man (that is as great a rogue) as any in the company' or 'a brisk hand', this being, as was explained to the court, 'a mild term used by the brotherhood for a rogue'. It was these brisk hands, young men of the sea who had so often proclaimed their disdain for death, who were likely to be sentenced to be taken 'to the place of execution without the gates of this castle, and there within the flood marks to be hanged by the neck, till you are dead, dead, dead'.[66]

# Maritime Mayhem Revived

# Maritime Mayhem Revived

The determined efforts of Captains Ogle and Solgard, Lieutenants Maynard and Bridge and other unsung naval heroes effectively cleared the seas of mass piracy for the best part of a century. The navy retained and indeed increased its presence on colonial stations and this naval threat, combined with the awful memory of the fate of those pirates captured in the 1720s, ensured that sailors no longer thought the game was worth the risk. Each of the three great naval wars of the middle years of the eighteenth century saw large numbers of privateers commissioned, but no longer did this lead to a resurgence of piracy once peace returned. The seas were now safe from predators, in peacetime at least, and this new security was reflected in a reduction in crews and armaments on merchant vessels and a resulting rise in maritime productivity.[1]

This is not to say that there was absolutely no piracy at all. In the Indian Ocean, there were dangers from Indian and Arab pirates on the Malabar Coast and in the Persian Gulf, though some historians say that the British only chose to term these seafarers 'pirates' in order to provide a good excuse to suppress them and so remove their commercial competition, a new twist on the old theme of piratical imperialism.[2] And elsewhere the occasional pirate appeared from time to time, mostly privateers in wartime exceeding or totally ignoring the terms of their commissions or mutineers who, once they had done the deed, had little choice but to engage in piracy in order to survive until their almost inevitable capture.[3] Some of these incidents were dramatic enough, such as the short-lived mutiny with piratical intent of HMS *Chesterfield* in October 1748, which provided a nice link with the past as one of its leaders had sailed with Bartholomew Roberts nearly thirty years before the mutiny.[4] However, this and other incidents amounted to very little against the background of an enormous expansion in the world's merchant shipping, which was able to carry peacefully and with little fear of pirates the products of the early Industrial Revolution.

Merchants, shipowners and sailors might then have been excused for believing that they would once again be able to go about their business in peace when the French Revolutionary and Napoleonic Wars at last came to an end in 1815, after nearly a quarter of a century of worldwide maritime warfare and privateering. But, alas, this was not to happen and there was probably more piracy and maritime mayhem in the first fifteen years of what has been labelled the Pax Brittanica than there had ever been in the so-called Golden Age of Piracy. None of these latter-day pirates has captured the popular imagination, and their names and indeed the very fact that they existed have been almost forgotten, so much so that most books on European and American piracy end in about 1730. Nevertheless, they certainly did exist, as can be seen in the most casual glance at the newspapers of the period which regularly record their depredations and atrocities.

The background to these years of anarchy at sea was provided by the Latin American Wars of Independence which effectively started in 1808 when Napoleon's conquest of Spain cut off the mother country from her colonies. Here is not the place to retell the story of this epic struggle in which great armies marched and counter-marched and fought great battles from Chile to Colombia and from what would later become Argentina to the borders of the United States. These heroic wars were decided principally on land, but there was also an important maritime element which is often forgotten. Most of the insurgent governments created navies, making full use of the abundance of American and European naval talent and shipping left unemployed after 1815. And most of them commissioned privateers to prey on the shipping of Spain and sometimes Portugal and therein lay the problem for the safety of world shipping.

These privateers were known generically as the Independent or

Patriot corsairs and they flew a variety of flags, which must have made life even more complicated for the ships' captains of the day than it does for the historian, especially as most of the privateer captains changed their flags and the names of their ships on several occasions in the course of their careers.[5] First to sea were the Buenos Aires or Argentine privateers who, once they had captured virtually all Spanish shipping off the River Plate, turned their attention to the West Indies and increasingly to the coasts of Spain itself. They were quickly followed into action by the corsairs of Colombia, who were known in English-language sources as the Carthagenian privateers after their base at Cartagena de Indias. This port was recovered by the monarchists in 1816, after which the Carthagenians found shelter and good friends in Haiti whose black republicans and slaves had successfully rebelled against their French masters in the 1790s, a major landmark in black history. The Haitians were now attempting to complete the job by recovering from the Spaniards the eastern part of the island, today's Dominican Republic, and they too commissioned corsairs to assist them in this enterprise. Other privateers flew the flags of Venezuela and of Mexico, the latter operating from Texan ports such as Galveston and Matagorda and from the island of Amelia in Florida until they were driven out when this became part of the United States in 1819. Other bases used by the corsairs included the Venezuelan island of Margarita, famous for its pearl divers, and many places once used by pirates, such as the island of Old Providence or Santa Catalina which had been the headquarters of puritan buccaneering in the 1630s.[6]

Last but not least there were the corsairs who from 1816 onwards flew the flag of General José Gervasio Artigas, the gaucho *caudillo* of the Banda Oriental, or what is today Uruguay. His commissions were especially valued since he was at war with both Portuguese Brazil and the Spanish province of the River Plate and so his privateers could legally attack the shipping of both countries. As a result, many independent privateers carried a commission from General Artigas in addition to one from, say, Buenos Aires or Mexico. There was no need to sail as far as Montevideo to acquire one of these, since 'near a hundred commissions signed by Artigas to cruise against Portuguese vessels are already on their way to North America', as the British commodore on the Brazil station reported in April 1818. Most of these commissions would be sold by agents in places such as the Swedish island of St Bartholomew's, one of many general clearing houses and prize markets for this privateering business. Ships sailing under the flag of Artigas, 'a convenient covering for every vessel with piratical intentions' as it was described in a dispatch from Jamaica, had the unenviable reputation of committing the worst excesses and these so-called commissions were for sale long after the general's death in 1821.[7]

Who engaged in this adventurous and violent occupation which both historians and contemporaries have considered a throwback to the days of Henry Morgan and Blackbeard?[8] The answer is that just about any unemployed sailor from any country in the world might find himself aboard one of these hundreds of privateering vessels preying on the shipping of Spain and Portugal, or to put it more colourfully, as *The Times* did in 1819, 'this villainous heterogeneous mass of ocean highwaymen are the very ejectment of the four quarters of the globe'.[9] One major source of captains, crews and ships was the United States which provided the majority of all corsair ships sailing under the flag of Buenos Aires, as well as contributing to other corsair fleets. The main centre of this activity was Baltimore and the vessels of choice were the famous Baltimore clippers, the fastest ships in the world at that time, 'with masts like the ears of a vicious horse thrown back on its neck', as a contemporary travel writer described them.[10] These ships had been developed during the War of 1812 against Britain and they were often commanded by former privateer heroes of that war. The United States was sympathetic to the Latin American struggle against Spanish imperialism, but these captains and their backers had little interest in politics and were strictly mercenary in their motivation. Their illegal efforts to bring back their prizes for sale in the United States, either by smuggling or after changes of packing, marks, bills of lading and supposed ownership in places such as St Thomas's or St Bartholomew's, recall the similar activities of those former Americans who backed the Red Sea men in the 1690s.[11]

Not all corsair captains were so mercenary as the Americans and the many former naval officers and privateersmen from Britain and Europe who took part in this lucrative business. The first corsairs to offer their services in the cause of Latin American independence were former French West Indian privateers who combined a Jacobin republican ideology with a consciousness of themselves as '*les garçons de la côte*', the heirs of the *flibustier* tradition of the seventeenth century, now savaging the Spaniards in a more honourable cause. Similar men were to be found as captains and officers in the fleet of Venezuelan privateers commanded by Louis Aury, French and Italian political adventurers who like Aury himself had served in the French revolutionary armies. It is doubtful, however, whether much of the revolutionary idealism of these white officers was shared by their largely black and mulatto crews, sailors and fishermen from Santo Domingo, Margarita, Guadeloupe and elsewhere who were often recruited by force and had little hope of great profit, however great the gains of the ship.[12]

This whole system of privateering with its cosmopolitan crews, most of them money-hungry, violent by nature and with no interest at all in Latin America, was a potential powder keg of trouble. Nevertheless, this trouble took some time to emerge. The governments of the major neutral powers, such as Britain, France and the United States, were all sympathetic to the cause of Latin American independence, partly for ideological reasons and partly because its success would open the ports of South America to a lucrative trade for their subjects. They therefore recognised the right of the independent privateers to attack Spanish and Portuguese shipping, so long as they respected the rights of neutrals and carried out their business properly by establishing courts where legitimate prizes could be condemned and where those who broke the rules could be tried and punished. The insurgent governments themselves were intent on not antagonising the great powers, whose support was essential to their cause, and so instructed their privateers to treat neutral shipping with the greatest respect. And, for a while, everything went along swimmingly. The British shipping papers reported the huge number of prizes taken by the independent privateers, some of them of great value, such as the *Esperanza* belonging to the Spanish Royal Philippine Company valued at a million dollars, and noted with pleasure (and some surprise) the great 'civility' with which their captains treated British merchantmen whom they had detained to check their papers.

But with so many privateers at sea and the Spanish and Portuguese merchant fleets rapidly declining in size, such civility was unlikely to last for ever. From 1816 onwards there was a crescendo of complaints against the rapacious and sometimes cruel behaviour of the privateers towards neutral shipping. Sometimes, this was fairly trivial, a hogshead of rum or some provisions or stores seized without payment, or the captain of a merchantman relieved of his watch and navigational instruments. But such depredations were to become increasingly frequent and serious. In May 1817, for instance, the British schooner *Hope* was attacked by a vessel under Carthagenian colours. 'The crew were principally blacks and mulattoes who behaved in the most outrageous and ruffianly manner,' it was reported in the shipping paper *Lloyd's List*. 'They stripped the *Hope* of all her provisions, excepting a piece of pork and a few biscuits; plundered 2,761 dollars; tortured the pilot to ascertain if more money was on board; took away the people's clothes and the shoes off their feet.' In the same month, the paper reported that the French brig *Le Lys* had been boarded by a small privateer schooner whose men relieved her of a considerable part of her cargo, jewellery, all the captain's private adventure, his stores, spyglass, compass and some of the vessel's sails. 'The commander was a Frenchman and behaved in the most brutal way to Captain Liebray and his crew, many of whom were severely beaten.'[13] Not even semi-official vessels were spared. In March 1818, the *Princess Elizabeth* packet boat carrying the mail from Rio de Janeiro to Falmouth was boarded by two vessels under Spanish colours, 'no common pirates' as they were described in *The Times*. They rifled the packet, taking money, watches, the baggage of the passengers 'and jewels which were reported to be very valuable', and then released her, 'having previously debated with earnestness whether they should not sink her, with her passengers and crew', a proposal which was fortunately vetoed by one of the privateer captains.[14] All this looked remarkably like piracy and it was certainly not the way that the crews of neutral ships expected to be dealt with, in the early nineteenth century at least. It was, however, the way that they were increasingly likely to be treated, as Captain Postlethwaite of the British ship *James* discovered in December 1818. He was boarded by the mainly English crew of a Venezuelan corsair vessel who proceeded to search for money and anything else in the most riotous manner. 'I must rob you',' said the privateer captain. 'Damn the British flag and all flags, all flags were alike to him . . . money he wanted and money he would have.' There was, in fact, not much money aboard and the corsair had to be content with liquor, chickens, a spyglass and sextant and the wearing apparel of the crew, all of which was collected while the sailors were herded below and the marauders drank their way through 'three dozen and a half of port wine'.[15]

Such incidents, which multiplied in the next few years, were the product of frustration at the growing absence of legitimate prizes and were not too different in kind from the illegal depredations of privateers in previous wars, though there were far more of them. Anarchy at sea was, however, to get much worse as a result of a spate of mutinies aboard the privateer ships in the years around 1820. Prominent among these were the black crews of many privateers based in the West Indies who, incensed by the racist inequality aboard and their derisory share of booty, murdered or otherwise disposed of their white officers and set off on piratical cruises against all comers, cruises which often ended in Haiti where their services were more than welcome.[16] The threat of capture, torture and possibly a sadistic death at the hands of black pirates stirred up predictable racial fears among travellers at sea, which were reflected in European and American newspapers. In May 1818, for instance, a report came in from Martinique that the French schooner *Emily* had been boarded by the former Independent privateer *Little Pelican*, whose black crew had mutinied and got rid of their officers at the island of Margarita. They robbed the passengers, captain and sailors of their money, clothing and everything else of value they could lay their hands on, 'even rings from the ears of some of the crew'. They 'tortured the boatswain to force him to confess where money might be concealed, and insulted the passengers (two of whom were ladies) in a most inhuman manner'.[17]

Mutiny was no monopoly of black sailors. Many of the corsair ships based at Baltimore also mutinied, some because they were terrified of the potential legal consequences of their captains' increasingly illegal behaviour, but most because these men too received only a small share of booty and wanted to make the most of the mayhem at sea while it lasted.[18] In 1819, for example, the mainly American crew of the Buenos Aires privateer *Luisa* mutinied off Africa while her captain was aboard a prize and set off on a cruise of murder and depredation. They plundered every ship at the Isle of May (Maio in the Cape Verdes), as ever a favourite target for pirates, robbed the customs house and inhabitants, murdering some of them, and then set off towards the United States, thieving from any ship they could capture and killing those who met their displeasure. They eventually ran their ship ashore in Carolina, where they were seized and their leaders tried and executed, after what *The Times* described as 'a series of atrocities of the most revolting description, particularly as relates to the mode in which Captain Sunby and his mate [of the British brig *Ann*] were put to death . . . stabbed in the act of supplicating for their lives'.[19] The *Luisa* was far from being alone in committing such atrocities and travelling at sea became alarmingly dangerous for neutral merchant shipping, as rogue privateers roamed the Atlantic and Pacific, the West Indies and West Africa, where the coast of Sierra Leone was described by a returning ship's captain as 'lined with pirates under every foreign flag, and their animosity towards the English is very great'.[20]

Bad though this situation was, it was to get very much worse, as can be seen from the computerised index to *The Times* which records three articles on piracy in 1818, three in 1819, twelve in 1820 and no less than twenty-eight in 1822. This sudden escalation in interest in piracy reflected the growing numbers of rogue privateers, but was principally focused on one incredibly dangerous part of the world – the coasts of Cuba and to a lesser extent of Hispaniola and Puerto Rico. Small-scale piracy was endemic in these regions but, from the second half of 1821 onwards, this was to grow into an epidemic of piracy more intensive and more terrifying to the victim than any other considered in this book. The epicentre was the north-west coast of Cuba, from Cape San Antonio, the most westerly point of the island, to Matanzas, a stretch of coastline studded with creeks and cays and other hiding places from which pirate vessels could attack merchant ships sailing through the Straits of Florida or the Old Bahama Channel, two of the busiest shipping routes in the world.[21]

These pirates were based ashore, where they had plenty of friends who would protect them if they were attacked and sell their booty in the markets of the island, even in Havana itself, the seat of the Spanish royal government of this 'ever faithful island', as Cuba which never rebelled was known. To begin with, they operated on a very small scale, using open boats with five or six men armed with muskets, pistols, cutlasses and long knives, quite sufficient to overawe the lightly manned and often unarmed merchant ships that were their prey.[22] Later, bigger crews of fifty or sixty, sometimes as many as a hundred, were reported. Their vessels were beautiful and very fast feluccas and schooners, all fitted with sweeps, and it was said by an American naval officer that they never went further out to sea than the distance which could be covered in four hours' rowing from the coast, so that if they were threatened by naval ships they could swiftly return to the almost impenetrable coastal maze of cays, creeks, shoals and mangrove swamps where pursuit was virtually impossible. These were classic pirates, lurking in their coastal redoubts, darting out and pursuing their prey 'with astonishing rapidity', boarding, driving captured crews below and ransacking their prizes with ruthless thoroughness. No merchant ship could compete with them in speed either with sweeps or sails and, just to weight the contest even further in the pirates' favour, there was a period of a few hours 'in the early part of every day [when] merchant vessels may be found becalmed near the land'.[23] Such vessels were sitting ducks and the pirates captured hundreds of them in their brief period of unrestrained success and glory.

The pirate crews were made up of 'the idle, vicious, and desperate of all nations', as was reported to the American House of Representatives in March 1822, former privateersmen, sailors and fishermen, escaped slaves, anyone black, white or mulatto who could wield a cutlass or a knife, but overall there was a very Spanish (or rather Cuban) feel about this 'fraternity of the most dangerous kind', as they were described in *The Times*.[24] Most of their vessels and captains had Hispanic names, the pirates were routinely described as swarthy and massively moustachioed, and they displayed a very *macho* Spanish combination of dignity, cruelty and love of the fiesta. Aaron Smith, an Englishman who claimed to have been forced to serve on one of their ships, described a party on board after the pirates had brought the product of a good prize to their well-hidden anchorage. 'A great deal of company from the shore' came aboard, including magistrates and their families, priests and pretty *señoritas*, who admired and bargained for the plundered goods laid out on deck, ate the plundered delicacies, drank the plundered wines and spirits, and then settled down to a fine fiesta, singing and dancing to the music of guitars. One cannot imagine Blackbeard or Bartholomew Roberts having such a party; nor indeed can one imagine them presenting a trunk full of stolen linen and silks to a priest whose prayers and intercessions with the Virgin had 'ensured their present success'.[25]

But clearly, these Cuban pirates did share some of the characteristics of their forebears. They drank to excess, they loved music aboard their ships and, according to a former American captive of the pirates, 'so great was their love of gambling that the captain would play cards with the meanest man on board'.[26] Some flew their own versions of the traditional pirate flags, 'a red flag forward and a white flag with death's head and marrow bones at main', 'a red flag with death's head and cross under it'.[27] And they seem to have shared the egalitarianism of the pirates of the golden age, though probably more in a disdain of authority than in an equal distribution of booty. 'Every man (of his crew) had a voice as well as himself,' said Aaron Smith of his pirate captain. 'The crews appeared all nearly on the same footing,' it was claimed at the trial of some Cuban pirates in Jamaica. 'No scramble for plunder; one person divided it, and gave it to the people as they presented themselves.' 'There was no idea of subordination on board, except when in chase of vessels, and even then but very little,' wrote Captain Barnabas Lincoln of his captors.[28]

It was, however, the cruelty of the Cuban pirates, rather than their egalitarianism, which most attracted the horrified notice of their contemporaries who ranted at the 'most bloodthirsty monsters that ever disgraced the name of man', as they were described in a report to the Secretary of the United States Navy.[29] These atrocities grew worse over time and were probably aggravated by the naval campaigns against the pirates which are described in the next chapter. Their favourite torture was to place a noose around the victim's neck and hoist him to the yardarm, only lowering him again at the point of death. This might be repeated several times to extract information, or could be varied by putting a grindstone round the victim's neck and throwing him into the sea attached to a rope which would (sometimes) be hauled in just before he drowned. But the pirates had many other little tricks to play. They beat their prisoners with cutlasses, cudgels and ropes' ends; they blindfolded them and fired off pistols behind their heads; they pinioned them and scattered gunpowder around their feet and then roared with laughter when it was ignited. Men were nailed to the deck, roasted on slow fires, slashed with knives and cutlasses and then exposed naked to the sun, mosquitoes and sandflies until they perished. More and more captives were murdered as time went on, sometimes whole crews at a time, the only evidence of their fate being a ship floating with nobody aboard and some indication of bloody massacre, like the sloop discovered in May 1822 by the US schooner *Alligator* 'in the neighbourhood of the pirates at sea, with only a dog on board, and marks of blood on her deck'. Some of these unfortunate captives were killed and thrown overboard; others were battened down in the forecastle or the hold while the ship was sunk or set on fire. Sometimes there would be just one survivor to tell the tale, as in the case of George Brown, a young sailor on the *Laura Ann* of New York who hid in the coal-hole while all his shipmates were murdered. Later, when the ship had been set on fire and the pirates had departed, 'he dropped overboard, under the vessel's bows, and swam ashore, distant about sixty yards, accompanied by two sharks, one swimming on each side of him'.[30]

Most of these horrors had long been within the repertoire of the more bloodthirsty pirates; even the gentlemanly Drake half hanged a prisoner in the manner described to extract information. But the Cuban pirates do have one claim to fame in pirate annals, apart from their splendid black schooners, luxuriant moustachios and *señoritas* which have been displayed in so many pirate films. For it was they who invented walking the plank, a form of punishment or execution never dreamed of by earlier pirates. The first we hear of it is on 18 July 1822 when the sloop *Blessing* was captured by a pirate schooner off the coast of Cuba, the story being reprinted in *The Times* from an original account in the *Jamaica Royal Gazette*. The pirates took the sloop's crew aboard their own vessel and 'demanded of the captain his money or his life'. On the following day, 'not producing any money, a plank was run out on the starboard side of the schooner, upon which [the pirate captain] made Captain Smith walk, and as he approached the end, they tilted the plank, when he dropped into the sea and there, while in the effort of swimming, the captain called for his musket and fired at him therewith, when he sunk and was seen no more'. A few years later, *The Times* printed another report which showed that the technique had been perfected. This time the victims were the crew of a Dutch brig who were captured on their way from Jamaica to Holland. Laughing at their captives' plight, the pirates 'proceeded deliberately to compel the wretched men to what is termed "walk the plank"'. One of the victims was, however, to have the last laugh even as he drowned. While he was being held 'by two of the pirates to pinion, blindfold, and fasten a shot to his feet, he made a desperate resistance, in which he fixed his grasp upon the throat of one of the ruffians, and they both tumbled over the side and were drowned'.[31] No doubt some of the tales of Cuban cruelty have grown in the telling, as survivors and newspapers combined to produce dramatic copy. There are, for instance, a suspiciously large number of cases where just one man survived to tell some grisly tale. But these pirates were certainly cruel, much crueller than such notorious monsters of the past as Ned Lowe, the worst of the golden age pirates. Such atrocities do not seem to have given them bad dreams. Aaron Smith described the horrible torture and death of one of the pirate crew who was suspected of treachery but, once the deed was done and the man had screamed his last scream, 'the guitar tinkled and the song went round, as if nothing had happened'.[32]

Cuban desperadoes and rogue privateers were not the only villains at work in these years of mayhem at sea, as maritime anarchy encouraged opportunist rascals to try their luck all over the world. One favourite sport was stealing ships, especially on the coast of Peru where royalist Spaniards facing defeat were desperately trying to get their money out of the country. Most of this was carried aboard British and American naval vessels, 'floating banks' whose captains greatly valued the freight money they received for carrying bullion, such as the $100,000 (about £20,000) brought aboard the United States naval brig *Cora* in September 1822 by the absconding master of the Peruvian mint.[33] But there was often plenty of money on merchant ships as well, as there was on the brig *Peruvian* of Liverpool, which was cut out of the harbour of Callao with $120,000 aboard by a boat's crew led by an adventurous Scotsman called Alexander Robertson. He dumped the brig's crew further down the coast and then headed out into the Pacific where he buried his share of the treasure for later collection on one of the uninhabited islands of the Northern Marianas. Piracy was now truly global, since even these distant islands were described by a British naval officer as 'the resort and rendezvous of numerous lawless and expatriated English sailors . . . ready for any and every desperate adventure which may present itself'.[34]

Other sailors took their stolen ships and treasures to islands nearer home, as did the crew of the British schooner *Jane* bound from Gibraltar to Bahia in Brazil in 1821. Discovering there was bullion aboard, they mutinied, murdering the captain and the helmsman. Then, kissing the Bible, they swore a terrible oath, 'May God Almighty never save their souls if they ever revealed what had passed', before setting sail to the Isle of Lewis in the Outer Hebrides where they scuttled the schooner and came ashore in a boat with some $30,000 in specie which they buried on the beach. However, even remote parts of the British Isles were no longer safe for pirates, and they were quickly apprehended by revenue officers and sent to Edinburgh, where the two ringleaders were tried and sentenced to hang on the evidence of their Maltese cabin boy.[35]

There was no need of mutiny to inaugurate a career of piracy, as we can see from the case of Charles Christopher Delano, master of the *William* of Liverpool, who was said by *The Times* to have been 'a desperate man who had lost money at cards'. In 1819, while sailing on a trading voyage to the Levant, he managed with little difficulty to persuade his crew to join him in a voyage of plunder, one of them predictably saying that 'what he desired was a short life and a merry one'. They disguised their ship and then boarded and seized the brig *Helen* of Dartmouth, transferring her cargo to their own ship before battening down her crew in the forecastle, smashing her boats and boring holes in her below the water line. The *William* then proceeded leisurely down the Mediterranean, selling off the *Helen*'s cargo to passing ships and ashore in Sardinia and Malta before arriving at her original destination in Smyrna.

No doubt they thought they had got away with it, as they divided the proceeds, but nemesis was on its way. The crew of the *Helen* managed to escape, 'by the aid of a hatchet and a chisel which were fortunately in the forecastle', and repaired the longboat sufficiently to stay afloat long enough to be picked up by a Greek brig which transferred them to HM Sloop of War *Spey* on her way to Malta, a British colony since 1800 and the headquarters of the Mediterranean fleet. The naval sloop's commander was sent to Smyrna where he quickly found and seized the *William* and her crew and brought them back to Malta for trial. Some idea of the seriousness with which this breach of maritime trust was regarded can be seen by the dramatic sentence imposed on the convicted men. The *William* was 'to be painted black, hauled out and anchored' in the middle of Grand Harbour, thus providing a splendid grandstand view for the thousands who watched the spectacle from the massive fortifications surrounding the harbour. Delano and five of his crew were then rowed out to their old ship, hanged from the yardarm till they were dead and then transferred to specially built gibbets outside Fort Ricasoli at the mouth of the harbour where their corpses were left hanging in chains.[36]

Such retribution was, however, not sufficient to prevent the

Mediterranean from being the scene of the last of the epidemics of piracy which sprang forth in these troubled years. The background to this was once again an independence movement, this time the Greek War of Independence which began in the spring of 1821 and lasted for the rest of the decade. Piracy on a small scale had long been endemic in many of the Greek islands and in the Morea, parts of which, such as the Maine peninsula, had never been fully conquered by the Turks. Such piracy, much of it at the expense of the Turks, was seen as an honourable occupation, as was the brigandage conducted by the robber chieftains called klephts who lorded it in the mountains of the mainland, and there were many pirates and klephts among the military and naval leaders of the Greek revolt.[37]

Former pirates could be found in the Greek navy, a large force of mainly small vessels such as brigs based in the three 'nautical islands' of Hydra, Spetsai and Psara. They could be found in even greater numbers among the privateers commissioned to search for the goods of Turks or for contraband of war being delivered to the enemy by neutral vessels. Such cruisers seem to have kept more or less to the terms of their commissions in the first few years of the war, though they were said by the British ambassador in Constantinople to be 'very imperfectly under the control either of their officers or of the government ... The search is usually effected by an overpowering number of the crew of the belligerent vessel armed and not over nice in their manner of executing the duty.' However, the British and indeed all the other Western powers looked very favourably on the Greek revolt and much could be excused in such a noble cause, even a certain amount of piracy by zealous patriots who were 'without the intention of doing wrong, but ignorant of the rights upon which they pretend to act'. The philhellene Captain Hamilton of HMS *Cambrian*, for instance, released two Greek vessels whose papers were irregular, 'as they did not appear to be of the worst class of pirates'.[38]

The Greeks were the masters of the sea in the early years of the revolt, but they were to lose this naval superiority from 1824 onwards with the arrival, as allies of the Turks, of a powerful Egyptian fleet under Ibrahim Ali, who had been promised the

Peloponnese for himself and Crete for his father Mehmet Ali in return for his assistance. It was now, with the Greek cause in disarray, that the 'worst class of pirates' began to make their appearance, as can be seen in shipping papers and the correspondence of the Admiralty which report an increasing number of out-and-out piratical attacks on neutral shipping. Some of these were conducted by former privateers and some by units of the Greek navy, such as the six large brigs which defected from the national fleet in September 1826. The mutineers declared that they were driven to piracy by lack of pay and when remonstrated with said, according to a British naval officer, 'Then give us to eat; if you do not, we will cruise.'[39] Most of the pirates, however, and there were many hundreds, possibly thousands, of them, were just pirates, operating from long-established bases in the islands of the archipelago and in the Morea. Here, like their Cuban counterparts, they had protection and support and a market for their plunder, whose low prices were ruining other fair traders trying to make an honest living. Piracy, wrote a merchant from Smyrna, 'is introducing a moral degradation amongst thousands who are either pirates, connivers, or purchasers of stolen goods'.[40]

Indeed, the depredations of the Greek pirates were on such a scale that they seemed likely to bring the trade of the eastern Mediterranean, fair or not, to a complete standstill. The Lloyd's agent at Constantinople reported in July 1826 that 'navigation is now become too dangerous to be attempted without convoy'. A year later, from the other extreme of the Greek pirates' cruising grounds, the Governor of Malta wrote that there had been so many attacks on the shipping of the island 'that all commercial operations are here suspended, from the conviction that any vessel leaving the port is sure to be plundered'. Altogether, British Admiralty records report 150 British vessels plundered by Greek pirates between March 1825 and October 1827 and the British had by no means a complete monopoly of the trade of the Levant. Ships from Italy, France, Austria and many other nations were just as much at risk.[41]

The vessel of choice of the Greek pirates was the *mistiko*, a fast, shallow-draught, three-masted vessel with large triangular sails and oars. These often operated in fleets such as the eight 'misticees', each armed with one large gun in the bows and forty men, who boarded and plundered the British brig *Mary* on 20 September 1827.[42] Few merchant sailors chose to resist such attacks and, in the majority of cases, it seems that little violence was used by the predators who simply herded the crew together and searched for those items of cargo and personal possessions which appealed to them. But, almost inevitably, there was some violence. 'It is melancholy to add,' wrote the Lloyd's agent in July 1826, 'that not content with pillage these wretched outlaws have in some instances accompanied it by the commission of horrid crimes on the unfortunate crews.'[43]

Such horrid crimes sometimes went as far as murder, occasionally of whole crews such as that of a Maltese brig captured by Mainiot pirates in April 1824. But the pirates usually contented themselves with savage beatings, such as that inflicted on the crew of the British ship *Elizabeth* who were beaten 'so unmercifully that we could scarcely crawl about the deck', as was reported in a letter written by her captain in Smyrna. Worse was to happen to the steward of the Maltese ship *Superba* which was captured in April 1827 by pirates from the island of Grabusa, a pirate stronghold off the north-west coast of Crete. 'They took the steward, beat him, and put him in the hold on the ballast, where several men committed an unnatural crime both upon him and a sailor, a passenger on board.'[44]

Contemporaries always made the most of pirate atrocities, since apart from making good copy they were a good way of getting the authorities to act. The Greek pirates certainly behaved badly on occasion, but their atrocities pale into insignificance when compared with those committed by the Cuban pirates or indeed with the barbarity shown by Greek to Turk or vice versa in the war itself, both sides priding themselves on their own cruelty and on their ability to bravely withstand the cruelty of their enemies. Slow deaths by impaling or roasting were the order of the day and victories were celebrated by the massacre of the vanquished – men, women and children – as at the Greek naval base of Psara, captured by the Turks in June 1824, where an English eyewitness saw eight thousand Greeks 'freshly butchered, their heads piled high in a ghastly pyramid'. The Greeks were, if anything, even more bloodthirsty. Maxime Raybaud, a French artilleryman, observed the aftermath of the Greek capture of the city of Tripolis, the capital of the Morea, on 5 October 1821. 'Everywhere too there were the screams of victims, competing with another sound which was to haunt Raybaud's memory – the guttural ululation of the Greek soldier in sight of his victim, and then the change of note as the *ataghan* (sword) was plunged in, an inhuman blood cry that was half scream, half laugh, "le cri de l'homme-tigre, de l'homme devorant l'homme."'[45] Some pirates may have been tigers in human shape, but most were pussy cats compared to a Greek or Turkish soldier.

It can be seen that there was not much peace at sea in the first fifteen years of the Pax Britannica and that piracy, which seemed to have been suppressed for ever in 1730, was back with a vengeance. From the mouth of the Mississippi to the Dardanelles, from Newfoundland to Ascension Island and far beyond, in the Pacific, the Indian Ocean and the South China Sea, piracy in various forms was rampant. This period did not throw up famous names who might later become the heroes or villains of children's books. It did, however, contribute to the composite legend which has formed the modern view of piracy. What pirate story worth the name does not employ a black schooner with tall, tapering, raked-back masts? How would the genre have survived if Cuban pirates had not invented walking the plank? What would central casting do if all pirates were northern Europeans and there were no swarthy, moustachioed Greeks and Cubans needed to swarm aboard a prize? European and American piracy has a long history and each part of it has contributed something to the legend, but it is a history which was to come to an end in the years around 1830. How that came about is the subject of the final chapter.

# CHAPTER TWELVE

# An End to Piracy

CHAPTER TWELVE

# *An End to Piracy*

Great Britain was truly mistress of the seas in the years after 1815 and, on the face of it, should have had little trouble in putting down the great epidemic of piracy which mocked the Pax Britannica, especially as the navies of almost every other power were engaged in the same activity. At the peak of the Napoleonic War, the Royal Navy had put to sea over a thousand vessels of war and, although the great majority of these were laid up, sold, or otherwise disposed of with the coming of peace, the peacetime navy was to remain extremely formidable. In January 1821, for instance, there were 143 vessels employing some 20,000 men in commission, numbers which could be speedily increased if any crisis loomed.[1]

Home waters were patrolled and protected by over fifty vessels, ten of them in the Irish squadron based at Cork, something of a change from the one weak ship deployed in these waters during the reign of James I. In the Mediterranean, there were eleven ships, numbers which would be doubled when Greek piracy became a threat later in the 1820s.[2] The East Indies squadron, which was just about to conclude a successful campaign against the pirates of the Red Sea and the Persian Gulf, comprised seven ships, while there was another squadron of twelve ships based at Cape Town (now a British possession), whose main function until his death in May 1821 was to ensure that no one rescued the former emperor Napoleon from his captivity in St Helena. The west coast of Africa was patrolled by a squadron of six vessels, which would tackle piracy if need be but was intended primarily to seek out and capture illegal slavers. This was a complicated and difficult task for, although Britain's abolition of the slave trade in 1807 had been adopted by several other countries, there was far from universal support of such a measure. As a result, the trade was still legal between some countries and some parts of the African coast despite intense diplomatic activity and numerous treaties. And there remained a huge demand for slaves, especially in Cuba and Brazil, so that the slave trade (legal and illegal), far from declining in the years after 1807, was to rise in the first three decades of the nineteenth century to reach a maximum of 135,000 slaves shipped a year in 1835. Britain's West African squadron, despite its unceasing vigilance along three thousand miles of African coastline, could do little to halt this growth, though it had its successes, such as the 3,500 slaves freed from seventeen captured vessels in 1825 or HM Schooner *Hope*'s capture in 1826 of the Brazilian brig *Prince of Guinea* with a cargo of 578 slaves, 'after a hard chase of twenty-eight hours and a most desperate action of two hours and forty minutes', a feat which was described by the squadron's commodore as 'one of the most gallant exploits performed since the peace'.[3]

Across the Atlantic, Britain had a 'Brazils' squadron of nine vessels based at Rio de Janeiro, which kept an eye on insurgent naval and privateering activity on both coasts of South America. In the West Indies, there were five ships in the Leeward Islands squadron based at Antigua and nine more at Jamaica, a number which had increased to seventeen by 1825 to cope with the crisis of Cuban piracy.[4] There were, of course, no longer any British station ships in Carolina, Virginia, New York and New England, but these were more than adequately replaced by the small but very effective United States Navy. And, finally, there was a North American squadron of six ships based at Halifax, Nova Scotia, and a further four vessels in Newfoundland.

This was a staggering array of peacetime naval might in comparison with the twenty ships assigned to duties outside Europe a hundred years earlier.[5] What was even more striking was that so many of these vessels were of exactly the type that naval commanders and colonial governors had previously pleaded for in vain. Most squadrons included at least one ship of real force capable of dealing with any privateer, such as a fourth-rate frigate, but the numbers were dominated by corvettes (sixth-rates), sloops, schooners, cutters and gun-brigs – small, fast vessels often equipped with oars and admirably suited for chasing pirates and privateers. Most important among these were sloops of war, of which there were fifty-five at sea in 1821 compared with just four in 1721. Some of these were quite small with ten guns and sixty-five men, but most had eighteen or twenty guns and around a hundred men, and these vessels were to be in the forefront of this last stage of the seemingly never-ending war against the pirates.

The Admiralty not only had more and more suitable vessels at its disposal than in the last great epidemic of piracy a century earlier, but it also had a more efficient and reliable intelligence service. This is not yet of course the age of the marine telegraph, let alone radio, and information transmitted by sea still relied on the vagaries of the winds, though the fastest sailing vessels were considerably faster than in the 1720s and steam vessels were just beginning to be used on short voyages or as tugs to tow sailing vessels out of harbour. News thus travelled more swiftly and there was much more of it, thanks to the existence of a worldwide information collecting service. This was partly supplied by the vastly increased merchant marine and the navy itself, but there were also institutions specifically designed for the collection of maritime information and its dissemination to London. Most important of these was Lloyd's, the leader in marine insurance, who had agents in every major port and produced the shipping paper *Lloyd's List* three times a week.[6] Lloyds' reports on piracy were routinely passed on to the Admiralty, as was information from a much enlarged consular service abroad. Supplementing these, and often carrying the reports, was the packet-boat mail service which had grown enormously since its modest beginnings in the late seventeenth century. By 1815, there were regularly scheduled services linking its headquarters at Falmouth in Cornwall with Lisbon, Malta, Rio de Janeiro and throughout the West Indies and North America.[7] All this incoming correspondence was carefully indexed by the Admiralty clerks and much of it was marked with the number 75, indicating that it included reports of piracy. The Admiralty certainly knew what was going on in the world, and reacted accordingly, though inevitably with some delay.

Knowledge of piratical or near-piratical plundering did not always lead to action, since there were serious diplomatic problems to be faced before ships of the Royal Navy could be unleashed on ships flying foreign flags or the flags of the various insurgent governments whom Britain had recognised and was pledged to support. This inevitably led to caution, despite the growing number of reports of illegal depredations, a policy derided by public opinion which believed that, if the country had a navy as large and powerful as the Royal Navy, it should use it. In September 1817, *The Times* demanded that decisive steps be taken against vessels of whatever flag exercising piracy between the continents of America and Europe. 'Till an example is made of villains of this description, the ocean cannot be navigated in safety by the honest trader.'[8] Similar pressure from many other quarters eventually forced the government to act and, on 8 June 1818, a circular was sent to the commanders of naval stations empowering captains to seize and detain any ship with commissions from Spain or the insurgent governments for which there was credible information that they had committed piratical acts against British ships or goods. The privateers, once seized, were to be brought, together with witnesses, to England or a colony where there was a court established for the trial of offences on the high seas.[9] Similar instructions were given to the navies of other powers, always with the proviso that they could only act to protect shipping or goods belonging to their own subjects, something that was not often easy to prove. On 3 March 1819, for instance, a growing number of complaints and demands for naval protection led to an Act of Congress authorising the President of the United States to employ a suitable naval force to seize and send into port privateers committing depredations against American merchant ships.[10]

Such orders certainly had a considerable impact and many suspect privateers were brought in, to French and British naval stations such as Martinique, Barbados, Rio and Jamaica, and to American ports.[11] Some of these were condemned and their officers tried and hanged, but in most cases it proved impossible to sustain a case against a privateer behaving irregularly. Reliable witnesses were hard to find (or easy to bribe by the defendant) and it was extremely difficult to prove the ownership of captured cargo, since these privateers were masters in disguising it. As a result, most cases were dropped for lack of evidence or, if they came to court, ended in acquittal for the defendants.[12] Nevertheless, the existence of these powers of seizure and the threat of a trial whose outcome was always dubious and could be fatal were sufficient to make the privateers more honest, so that complaints against them began to decrease and then disappeared completely as the wars of independence drew to a close and no more commissions were issued.

There was, however, to be one last outburst of rogue privateer activity before this happy situation was achieved. In 1825, Brazil and Argentina drifted into a war whose eventual outcome would be the creation of an independent Uruguay as a buffer state between them.[13] Once again, large numbers of privateering commissions were issued by both sides and by May 1827, as peace loomed, Rear Admiral Otway on the Brazil station feared the likely consequences. 'Great numbers of men of all nations, and of lawless habits and character, being turned adrift by both parties, will most probably have recourse to piracy for subsistence, to which practice, their previous predatory habits, the extended coasts and the few vessels of war to protect the encreasing trade will invite them.'[14]

This proved only too true and the next couple of years saw an orgy of illegal attacks, not just on the coast of South America, but throughout the Atlantic and West Indies and on the African coast as well. Several of these predators were captured, such as the *Convención Argentina* which was 'gallantly carried, sword in hand' by Lieutenant Fitzgerald RN in the River Plate, the schooner *Presidente* seized by HMS *Black Joke* on anti-slavery patrol off West Africa after a fight throughout the night in which the privateer had twenty men wounded and six dead including her English captain, and *Las Damas Argentinas* captured by HM Sloop *Victor* at the Dutch island of St Eustatius.[15] Once again, the results of the trials which followed were not easy to predict. *The Times* got quite excited about the 'Forty Pirates' captured aboard the *Presidente* and brought back to London for trial. But the jury were not convinced that they had exceeded their Buenos Aires commission and found them not guilty. The crew of *Las Damas Argentinas*, by contrast, were tried in Jamaica and found guilty and most of them hanged, while the Baltimore-built privateer schooner herself was taken into the navy, being 'well suited to HM service'. Such trials were a lottery, in which the odds were in the favour of the privateer/pirates but not by very much.[16]

Peace was eventually signed between the two warring nations, the privateers were called in and determined efforts by the navies of the great powers and by the Brazilian and Buenos Aires governments themselves brought this last rampage of the rogue privateers to an end. In April 1829, Captain Wilson of HMS *Tribune* sailed south along the Argentine coast and out to the Falkland Islands and found 'no privateers or prizes about these islands or anywhere else in his cruise. I believe therefore that part of the coast is now free from piratical vessels.' He did, however, discover on East Falkland some settlers from Buenos Aires, about fifty men, women and children with about 17,000 head of cattle. These and other Argentine settlers were cleared out in December 1832 by HMS *Clio* who raised the Union Jack over the islands. But that, of course, is another very long story.[17]

While the policing of the oceans was mainly left to the ships cruising in the various stations overseas, there was also a pool of vessels based in England which could be quickly sent out on particular anti-piratical duties. When the Admiralty heard of the piracies committed by the former privateer *Luisa*, for instance, they immediately dispatched Captain Stewart Blacker in HM Sloop *Lee* in pursuit of her. He sailed first to Madeira where the pirate had last been seen, arriving on 20 January 1819. Finding nothing there, he decided to try and track her down by visiting places where she might have gone to sell her plunder, calling first at 'the ports of Mogodore and Sallee on the Morocco shore (so notorious in ancient and modern history for their piracy)'. He then tried the Canaries and the Cape Verde Islands where he received information that the *Luisa* had committed many depredations and was headed either to Margarita or Santo Domingo to dispose of her loot. He had no luck in either of these places, nor in Puerto Rico, while in Port Royal, Jamaica, he was to learn that further pursuit was futile as the *Luisa* had been destroyed by her own crew on the coast of Carolina. Captain Blacker arrived in Charleston on 31 April, after three months of frustrated but determined search, only to meet frustration again as the American authorities refused to hand over for trial in England the British members of the *Luisa's* crew who were languishing in the local gaol. Captain Blacker's cruise may have been fruitless, but there was a remorselessness about his search that suggested that had the *Luisa* stayed at sea she would have been caught sooner or later.[18]

There is the same sense of impending doom in the story of the last ship to engage in large-scale piracy in the Atlantic. This was not a privateer turned pirate but a slaver, the schooner *Panda* which set sail from Havana for the coast of West Africa in August 1832. On her way she encountered the American brig *Mexican* on a voyage from Salem, Massachusetts, to Rio de Janeiro. The crew of the slaver boarded the American vessel, robbed her of $24,000 in specie and anything else they could find, cut the rigging, slashed the sails and cut down the yards. They then cooped up the American crew in the forecastle and set fire to the brig before continuing on their slaving voyage. However, on this occasion, there were to be no dead men and the tale could be told, for the crew of the *Mexican* escaped from their prison quite easily, though they did not dare to put the fire out too quickly lest the pirates realised they had survived and came back to finish the job. But once the pirates were safely out of sight, they set to work, repaired the brig and made their way back to Salem, since with no money they were unable to continue their trading voyage.

Detailed descriptions of the *Panda* and her officers were now dispatched throughout the world's shipping lines and she was eventually tracked down to a river in West Africa, where she was captured by forty men in boats from the British brig-of-war *Curlew*. The pirates escaped ashore, but sixteen including the captain and first mate were rounded up and brought back to England. The Admiralty waived jurisdiction, since their crimes had been against subjects of the United States, and sent them off in another British warship to Salem where the *Mexican* was fortuitously in harbour. Members of the plundered crew were thus able to testify to the *Panda's* piracy and five of her men were condemned and hanged in Boston on 11 June 1835, including her Catalan captain Don Pedro Gibert, a man described as 'exceeding handsome . . . and a great favorite with the ladies'. The equally guilty mate, Bernardo de Soto, was pardoned because of his previous humane conduct in saving the passengers and crew of an American ship wrecked in the Bahamas, a plea given added emotional appeal by the desperate journey made by his wife from Spain to Washington to beg for his life. And so ended the last pirate 'that has ever troubled the course of navigation upon the high seas', as wrote Edward Battis, son of one of the crew of the *Mexican,* in his excellent telling of the story which was published in 1898.[19]

Policing the high seas against the rogue privateers presented naval commanders with a whole range of problems of identification, proof and diplomatic tact, not to mention the considerable difficulty of catching up and seizing some of the fastest vessels in the world, and the problem was only really resolved with the final independence of the Latin American nations. By contrast, stamping out the Cuban pirates should in theory have been quite easy to achieve, given the naval power available. Naval intelligence was well aware of the general area in which the bandits had their bases and the pirate schooners were individually no match for even the weakest naval vessel. Nevertheless, the campaign against the Cuban pirates was to take several years before it could be said to have been completely successful, as the pirates had many advantages on their side.

Most important of these was the sheer difficulty of following them through the coastal maze of cays and shoals or finding them in their well-concealed hideaways. Aaron Smith recalled being aboard a pirate schooner within musket-shot of British and American men-of-war which were searching for it. 'We could plainly perceive the men in their tops from the mast-head of the corsair, without being perceived by them; the vessel being completely screened from observation by the trees.'[20] But even if these difficulties were successfully negotiated and a pirate vessel located at anchor, the rovers themselves were to prove far from easy to capture. If their firepower was insufficient to do much damage to their naval attackers, as was usually the case, they simply retreated to the land, leaping overboard and swimming ashore where they often kept horses ready saddled to take them to safety. And pursuit was impossible, given the Spanish determination not to allow foreigners to set foot on Cuban soil. This would not have mattered too much if the Spanish authorities had cooperated with the foreign navies by employing some of the 40,000 soldiers garrisoned on the island to pursue the pirates when they had been driven ashore. But this they did not do, in the early years at least, and the pirates found welcome asylum in this largely lawless island before setting out to plunder once again when the thwarted naval vessels had gone away. These Cuban pirates, then, were going to take some beating as they had skills which might be the envy of a pentathlete. They could ride and swim, sail and row, shoot straight with cannon or musket and were formidable close-quarters fighters with a cutlass or a knife.

The first serious efforts to eradicate them were made by the United States whose shipping had been very seriously hit, so much so that the House of Representatives was informed 'that the intercourse between the northern and southern sections of this Union is almost cut off'.[21] Individual ships were sent out in pursuit of pirates late in 1821 and, in 1822, a regular West Indian squadron of thirteen vessels was established under the command of Commodore James Biddle. This had considerable success. In the second half of January 1822, the US schooner *Porpoise* swept the north-west coast of Cuba, capturing or destroying twelve pirate vessels, together with two more on the stocks and three establishments ashore, a cruise which won warm praise from the commodore. 'Nothing could exceed their ardor in pursuit, but their enthusiasm in attack.' Two months later he reported the remarkable achievement of Lieutenant Lawrence Kierney in the US brig *Enterprise* who captured in a single day 'eight sail of piratical vessels, whose united crews amounted to about 160 men. This must be pretty nearly a finishing stroke to the desperadoes.'[22]

More successes were to follow, usually without any serious American casualties, though in November 1822 the heroic (or foolhardy) Lieutenant Allen of the US schooner *Alligator* was killed when leading an attack through shoal water in the ship's boats. The pirates 'opened a heavy fire on the pursuing boats. One of the musket shots struck Lt. Allen in the head while he was standing in his boat (which was in advance of the others), animating his men by his example, and soon afterwards another ball entered his breast.'[23] The Americans were to remember Allen who was later to become the hero of pirate novels.[24]

Altogether, the Americans claimed to have captured, sunk or burned twenty-nine pirate vessels in the waters of Cuba and Puerto Rico between October 1821 and September 1822, a typical action being that of the US schooner *Peacock* whose cruise is described by a British naval officer in a letter from Havana. Her boats pursued pirates within the reefs and forced aground and burned five pirate vessels 'with the whole of their settlements, houses, huts, and every thing which appeared to belong to the pirates'. Plundered property, mainly coffee, lay strewn about on the shore, as did letters and bills of lading belonging to seven captured merchant ships. The one thing missing was any pirates, every man of whom had escaped ashore, and this was sadly too common an outcome of these 'successes'.[25]

The frustrated Commodore Biddle wrote to the Cuban authorities in April 1822, begging them 'to sanction the landing, upon the coast of Cuba, of our boats and men, when in pursuit of pirates'. The answer of the captain-general was received a few days later. 'I cannot and must not consent to it.'[26] The Spanish fear of any breach of their territorial jurisdiction was in the American case compounded by a genuine fear that the anti-pirate campaign was merely a cover for invasion, since there were many, both in Cuba itself and in the American slave states, who would have liked to see the largest sugar colony in the world annexed to the United States.[27] Many people also believed that the Cubans welcomed and protected the pirates because their depredations could be seen as reprisals for the attacks on Spanish shipping by the crews of privateers operating out of Baltimore. There may have been some truth in this, but in fact by 1822 the Spaniards were beginning to act against the pirates themselves, even if they were not yet prepared to let Americans land in pursuit of them. A descent was made on a gang based at Cape San Antonio in March which led to many captures and the execution by shooting of the captain and lieutenant of the gang. Another pirate crew was captured by a vessel fitted out at Trinidad de Cuba, the commander being condemned to hang and the men to work in chains on the streets for two years, a punishment which shows a degree of imagination unknown in Britain or the United States whose judicial systems knew no outcome between death and acquittal or pardon.[28]

American successes predictably upset British public opinion which felt humiliated that British shipping was being protected by the men-of-war of a nation that had so recently been an enemy, while 'the far-famed Mistress of the Seas was nowhere to be seen', as a speaker in the House of Commons declared. Nor were people very impressed by the British government's claim that 'it would be disrespectful to Spain if our cruisers were to disturb [the pirates]'. Abuse in the press of the navy and government policy was soon followed by the old allegation that the reason that the Jamaica squadron was not chasing pirates or protecting trade was because, according to *The Times*, they had 'turned a sort of traders themselves', by concentrating on the profitable carriage of bullion for merchants fearful of its capture by pirates. 'We can hardly expect from those officers any attempt to crush the system of piracy, the indirect source of their profits.' The final straw was the news that the Royal Navy schooner *Speedwell* had been attacked by four piratical schooners off the north coast of Cuba and 'being overwhelmed by numbers would have been taken, had not the U.S. sloop of war *Peacock* come to her assistance'. This was too much. 'A British man of war captured by a gang of highway robbers!' thundered *The Times*. 'But she was not in the end made prize of: from the humiliation of capture she was rescued, that she might encounter that of — being saved by a cruiser of the United States!'[29]

As this torrent of abuse reached its height, 'a thousand ships of Britain remain inactive',[30] negotiations with Spain and the Cuban authorities were in fact being successfully concluded. On 5 September 1822, Admiral Sir Charles Rowley in Jamaica received a letter from the Captain-General of Cuba saying that he would be happy to cooperate in 'the extirpation of a band of men without principles'. He had given the necessary orders 'towards the pursuing and annihilating those men wherever they will be met with' and would give every assistance to the Royal Navy 'compatible with the national dignity and territorial jurisdiction'.[31] This was somewhat ambiguous, but it was sufficient for Admiral Rowley to send five ships to Cuba early in October to root out pirates, with permission to land if they were absolutely certain there were pirates in the vicinity. Some twelve weeks later he was able to report that his ships, or in most cases their boat crews, had captured or destroyed nine pirate vessels, killed twenty pirates and captured another fifty-seven, some of these with the assistance of the Spanish forces ashore.[32] In February 1823, his replacement as commander in Jamaica, Commodore Sir Edward Owen, forwarded to the Admiralty the reports of the officers who had been engaged in these actions. 'Their Lordships will receive with satisfaction the additional proof . . . that the meritorious exertions of H.M. officers, in conjunction with the officers of the United States of North America . . . have had complete success; and that the name of pirate is scarcely now remembered in the ports of Cuba.'[33] But this was wishful thinking and it was to be some time yet before the pirates of Cuba really were eradicated.

The United States sent out a second pirate-hunting squadron in 1823, this time under the command of Commodore David Porter, a naval hero who had captured the first British warship taken in the War of 1812. There had been a debate during the winter as to the best method of combating the pirates and it was decided that, to be fully effective, the squadron 'will require a particular kind of force, capable of pursuing them into the shallow waters to which they retire', as President Monroe informed the Senate. And so, in addition to the ships which had sailed with Biddle in 1822, Commodore Porter was supplied with a fleet of vessels specifically tailored to the task in hand, the first time that such a sensible policy had been adopted in pirate-hunting history. These included ten fast schooners, with a draught of less than seven feet and fitted with twenty or twenty-four sweeps, and five light double-bank cutters or barges, each to row twenty oars and adapted to carry forty men, well armed with muskets, pistols, boarding pikes and cutlasses.[34] The squadron was also graced by the presence of the US steam brig *Sea Gull*, the first naval steamer of any country to serve in action. She was originally built as a New Jersey ferry and 'the croakers predicted that she would founder at sea in the first blow', as Porter told his son who later wrote his biography. But in fact the *Sea Gull* did good service, mainly as a mother ship to the rowing vessels, though she had a chance to use her powerful guns on occasion and in May 1825 was reported to have sunk a pirate ship after a two-hour gun battle off Matanzas.[35]

Porter chose as his base Key West, American since 1819 and only a hundred miles from the coast of Cuba. The United States was now at last getting cooperation from the Spanish authorities in Cuba and his orders permitted him to pursue pirates ashore, having first given notice of his intentions, orders which shared the ambiguity of those given to the British commanders.[36] American relations with these British counterparts were excellent, the British going so far as to replace the normal admiral commanding the Jamaica station by a commodore so that Porter would not be outranked and 'we might meet on equal terms', as the American commodore recorded with gratitude.[37] There was a certain amount of division of labour, the British concentrating their searches on the south coast of Cuba and the Americans on the north, but men of the two navies also hunted together, as in March 1825 when the boats from the British frigate *Dartmouth* and the schooners *Union* and *Lion* joined up with boat crews from the *Sea Gull* in a successful pursuit of the pirate schooner *Socorro*. 'I am happy to say,' reported the British commodore Sir Lawrence Halsted, 'the greatest harmony prevailed throughout the service, the men of either nation receiving orders from the officers of the other and obeying each with equal alacrity.' This harmony was echoed by Lt. Com. McKeever of the *Sea Gull*, who praised 'the handsome manner in which we were seconded by the officers and crews of the boats of HMS *Dartmouth*'.[38] There had been a certain amount of cooperation between the British and French in previous anti-pirate campaigns, in both the Leeward Islands and West Africa, but nothing on the scale of this Anglo-American camaraderie, this being nicely epitomised by the kind and friendly treatment given to sick British sailors at Key West which included taking convalescent men for a trip round the Florida Keys in the steam brig.[39]

Such cooperation, along with Spanish assistance and the choice of the right sort of vessels for the job, was to prove the doom of the Cuban pirates, but the service was quite incredibly arduous for the British and American sailors and marines involved. Nearly all the close-up work was done by men rowing in open boats who pursued the elusive pirates from cay to cay, through shoals and reefs and into hidden passages through the mangrove swamps, such close pursuit often being done under fire from the retreating pirates. Captain Godfrey of HMS *Tyne* reported a successful cruise by his men who had chased pirates 'in open boats without any kind of shelter for thirty days and thirty nights', a record beaten by Lieutenant Platt of the United States Navy who was employed for sixty-eight successive days in an open boat on the north-west coast of Cuba, 'in the examination of the inlets, bays, keys, and other places of piratical resort'.[40] A report to the House of Representatives in January 1825 stressed the perilous service being imposed on Americans engaged in anti-pirate duty, who faced disease as well as danger in vessels too small to maintain health on long cruises. But such sacrifice was justified by the result. 'They enabled the commanders to scour the coast, to penetrate into the shoal waters of the creeks and inlets, to the very margin of the land.'[41] No pirate hunters in the past had ever shown such zeal, determination and courage as these truly professional British and American sailors and marines.

At the end of these exhausting pursuits there was likely to be a battle against a pirate schooner which would often be anchored broadside on to the narrow entrance of its hideaway, as was the *Zaragozana* when she was attacked by boats from HMS *Tyne* and *Thracian* in March 1823, an action which was reported with great enthusiasm in *The Times*. As the boat crews rowed in, they were greeted by incessant, galling fire for three-quarters of an hour from both the schooner and from men in a thicket on one side of the harbour entrance, until 'at length the opportunity for boarding arrived and, with three cheers, our gallant fellows rushed in under a heavy shower of grape and musketry. The panic on board was instantaneous and, with trifling exception, the entire of her crew threw themselves into the sea.' The pirates had ten killed, fifteen wounded, sixteen taken by the Spaniards ashore and twenty-eight brought to Port Royal for trial. The naval boat crews also had casualties, two men killed and seven wounded, but they were prepared to praise their daunty opponents who 'fought the vessel with a skill, and until the moment of panic with a desperate courage, worthy of a better cause'.[42]

A similar but even more bloodthirsty action was fought a few months later by the United States barges *Gallinipper* and *Mosquito* against the notorious pirate Diaboleto (Little Devil) in his schooner *Catilina*. She was anchored in shoal water in the same place where 'the gallant' Lieutenant Allen had been killed the previous November, a coincidence which had a galvanising effect on the heavily outnumbered twenty-eight men in the American barge crews as they rowed in to give battle. 'The word was "Remember Allen. Do your duty, boys, with a will and show no quarters".' They rose from their seats, pulled off their hats and gave three hearty cheers, when the pirates jumped overboard . . . like frogs from a bank.' The slaughter was immense as the Americans shot the pirates in the water or in the woods where they pursued them and many were killed after orders had been given to grant quarter. 'The greater part were sent to eternity in less than half an hour, a fit ending for such wretches.' Only five pirates survived, desperately wounded, and these were sent to the Captain-General of Cuba to be tried by the laws of Spain. The Americans did not have a single man killed or wounded, a sure sign that God was on their side according to Commodore Porter. 'Nothing less than providential influence and protection could have occasioned consequences so fatal to the pirates, and so exempt from injury on our side, as to appear almost miraculous.'[43]

Such actions, and there were many others, and the continuous patrolling of their hideaways, drove the Cuban pirates from the sea, so much so that they took to robbery on the land. 'When I left Matanzas,' wrote Porter to the Secretary of State, 'the country was alarmed by large bands of robbers, well mounted and armed, who had plundered several estates, and committed some murders in the neighbourhood of the city . . . These bands were composed of the freebooters who lately infested the coast and who, being compelled to abandon the ocean, had taken up this new line of business.' Other pirates left Cuba to follow their trade in Campeche, Yucatan and Puerto Rico where they were just as ruthlessly hunted down by the British and American navies and the Spanish authorities. In March 1825, for instance, Lt. Com. John D. Sloat obtained two small sloops from the Governor of St Thomas to cruise against rovers based in Puerto Rico. He soon brought a pirate sloop to battle and, after forty-five minutes' action, the surviving pirates ran her ashore and jumped overboard, only to be taken by Spanish soldiers. Among the prisoners was 'the famous pirate chief Cofrecinas who . . . has for years been the terror of this vicinity', Sloat reported in a letter to the Secretary of the Navy. 'His career has been marked by the most horrible murders and piracies . . . Although wounded when he got on shore, he would not surrender until he received the contents of a blunderbuss which shattered his left arm and he was brought to the ground with the butt of it.' The Spaniards executed the eleven captured pirates by shooting, a spectacle which was described in the American newspaper *Niles' Weekly Register*. 'They all except one met their fate in the most hardened manner. The celebrated Cofrecinas refused to be blindfolded, saying that he himself had murdered at least three or four hundred persons and it would be strange if by this time he should not know how to die.'[44]

By this date, the desperadoes were on their last legs but any relaxation of naval vigilance tended to be followed by a fresh upsurge in pirate activity, as happened when the Americans were forced to sail into healthier waters to recuperate from an epidemic of yellow fever. As late as April 1829, there were still pirates in the Colorados shoals, a much favoured hideaway, from where one of their schooners was brought into Havana with five prisoners. One of these, who claimed to have been a forced man, 'stated to the authorities that during the cruise the pirates had murdered one hundred and fifteen souls'.[45] But there were few of these murderous marauders left, hardly surprisingly since a total of ninety-seven pirate vessels had been destroyed or captured by the Americans, British and Spaniards, the bulk of them by the Americans, and 1,741 pirates had been killed or captured.[46] And many of those captured had suffered 'the just retribution' reserved for pirates, one who was hanged in Richmond, Virginia, being reserved for a posthumous notoriety in the service of science. According to a report in *The Times*, his head was cut off and dispatched to Baltimore in order that a pirate's brain might be examined by the phrenologists of that city. 'They will probably find the organs of destructiveness finely developed.'[47]

In 1826, as the campaign against the Cuban pirates dwindled to very little, the attention of the Admiralty and the newspapers switched to the eastern Mediterranean where an intense campaign against the Greek pirates was to be waged for the next two or three years. Most of this action was carried out by sloops under the command of Captain Hamilton, 'the senior officer of His Majesty's ships in the Archipelago', or by the sloop attached to the small separate command in the Ionian Islands, in these years a British protectorate.[48] These sloops had many other duties such as convoying and carrying dispatches, so there were rarely more than three or four vessels actively engaged in chasing pirates and these were to be kept very busy. In July 1827, Commander Charles Cotton reported to Hamilton the capture by his men of two pirate *mistikos* near Cape Matapan. 'I take the liberty of remarking,' he wrote, 'that this is the twelfth time the officers and men of H.M. sloop *Carnelian* have been differently engaged with pirates, since having the honour of being under your orders.'[49]

Although the waters of the Aegean are very different to those of northern Cuba and the Greek pirates were scattered over a much wider area, the two campaigns showed many similarities. Once again, nearly all the close-quarter chasing was done by boat crews rather than the sloops or frigates themselves and, although this never amounted to the weeks in open boats in unhealthy waters endured by the crews in Cuba, it was often an arduous and of course dangerous duty. In another report from Commander Cotton, describing the pursuit of five pirate vessels off Andros by the boats of the *Carnelian* in February 1827, he remarked that it had been 'a most severe chase, my men greatly fatigued, having pulled the distance of eighteen or twenty miles in a calm'.[50]

These strenuous rowing performances and the tactics of fighting and boarding from the ships' boats were a striking feature of the anti-piracy campaigns of the 1820s. They reflected skills learned and developed in the innumerable cutting-out actions and raids ashore of the Napoleonic Wars and they were very effective, allowing a remorseless pursuit ending in several different points of impact on the target. The marines and sailors toiling at the oars nearly always managed eventually to drive the pirate vessels ashore and did so with remarkably few casualties. It is unlikely that the oarsmen welcomed boat duty, but it provided a wonderful opportunity for the lieutenants and midshipmen who commanded the boats and urged their men on. Chances of glory were few and far between in the peacetime naval service and had to be seized when opportunity offered, and many of these young officers had their careers furthered by their captains' generous praise of their gallantry and perseverance.

But, as in Cuba, it was much easier to capture or destroy the pirate vessels than it was to capture or kill the pirates themselves, as can be seen in the reports made by the naval commanders. Like the Cubans, the Greeks were adept at leaping overboard and swimming ashore with their arms, as Commander Irby of HM Sloop *Pelican* reported in April 1827.[51] Once ashore, they usually retreated to well-prepared defensive positions from which they could make life very difficult for the sailors and marines landing and attacking them, the pirates often being reinforced by locals friendly to their cause. Early in 1827, the *Carnelian* chased a pirate *mistiko* 'into a small cove, high rocks on each side. The crew immediately left her, formed in two parties and took up their positions on each side of the entrance to the cove.' The Greeks were eventually forced from these defensive positions by landing parties advancing on them from both sides, but all they did then was retreat again and vanish into the impenetrable mountains.[52] A few months later the *Rose* forced a pirate vessel ashore on Samothrace. The marauders retreated to an old Venetian castle and 'posted themselves in such an advantageous way and appeared so determined on an obstinate defence as to render it prudent for our boats not to pursue them on shore'.[53]

The men of the *Rose*, still cruising off Samothrace, were to be in difficulties again a few weeks later, as we learn from a letter written by the Lloyd's agent at Smyrna. 'The pirates to the number of three hundred defended the beach, and prevented the *Rose's* boats from landing till she could be brought sufficiently close to make the guns bear. The boats' crews pursued the pirates into a wood but made no prisoners, while they unfortunately had one man killed and another wounded by the fire of the pirates.'[54] Far worse was to happen to the boats' crews of the frigate HMS *Sybille* when they attacked pirates from two *mistikos* on the south coast of Crete in June 1826. The pirates 'kept up a most tremendous fire of musketry upon the boats from upwards of two hundred armed men behind a succession of stone walls they had erected for their protection in case of being at any time attacked'. The frigate managed to anchor close in and force the pirates to flee with 'a most destructive fire . . . the walls not proving any protection against round shot and grape', but before they fled they had killed seventeen and wounded twenty-nine of the naval crews. The pirates' own losses were estimated by the frigate's captain at between fifty and sixty.[55]

The Greek pirates then, like so many pirates before them, were no pushover. They were brave and well trained in the use of their arms and, if the worst came to the worst, they nearly always had mountains behind them to which they could flee and hide with little fear of being captured. The Royal Navy, and the navies of Austria and France which were also active against the pirates, took or destroyed scores of their vessels, but only a few hundred of the pirates themselves. Some of these were taken to the Ionian Islands for trial or to Malta where there were complaints of the nuisance of dealing with the large number of Greeks sent there to be tried for piracy.[56] Sir Frederick Ponsonby, the Governor of Malta, reported in June 1827 that 131 persons accused of piratical acts had been detained there since May 1824. However, most of these had been discharged for want of evidence and he had been able to bring to trial only twenty-six. 'Unless the most complete evidence is obtained, conviction is impossible before a jury of this island.' Like Jamaicans in the 1670s and 1680s, it would seem that the inhabitants of this former corsair island were reluctant to see their fellow spirits swinging from the gallows.[57]

On 5 July 1827, the Treaty of London was signed by representatives of Britain, France and Russia. This empowered these countries to resolve the Greek War of Independence by sending a joint squadron to enforce an armistice pending negotiations with the Sultan regarding the future of Greece. And, on 20 October, the Turco-Egyptian fleet was deemed to have broken the armistice by opening fire at Navarino Bay on the allied fleets commanded by Admiral Sir Edward Codrington. There then followed one of the most terrible exhibitions of gunfire in the history of naval warfare. At least sixty Turkish and Egyptian ships were totally destroyed and nearly half of their crews were killed and wounded, while the allies did not lose a single ship.[58]

The battle of Navarino ensured that Greek piracy would not survive for very long. Admiral Codrington had written in September 1827 to 'the Persons exercising the Functions of Government in Greece', telling them to put their house in order. 'And if, instead of the encouragement now given to [piracy], you do not exert yourselves to destroy it, I shall consider Greece as without a Government, and act as I myself think best for commerce under these circumstances.'[59] No Greek government could afford to ignore such a warning after the salutory example provided by Navarino of what might happen to those who defied the Great Powers. The Greek navy, now once again master in their own waters, buckled to and conducted a very successful campaign under the command of Admiral Miaoulis, which more or less eradicated piracy from the upper archipelago. Meanwhile, Admiral Codrington was able to devote more of the vessels under his command to the same task. In January 1828, an Anglo-French squadron under the command of Sir Thomas Staines wiped out the formidable pirate stronghold of Grabusa with some assistance from the Turkish Governor of Crete. Lesser successes were to follow, sufficiently so for a notice to be posted up in the Commercial Rooms in Malta in the autumn of 1829, stating: 'Piracy is no more talked of.'[60] And this was not one of those false dawns which punctuate the history of piracy. It really had been eradicated, not just in Cuba and the Aegean but throughout the Atlantic and Mediterranean world, a major landmark in maritime history which was given its final, crowning endorsement with the French occupation of Algiers in 1830, marking the effective end of the centuries-long threat of the Barbary corsairs.

The Muslim corsairs had enjoyed a renaissance during the confused era of the French Revolutionary and Napoleonic Wars. The fleets grew in size, prizes were plentiful and new enemies were created to swell the potential booty. Among these were the United States whose merchant shipping was attacked by Algerian corsairs after the American government failed to send the regular annual tribute in 1813. The Americans were busily engaged in war against Britain at that time but, barely a fortnight after this war was concluded in 1815, a powerful squadron was sent to the Mediterranean under the command of Commodore Stephen Decatur, one of the great heroes of the young American navy. They quickly captured the Algerian flagship and another corsair vessel and then sailed for Algiers itself where the Dey immediately made peace, only forty days after the squadron had set sail from the United States. This was swift retribution but the expedition, like so many before it, did no more than restore the status quo.[61]

Meanwhile, a more constructive, long-term approach to the problem of the Barbary corsairs had been discussed at the Congress of Vienna in 1814. The British Admiral Sir Sidney Smith, in the midst of a discussion about the abolition of the West African slave trade, drew the attention of the Congress to the continued existence of Christian slavery in North Africa and the continued depredations of the corsairs. He suggested an international combination of naval forces to eradicate these shameful institutions which should have no place in the nineteenth-century world. His proposals were heard with approval but in fact, once again, no such combination was ever set forth.[62]

The nearest to combined action was the powerful Anglo-Dutch fleet which, under the command of Lord Exmouth, bombarded Algiers for nine hours on 27 August 1816 after the Dey had refused to listen to demands that he free the Christian slaves. The destruction was immense, with the fortifications in ruins and all but two of the Algerian fleet sunk, and the Dey was forced to free the 1,200 mainly Italian slaves then in captivity. But that was as far as it went. The fortifications were quickly rebuilt, new ships were provided by the Sultan and on 22 August 1817, less than a year after the battle, a letter to Lloyd's from Algiers reported that 'our navy consists of a frigate of 44 guns, five corvettes with 18 to 24 guns each, five swift-sailing brigs and a schooner'.[63]

The Algerian and Tunisian corsair fleets were both still active in the 1820s but by now the writing really was on the wall. European public opinion and government policy were united in the desire to suppress both the corsairs and the institution of Christian slavery. The only question was who would bring this about and when and how. Would it be Britain, who sent a squadron to Algiers in 1824 after a supposed slight to the British consul? Not on this occasion, as we hear from an officer of the Royal Marines who took part in 'this unfortunate war, out of which we have extricated ourselves with so little honour. It appears to have been a ridiculous business from first to last.'[64] Another ridiculous business, this time a supposed insult to the French consul in 1827, was to have more far-reaching results. After a desultory and ineffective three-year blockade, a massive French armada carrying 37,000 infantry set sail from Toulon for Algiers to impose what was supposed to be a 'temporary' occupation. Many such armadas had sailed in vain in previous centuries, but this time there was to be no problem and, on 5 July 1830, the city was occupied and the Dey capitulated, though it was to be several decades before the French were able to conquer the tribes of the interior. Such an example soon induced Tunis and Tripoli to end all acts of hostility against European nations and restore to liberty the few remaining slaves. A month after the French conquest of Algiers, the Bey of Tunis renounced corsair activity 'entirely and for ever' and abolished the institution of Christian slavery. A few days later the Pasha of Tripoli followed suit.[65]

The holy war in the Mediterranean was over and so was piracy throughout the Western world. In the Far East, however, pirates were to remain rampant and the navies of the world were to be busy chasing, chastising and destroying them in the waters of Borneo, Malaya, South China, the Sulu Sea and elsewhere until well after the Second World War.[66] But that is another story, as indeed is the alarming revival in piratical attacks on shipping since the early 1980s, mainly in Eastern waters, a revival which reflects the maritime dangers of a post-imperial world in which the navies of the Great Powers can no longer patrol where and how they wish and former colonies have neither the naval power nor the resources and will to eradicate the problem.[67]

But in those seas which have been the main arena of the pirates in this book – the Mediterranean, the Atlantic and the Caribbean – there has been very little piracy since the assault of the *Panda* on the *Mexican* in 1832. Every now and then, a crew has mutinied, murdered its officers and tried to seek a safe haven, or the inhabitants of formerly piratical regions have remembered their heritage. In 1846, for instance, *The Times* reported that piracy had been prevalent of late in the Greek archipelago, while in the following year a number of attacks on grain ships were made by men from the famine-torn west coast of Ireland.[68] Morocco, too, remained a potentially dangerous part of the world, especially the coast of the Rif whose warlike inhabitants the Emperor admitted 'were his subjects but not under his control'. As late as 1896, members of the crew of the *Saint Joseph* were to discover that Christian slavery had not been totally eliminated in this region when they were 'tied together in couples and sold by auction'.[69] But these were isolated incidents in seas almost completely free of piracy, seas which were patrolled by navies increasingly well equipped to run down maritime miscreants. As Philip Gosse wrote in 1932 in his *History of Piracy*, 'there is no doubt that the type of man who once turned to piracy still exists, but is compelled to find other channels for his talents.' The days of Blackbeard, Bartholomew Roberts and Diaboleto were over and, as *The Times* remarked in 1919, 'the life of any future pirate would be too short to be even merry'.[70]

# Notes

The notes normally refer only to the surname of the author, or the first word or words of anonymous works, with the date of publication given for authors with more than one work listed in the Bibliography. For full details of references, see the Bibliography, pp. 277–89.

## Preface

1. Johnson, p. 54.
2. For more on Blackbeard and his last fight see below pp. 165–6, 193–4.

## Chapter One: Pirates of Fable

1. Thoreau, p. 78.
2. Thornton (1968), p. 81; Rediker (1997), p. 33; Deschamps, p. 30.
3. Pennell (1998), pp. 65–8.
4. Burg (1983); Turley; Pennell (1998) p. 65; for a discussion of pirate homosexuality see below p. 107.
5. Clifford, p. 165; Rediker (1997), pp. 34–6, and see below pp. 170–2.
6. For trial, see CO 137/14 ff. 16–18; Johnson, pp. 130–41; for a brief discussion of Johnson, see below pp. 129–30, 163.

7. For example: Stanley; Rediker (1996); Pennell (1998), pp. 67–8.
8. Lorimer, Internet publicity on www.booty.pirate-women.com.
9. Griffin; Larsson.
10. Harte, p. 14.
11. Parish; see also Rogoziński (1995) for plot summaries of pirate films.
12. Parish, pp. 1–3; Thornton (1968), p. 79.
13. Parish, pp. 1, 19, 68.
14. *CSPAWI* 1669–74, #729, 13 January 1672.
15. Rodger (1986), p. 113.

*Chapter Two: A Nation of Pirates*

1. The following section on local piracy in the British Isles relies mainly on Mathew, Andrews (1975) and Ewen (1949).
2. Ewen (1949), pp. 39–40.
3. *APC,* xiii, 227–9, 272, 355.
4. Ewen (1939), p. 10.
5. HMC *Hatfield,* v, 519; Mathew, pp. 339–41.
6. Mathew, p. 337; Ewen (1949), pp. 37–8.
7. Andrews (1975), p. 200.
8. Ibid., p. 207.
9. Andrews (1970), p. 81, quoting Stow.
10. Manwaring and Perrin, ii, 18.
11. Rodger (1997), p. 345.
12. Barker, p. 4.
13. Quoted in Senior (1976), p. 7.
14. Quoted by Tenenti, p. 58.
15. Andrews (1972).
16. *CSPV* 1607–10, 27 May 1608.
17. *VCH Suffolk,* ii, 215; *APC* 1599–1600, 10 March 1599/1600.
18. *CSPD* 1603–10, 8 August 1609; *CSPV* 1607–10, 5 November 1607, 18 June 1608; Barker; Senior (1976), pp. 39–40, 87–94.
19. *CSPV* 1607–10, 6 June, 11 June 1607.
20. *CSPV* 1610–13, 3 March 1613.
21. *CSPV* 1603–7, 28 May 1603; 1607–10, 14 May 1608.

22. *CSPV* 1603–7, 18 May, 17 November 1603.
23. *CSPV* 1610–13, 24 August 1611.
24. *CSPV* 1617–19, 31 January 1618.
25. *CSPV* 1613–15, 8 July 1615.
26. Senior (1975) and Senior (1976).
27. Mainwaring, ii, 15–16.
28. For Leamcon, see Moore (1912).
29. *CSPI* 1611–14, p. 305, 18 November 1612.
30. Edwards, p. 62, 31 October 1612.
31. *CSPI* 1611–14, p. 99, 23 August 1611; Mainwaring, ii, 39–40.
32. *CSPI* 1608–10, p. 100, 20 November 1608.
33. Edwards, p. 120, 4 August 1613.
34. *CSPD* 1611–18, 5 July 1611, examination of John Collever.
35. Edwards, p. 120, 4 August 1613.
36. Manwaring and Perrin, i, 21.
37. *CSPI* 1608–10, p. 100, 20 November 1608.
38. Caulfield, pp. xlix–l.
39. Senior (1976), p. 37.
40. Ibid., p. 25.

## Chapter Three: *God's Plunderers*

1. The following section on the Barbary corsairs relies mainly on Bono, Earle (1970), Sebag, Spencer, Turbet-Delof and Wolf.
2. Pennell (1989) p. 59.
3. Pignon, p. 208.
4. Des Boys, x, 91–9.
5. Grandchamp, pp. 473–6, 495.
6. Hebb, p. 139.
7. Lewis, p. 125; D'Aranda, p. 238.
8. Earle (1970), p. 93; Stirling-Maxwell, p. 86; Defoe, p. 148.
9. De Paradis, p. 57.
10. Belhamissi, p. 101.
11. This section on Sallee is based mainly on: Coindreau; Lloyd (1981), ch. 8; Wilson.
12. Wilson, p. 82.

13. The following section on the Maltese corsairs is based mainly on Earle (1970) and Fontenay and Tenenti.

14. For a discussion of the relative income of the Order from its estates and from the *corso*, see Fontenay.

15. Dumont, p. 342.

16. Engel, ch. 4.

17. Marryat, pp. 71,94; Pérez-Reverte, p. 162.

18. Des Boys, x, 266.

19. National Library of Malta, MS 152, Rubric 49.

20. For the Jewish involvement in the ransom business, see Eisenbeth.

*Chapter Four: Cleansing Home Waters*

1. Barnby.

2. Mathew, pp. 347–8.

3. Hebb, p. 9; Berckman, p. 15.

4. Senior (1976), ch. 6.

5. *CSPI* 1603–6, pp. 382–3, 2 January 1606; 1608–10, pp. 105–6, 20 November 1608; on the anti-piracy statute of 1536 (28 Henry VIII c.15), see Ritchie, p. 141.

6. *CSPI* 1608–10, p. 495, 21 September 1610.

7. Ibid., pp. 277–8, 22 August 1609.

8. Senior (1976), p. 68.

9. *CSPI* 1611–14, pp. 89–90, 29 July 1611.

10. Edwards, p. 65, 24 December 1612.

11. *CSPV* 1610–13, #663, 15 October 1612.

12. Ibid., #780, 791, 798, dated 3, 16 and 24 March 1612/13.

13. *CSPV* 1607–10, #712, 17 November 1609, #724, 1 December 1609.

14. Hannay, p. 41.

15. For the capture of Mamora, see De Castries, ii, 566–72.

16. *CSPI* 1606–8, 16 July 1607.

17. *CSPI* 1611–18, 26 March 1613.

18. HMC *Downshire*, iii, 169–70.

19. Quoted in Senior (1976), p. 141.

20. Rodger (1997), p. 367; Woodward.

21. ADM 2/48, pp. 77–8, 236.
22. ADM 2/367, pp. 412–13, 16 February 1724/5.
23. For Solgard, see below pp. 202–3.
24. ADM 2/51, pp. 172, 180–2, 192; for Gow's piratical career, see Johnson, pp. 323–33.

*Chapter Five: Containing the Corsairs*

1. Corbett, i, 52.
2. Spencer, p. 124.
3. *CSPV* 1610–13, 2 September 1611.
4. Quoted by Mathiex, p. 89.
5. Quoted by Hebb, p. 91.
6. Molloy, p. 61.
7. Davis (1961), p. 130.
8. For the Algiers expedition, see Hebb, ch. 5.
9. For Roe's embassy, see Hebb, ch. 8.
10. Hebb, p. 185.
11. For the Sallee expedition, see Hebb, ch. 11.
12. Hebb, pp. 253–5.
13. Corbett, i, 226; Capp, p. 71.
14. On convoy, see Hornstein, ch. 3.
15. Capp, pp. 233–4; Middleton, p. 96.
16. Fisher, pp. 210–14; Baumber, pp. 203–5; Earle (1970), p. 39.
17. Anderson, p. 100.
18. Hebb, p. 91; Hornstein, p. 144 and see ch. 4 for these campaigns.
19. Belhamissi, p. 101.
20. Panzac.
21. Shaw, p. 256.
22. For treaties, see Bono, pp. 56–66.
23. Macintyre, pp. 2–3.
24. Spencer, pp. 132–4.
25. Macintyre, pp. 2–3; for the war between the USA and Tripoli, see Allen (1905), pp. 88–266 (quotation from p. 249).
26. Cavaliero, p. 20.

27. Earle (1970), pp. III–21, and 265–7; Cavaliero; Fontenay and Tenenti, p. 106.


*Chapter Six: The Buccaneers*

 1. Thornton (1968), p. 81; the early part of this chapter relies for general background mainly on Andrews (1978), Barbour, Haring, Newton (1933).
 2. Hickeringill, p. 33.
 3. For this episode in imperial history, see Newton (1914).
 4. Leslie, p. 91.
 5. *CSPV* 1667–8, p. 253; Mattingly.
 6. Blank commission quoted in Earle (1981), p. 26.
 7. De Lussan, p. 89.
 8. Haring, p. 267; Zahedieh, p. 154.
 9. For L'Ollonais and other buccaneer captains, see Exquemelin, and Marley (1994), which is a biographical dictionary of the buccaneers.
10. For Morgan's campaigns as admiral, see Earle (1981).
11. Exquemelin, p. 203. For a discussion of Exquemelin's reliability as a source, see Earle (1981), pp. 265–6.
12. Thornton (1952), p. 37; and for the buccaneers as 'agents of empire' see Thornton (1968); for general background to the buccaneers after 1670, see: Crouse; Haring, chs 6 and 7; Newton (1933), ch. 22; Thornton (1956), ch. 6; Zahedieh.
13. *CSPAWI* 1669–74, #367, 31 December 1670.
14. *CSPAWI* 1675–6, #863, 4 April 1676.
15. *CSPAWI* 1669–74, #729, 13 January 1672.
16. *CSPAWI* 1681–5, #668, 29 August 1682.
17. Uring, p. 355; *CSPAWI* 1669–74, #1115, 8 July 1673; Add. 39946, pp. 19–20; for the logwood trade, see Wilson (1936).
18. *CSPAWI* 1681–5, #712, 29 September 1682.
19. Newton (1933), pp. 327–8.
20. Haring, pp. 262–6.
21. Zahedieh, p. 157.
22. Céspedes del Castillo, p. 243; for a general account of the

South Sea men, see the chapter on the buccaneers in Gerhard; Kemp and Lloyd.

23. BL Sloane 3820 p. 54.
24. *CSPAWI* 1681–5, #668/1, 29 August 1682; #1188, 15 August 1683; #1845, 25 August 1684; 1685–9, #210, 4 June 1685.
25. *CSPAWI* 1681–5 #1313, 18 October 1683; 1685–9 #226/1, 12 June 1685; 1681–5 #1862/4; Ritchie (1986) pp. 23–5.
26. Charlevoix, pp. 42–6; Vaissière, pp. 13–19.
27. Earle (1981), pp. 41–2, which is based on Morgan's articles of agreement with his captains in AGI IG 1600.
28. BL Sloane 49 f.42.
29. Exquemelin p. 60; Charlevoix, p. 52; Labat, p. 37.
30. Labat, p. 37; cf. Exquemelin, p. 60; Morgan in AGI IG 1600.
31. AGI IG 1600; Dampier, p. 55; Labat, p. 37.
32. De Lussan, p. 121.
33. Dampier p. 30, and see below p. 168.
34. Wilkinson, p. 24; Betagh, pp. 148, 186–7.
35. Dampier, p. 195.
36. Dampier, p. 28.
37. Le Golif, p. 191.
38. Charlevoix, pp. 44, 55; Labat, p. 175; Vaissière, p. 13.
39. BL Sloane 239; and for copies, see Sloane 44, 46A, 46B, 47.
40. Callander, ii, 552.
41. BL Sloane 3820, pp. 71, 84, 171.
42. Exquemelin, pp. 85, 102–3.
43. Earle (1981), p. 79.
44. De Lussan, pp. 187, 214.
45. Labat, p. 127.
46. Burg (1983), pp. xvi, xxiii; cf. Turley for a book with a similar argument.
47. Exquemelin, p. 44.
48. Le Golif, p. 110.
49. Burg (1983), p. xvii.
50. Exquemelin, p. 59; Dampier, p. 106.
51. For some examples, see de Lussan, pp. 202, 227, 256.
52. BL Sloane 3820, p. 150.
53. CO 1/25 f. 160. Browne to Williamson, 12 October 1670;

quoted in Earle (1981), p. 66.

## Chapter Seven: The Red Sea Men

1. Hamilton, i, 89.
2. Information from an unpublished paper written by Dr D.D. Hebb based on material in HCA 15/15.
3. OIOC E/3/56, #6930.
4. For this period of piracy in the Indian Ocean, I have relied for background mainly on Grey, Deschamps, Ritchie (1986), Bruijn and Gaastra, Rogoziński (2000), Barendse.
5. *CSPAWI*, 1693–6, 10 June 1693, 13 June 1695.
6. For the voyage of the *Jacob*, see: Ritchie (1986), pp. 34–8; Rogoziński (2000), pp. 14–17, and see these two books *passim* for this whole episode in pirate history.
7. *CSPAWI* 1693–6, 25 June 1695; quoted in Hill (1923), p. 50; Shelvocke, p. 7.
8. Barlow, ii, 473.
9. For the story of Avery, see: Ritchie (1986), pp. 85–9; Rogoziński (2000), pp. 79–92.
10. OIOC E/3/52 #6205; the Muslim historian Khafi Khan quoted by Hill (1923), p. 102.
11. Ritchie (1986), p. 88.
12. Ibid., pp. 85–9; Rogozinski (2000), pp. 79–91.
13. *CSPAWI* 1696–7, 17 August 1696, Edward Randolph to the Commissioners of Customs.
14. OIOC E/3/52, # 6230; E/3/55 #6809.
15. OIOC E/3/55, #6642, 10 April 1699.
16. ADM 1/1588/8, 24 August 1698, depositions of John Graham and Richard Brookes.
17. *CSPAWI* 1696–7, 22 June 1697.
18. *State Trials*, v, 324.
19. For the story of Kidd, see, in particular, Ritchie (1986).
20. OIOC E/3/51 #6113, 16 November 1695.
21. For this episode, see Wright, ch. 8.
22. OIOC E/3/51 # 6113, 16 November 1695.
23. Keay, p. 189; OIOC G/3/17, 23 July 1700.

24. *CSPAWI* 1697–8, 28 November 1697, 1 September 1698; Leibbrandt (1896a), pp. 228–32.

25. Grey, p. 123.

26. *CSPAWI* 1697–8, 1 September 1698.

27. ADM 1/2636/16, 10 March 1700; OIOC E/3/57 #7055, 10 May 1700; #7316, 28 December 1700.

28. Hill (1923), pp. 138–41.

29. For depositions relating to this, see: ADM 1/2650/1, 23 June 1721; OIOC E/1/13 #72, 8 February 1722; #184, 22 August 1722.

30. For this period of Indian Ocean piracy, see Rogoziński (2000), ch. 15.

31. Bernardin de Saint-Pierre quoted in Grandidier, v, 66.

32. ADM 1/2096/11, 30 September 1721; ADM 1/1597/16, 28 October 1723; and for a good description of the campaign, see Biddulph, pp. 169–200.

33. Furber, pp. 144–5; Hill (1920) p. 67; Grandidier, v, 113.

34. Leibbrandt (1896a), p. 137.

35. OIOC E/3/52, #6253, 31 July 1696.

36. OIOC E/3/51, #6039, 28 May 1695.

37. OIOC E/3/53, #6467, 11 December 1697; Hill (1920), p. 61.

38. *State Trials,* v, 10.

39. *State Trials,* v, 10, 14.

40. OIOC E/3/52, #6253, 31 July 1696. For sailors' wages in the 1690s, see Davis (1962), p. 136.

41. Ritchie (1986), p. 120.

42. *CSPAWI* 1696–7, #517 iv, 18 December 1696.

43. Earle (1981), p. 90; see above p. 98.

44. Rogoziński (2000), pp. viii–x, xx–xxi.

45. For debate on authorship, see Moore, ch. 8 and Furbank and Owens, pp. 100–13; for the bibliography of Johnson's book, see Gosse (1927).

46. For Captain Misson, see Johnson, pp. 340–72, and 397–416; see also Atkinson (1920 and 1922).

47. For example, Rediker (1997), p. 31.

48. Hill (1923), p. 97.

49. Rogoziński (2000), p. 57.

*Chapter Eight: War Against the Pirates*

1. Thomson, p. 106; *CSPAWI*, 7 June 1699.
2. Data on ships from the Admiralty list book, ADM 8/1, and for Jamaica, see Pawson and Buisseret, ch. 5. For detailed information on the ships see Lyon.
3. *CSPAWI* 1681–5, 22 February 1683.
4. *CSPAWI* 1675–6, 10 April and 30 September 1675.
5. *CSPAWI* 1681–5, 6 November 1682.
6. ADM 51/3870, 29 May 1680; Add. 12424, 29 May 1672.
7. *CSPAWI* 1681–5, 22 February 1683.
8. Add. 12424, 27 December 1671; ADM 51/3870, 13 February, 20 March 1678/9.
9. Earle (1979), ch. 16.
10. ADM 51/3926, log of *Norwich*, 19–26 June 1682; *CSPAWI* 1681–5, 15 November 1682.
11. ADM 2/1727, p. 142. Orders of 15 July 1686.
12. ADM 51/3926, 3–5 August 1681.
13. ADM 51/3926, 29–30 January 1681; *CSPAWI* 1681–5, 1 January and 2 July 1681; Marley, p. 139.
14. *CSPAWI* 1669–74, 17 December 1671 and 27 January 1672; for Morris's career, see Marley, pp. 270–4.
15. Add. 12424, 20 February 1672.
16. Add. 12424, 10, 20–21 February, 7, 20 March 1672.
17. *CSPAWI* 1681–5, 18 October 1683, deposition of Thomas Phips; Marley, pp. 177–80.
18. *CSPAWI* 1681–5, 15 August 1683; and for St Thomas, see Westergaard.
19. *CSPAWI* 1681–5, 12 September 1684.
20. Bodleian, Rawlinson A 300, journal of *Bonetta Sloop*, 27 July 1684; Marley, p. 23.
21. *CSPAWI* 1681–5, 30 August 1684.
22. ADM 51/345/4 and 5, 12–13 June 1686.
23. *CSPAWI* 1685–9, 9 February 1687; ADM 51/345, 28 January 1687; see also Pawson and Buisseret, pp. 53–5; Marley, pp. 23–5.
24. Zahedieh, pp. 160–1.
25. For this paragraph and what follows, see, in particular, Steele (1968), ch. 3; Ritchie (1986), pp. 127–59; Baugh (1994);

Thomson; and for an excellent recent study of the relations between merchants and government, see Gauci.

26. II Gull. III, c. 7.
27. *State Trials,* viii, 208; *CSPAWI* 1704–5, 13 July 1704.
28. *CSPAWI* 1697–8, from 6 June 1698 onwards, and 1699–1700 *passim.*
29. ADM 1/1871/8, 4 April 1699.
30. ADM 1/1435/5, John Aldred to Admiralty, 4 August 1699.
31. Ships from the list books, ADM 8/6–7.
32. Numbers from the list books. For details on royal ships, see Lyon.
33. *CSPAWI* 1700, 7 May.
34. ADM 1/1462/4, 29 April 1700; ADM 1/1588/27, 1 November 1699, 3 June 1700; ADM 1/2033/4, 17 April 1700; ADM 1/1462/18, 28 January 1701; 1/2277/4, 14 April 1700.
35. For details, see Hepper, pp. 21–2.
36. For the fight, see ADM 1/2277/5, 3 May 1700, Passenger's report; *CSPAWI* 1700, 6 and 7 May, 5 June 1700.
37. ADM 1/2215/6, 16 June 1701.
38. ADM 1/1871/11, 12 June, 30 July and 29 August 1698.
39. ADM 1/1589/25, 18 July 1700.
40. ADM 1/1589/25, 18 July 1700; Hill (1923), p. 146; Sloane 3820 pp. 6–7, 151. For a general discussion of pirate flags, see Cordingly, pp. 138–43, and see Rediker (1989), pp. 278–80, for the iconography of the 'Jolly Roger'.
41. ADM 1/1589/21, 6 November 1701; 1/1590/5, 2 April 1702; 1/1754/6, 12 June 1702; 1/2033/19, 5 February 1700; *CSPAWI* 1701, 14 October 1701.
42. Hughson, p. 46.
43. *CSPAWI* 1702, 10 July, 19 August 1702.

*Chapter Nine: The Golden Age of Piracy*

1. Quoted in Bourne, p. 183.
2. The following general description of the rise of piracy rests mainly on colonial papers in *CSPAWI*, naval correspondence in ADM 1 and Johnson.

3. Craton, p. 95.
4. *CSPAWI* 1712–14, 22 April 1714.
5. For an account of this disaster, see Wagner, ch. 4.
6. ADM 1/1471/24, 13 May 1716; Wagner, p. 65.
7. Saiz Cidoncha, p. 376; Uring, p. 355; *CSPAWI* 1716–17, 3 July 1716.
8. PRO SP 42/16, f. 8, 5 August 1716.
9. Rediker (1987), p. 256.
10. ADM 1/1472/11, 22 May 1718; ADM 1/1473/13, 22 August 1725.
11. Rediker (1987), p. 256; for Easton, see above pp. 31, 62.
12. ADM 1/2624/6, 18 April 1721.
13. Johnson, p. ix.
14. Moore (1939), p. 127.
15. Snelgrave; French translation of de Bucquoy in Grandidier, v, 103–39.
16. ADM 1/2242/5, 17 May 1723.
17. Burg (1977), pp. 46–7.
18. For this captain/mate problem, see Earle (1998), p. 162
19. *CSPAWI* 1717–18, #807, 24 December 1718.
20. Snelgrave, pp. 199, 226, 284.
21. Johnson, p. 85.
22. Snelgrave, p. 199.
23. CO 152/14, f. 286.
24. CO 152/12, #67 (iii), 19 December 1717; Johnson, pp. 55–7.
25. Grandidier, v, 107, 117–18. Snelgrave, p. 272, also admired Taylor.
26. See above, p. 33.
27. Numbers in ADM 1/2242/6, 14 October 1719, 'an account of the fishery of Newfoundland 1719'; Deschamps, p. 10; HCA 13/82, f. 316, 18 June 1701; ADM 1/2097/11, 12 July 1723.
28. Snelgrave, p. 203.
29. Earle (1998), pp. 130, 133–4, 226; Flavel, intro. A3.
30. Snelgrave, p. 227.
31. HCA 1/99/3, p. 28.
32. Grandidier, v, 115; HCA 1/99/3, p. 48.
33. ADM 1/4102, #76, 22 September 1719.
34. CO 152/11, #45, 14 December 1716.

35. Snelgrave, p. 220.
36. Johnson, p. 182.
37. HCA 1/99/3, p. 59; CO 23/1, #18, f. 78v.
38. Johnson, p. 212.
39. CO 5/867 #4/1, p. 11; Johnson, p. 482; HCA 1/99/3, p. 102; Snelgrave, p. 225; ADM 1/2649/16, 21 October 1720.
40. ADM 1/1598/12, 20 October 1721.
41. See ship names in Johnson, pp. 45, 71, 86–7, 147 etc.; other ships such as *Flying King, Royal Fortune, Royal Rover* may have been named for the same reason; Craton, p. 100; Snelgrave, p. 216; *CSPAWI* 1717–18, #551–1, 31 May 1718; HCA 1/99/3, p. 98; ADM 1/4102 #70, 28 August 1719.
42. Dampier, pp. 15–17.
43. Clifford, p. 165.
44. Clifford, p. 165.
45. Bolster, ch. 1.
46. CO 23/1, #49 (xi).
47. Bolster, p. 5.
48. Leibbrandt (1896a), p. 309; Rediker (1997), pp. 34–6.
49. CO 152/14, f. 292; Roberts, p. 80.
50. Roberts, Lowther, Phillips in Johnson, pp. 182–4, 274–5, 307; Low in Dow and Edmonds, pp. 146–7; Anstis in ADM 1/4104, #75.
51. Grandidier, v, 115.
52. Grandidier, v, 115; Dow and Edmonds, p. 232.
53. Grandidier, v, 115; Snelgrave, p. 256; Johnson, p. 308; ADM 1/4104, #75.
54. Roberts, p. 61.
55. Grandidier, v, 115.
56. HCA 1/99/3, p. 45.
57. For example, John Phillips in Johnson, p. 307; Anstis in ADM 1/4104, #75.
58. See, for instance, Johnson, pp. 144, 185.
59. Roberts, pp. 63, 86; Grandidier, v, 118; Snelgrave, pp. 236–7; Johnson, p. 300; ADM 1/1472/11, 28 January 1722.
60. CO 152/12, #136 (vi), 24 February 1719.
61. Snelgrave, pp. 207–8; *CSPAWI* 1724–5, 16 June 1724; Johnson,

p. 437; Betagh, p. 26; Rediker (1989), pp. 270–1.

62. Add. 39946, p. 28.
63. PRO SP 42/123, deposition of John Carleton, 18 December 1717.
64. CO 152/13, deposition of Robert Dunne, 25 September 1720.
65. Quoted in Jameson, p. 314.
66. Snelgrave, pp. 223, 233–4, 242.
67. Roberts, pp. 59–60.
68. *CSPAWI* 1720–21, 20 May 1720; Roberts, pp. 62–3.
69. Snelgrave, p. 265.
70. Johnson, p. 104; HCA 1/99/3, p. 152.
71. ADM 1/1879/22. His relation is enclosed in a letter of 13 April 1723.
72. Dow and Edmonds, p. 339.
73. HCA 1/99/3, p. 116.
74. Johnson, pp. 107–8; Deschamps, p. 15.
75. Johnson, pp. 189, 88, 105.

*Chapter Ten: Extermination*

1. Johnson, pp. viii–ix.
2. *CSPAWI* 1716–17, #484, 1 March 1717; ADM 51/865/1, log of *Scarborough* 13–21 January 1717.
3. *CSPAWI* 1716–17, 20 July 1717; for Bellamy's shipwreck and the recovery of pirate artefacts from it, see Clifford.
4. Philip Ashton's *Memorial* in Dow and Edmonds, p. 238.
5. ADM 1/1597/1, 16 August 1719.
6. *CSPAWI* 1722–3, #382, 10 December 1722. The disposition of naval vessels here and elsewhere in this chapter is based on ADM 2/46–51; ADM 1/4097–106; SP 44/218.
7. For example, ADM 2/48, pp. 174–8, orders for HMS *Diamond*.
8. ADM 3/31, 19 June 1717; ADM 2/49, pp. 263–5, orders to Captain Pearce of *Phoenix* of 19 June 1717.
9. ADM 1/1438/9, 20 March 1728.
10. ADM 1/2282/8, 4 January 1723, 20 November 1724.
11. ADM 2/46 pp. 279–80, orders for *Ruby*, 19 May 1713.

12. ADM 1/1880/16, 20 January 1723, 3 November 1723.

13. Quoted by Dow and Edmonds, p. 136; Baugh (1965), pp. 7, 109.

14. For some examples, see ADM 1/4101 #14, 18 September 1718; ADM 3/31, 9 April, 30 July 1718; SP 44/220, pp. 252–3, 4 February 1720; *CSPAWI* 1722–3, #659–8, 25 July 1723.

15. ADM 1/4101, #14, 18 September 1718; ADM 1/2096/10, 5 May 1722.

16. Quoted in Bourne, pp. 186–7.

17. ADM 3/31, 24 September 1717.

18. *CSPAWI* 1717–18, 29 March 1718.

19. Ibid., 3 February 1718.

20. ADM 1/2282/13, 4 February, 4 March, 3 June 1718, including a list of the surrendered pirates; *CSPAWI* 1717–18, 29 March 1718.

21. ADM 1/2282/2, 3 September 1718; Johnson, p. 558.

22. Craton, pp. 100–9, and see Rogers' letters in *CSPAWI* 1717–18, 31 October, 24 December 1718; 1719–20, 30 January, 3 March, 29 May 1719, etc.

23. ADM 1/2646/6, enclosure in letter of 17 June 1720.

24. Johnson, p. 14.

25. ADM 1/1597/1, 20 November 1718; ADM 1/1982/4, 27 March 1718; *CSPAWI* 1717–18, 31 October 1718.

26. *CSPAWI* 1717–18, 31 May 1718.

27. ADM 1/1879/5 3, 26 July 1718; ADM 51/865/2, 13 June 1718; *CSPAWI* 1717–18, 9 November 1718.

28. Johnson, p. 67, 70–7; *CSPAWI* 1717–18, 21 October 1718.

29. Johnson, p. 15, 561–75; *CSPAWI*, 24 December 1718.

30. Good accounts in Cordingly, pp. 226–33, and Johnson, pp. 48–55.

31. ADM 1/1472/11, 26 January 1720; ADM 1/1826/2, August 1721.

32. War was declared in December 1718 and orders to commit hostilities against the Spaniards in the West Indies had arrived by March 1719. *CSPAWI* 1717–18, 24 December 1718; ADM 2/49, p. 564, 3 January 1719; ADM 1/2648/6, 30 March 1719.

33. *CSPAWI* 1717–18, 24 December 1718; 1719–20, 24 March 1719; ADM 1/2624/6, 28 October 1719.

34. ADM 1/2649/5, 3 February 1719; orders for the suspension of arms left England on 1 March 1720. ADM 2/50 p. 178, 1 March 1720.

35. ADM 2/50, pp. 154, 250, 531, orders for *Royal Ann Galley* (17 November 1719), *Swallow* (21 July 1720) and *Guernsey* (26 June 1722).

36. For Ogle's cruise and the battle, see: ADM 2/50 pp. 290–3, 24 November 1720 (orders); ADM 1/2242/6 (letters); HCA 1/99/3 (trials); and excellent descriptions in Johnson, pp. 196–215 and Cordingly, pp. 243–51.

37. Dow and Edmonds, p. xxii.

38. Snelgrave, p. 260.

39. For historical studies of women pirates and seafarers, see among other works: Stanley; Creighton and Norling; Rediker (1996); Pennell (1998), pp. 67–8.

40. *CSPAWI* 1719–20, 13 November 1720; CO 137/14 ff. 17v–18.

41. ADM 1/2624/6, 18 April 1721; *CSPAWI* 1720–1, 20 April 1721; Johnson, pp. 109–10.

42. *CSPAWI* 1720–1, #527(i), letter from Vernon, 8 March 1721.

43. ADM 52/436, 25 April 1722; ADM 1/1598/3, 17 May, 11 July 1722; ADM 1/1880/16, 28 April, 17 May 1722; Saiz Cidoncha, pp. 378–9.

44. ADM 1/4104, #75, 13 May 1723; ADM 1/2242/5, 17 May 1723.

45. ADM 1/1472/11, 16 June 1723; Johnson, p. 262.

46. ADM 51/354/8, 25 February–4 March 1723.

47. ADM 51/4394/2, 7–30 April 1723; ADM 1/2242/5, 17 May 1723.

48. ADM 51/533/10, 16 June 1723; *CSPAWI* 1722–3, 8 June 1723.

49. CO 152/14 f. 289; Johnson, pp. 282–3.

50. ADM 1/2452/4, 12 June 1723; Cordingly, pp. 252–4; Johnson, pp. 294–6.

51. ADM 1/2452/4, 12 June and 25 November 1723, 25 May 1724; Dow and Edmonds, p. 210.

52. ADM 1/2452/4, 29 March 1725; ADM 1/2242/6, 13 May 1725.

53. Rediker (1989), p. 256.

54. ADM 1/2650/15, 27 October 1723.

55. ADM 1/2242/5, 18 June 1724; ADM 51/4161, 31 August 1724.

56. ADM 1/2282/1, 5 March 1726; ADM 1/1472/11, 7 April 1726.

57. ADM 1/1598/19, 6 March 1726; Johnson, p. 302.

58. CO 5/869 ff. 381–406v; Johnson, pp. 488–95.

59. Black, pp. 121–3; Cordingly, p. 232.

60. Grandidier, v, 66.

61. Ritchie (1986) p. 236; Rediker (1989), p. 283.

62. See above pp. 147–8.

63. CO 5/869, f. 401v.

64. ADM 1/2242/6, 5 April 1722.

65. HCA 1/99/3 *passim.* Quotations from pp. 65, 54–5, 151.

66. HCA 1/99/3, pp. 121, 133, 157, 56.

## Chapter Eleven: Maritime Mayhem Revived

1. Shepherd and Walton, pp. 80–5.

2. Gosse (1932), pp. 244–64; Course, pp. 62–83; Risso.

3. For some examples, see: Hill (1923), pp. 159, 176; *Gentleman's Magazine* xix, 295–6; xxviii, 92; xxix, 604; xxxi, 236.

4. May.

5. The following is based mainly on Pérotin-Dumon, Currier, Griffin.

6. See above p. 91.

7. Beraza; Pérotin-Dumon, p. 670; Graham and Humphreys, pp. 231–2; ADM 1/271, 23 April 1821.

8. Griffin, p. 2.

9. *Times*, 31 December 1819, p. 4b.

10. Griffin, p. 2; Alexander, i, 322–3.

11. Griffin, pp. 18–21.

12. Pérotin-Dumon; Ferro, pp. 171–7.

13. *LL*, 8 and 22 July 1817.

14. *LL*, 21 April 1818; *Times*, 24 April 1818, p. 3c; Howat, p. 18.

15. ADM 1/270, deposition of Thomas Postlethwaite, 21 December 1818; *Times*, 17 February 1819, p. 3e.

16. Pérotin-Dumon, p. 674.

17. *LL*, 7 and 17 July 1818.

18. Currier, pp. 39–42.

19. Currier, p. 41; *LL*, 19 and 23 February 1819; *Times*, 12 June 1820, p. 3a.

20. *LL*, 4 August 1818.

21. This description of the Cuban pirates is based mainly on reports in *The Times*, *LL* and in *NA* vols i and ii.

22. *LL*, 16 November 1821.

23. *NA* i, 1004, 7 December 1824; i, 1009–10, 8 April 1824.

24. *NA* i, 787; ADM 1/279, 13 November 1828; *Times*, 14 February 1823, p. 2d.

25. Smith, pp. 38–47.

26. *Narrative*, p. 10.

27. *Times*, 28 May 1823, p. 3c; Allen (1929), p. 29.

28. *Times*, 20 December 1823, p. 3d; ADM 1/273, 3 February 1823; *Narrative*, pp. 19–20.

29. *NA* i, 1120–1, 19 November 1823.

30. *Times*, 5 November 1822, p. 2d; 20 December 1823, p. 3d; *LL*, 27 May 1825; Goodrich, p. 320; *NA* ii, 26, 21 October 1824.

31. *Times*, 28 September 1822, p. 2d; 23 July 1829, p. 3f; Cordingly, p. 155.

32. Smith, p. 78.

33. Billingsley, pp. 166–7.

34. ADM 1/194 #85, 1 February 1830.

35. *Times*, 7 August 1821, p. 3d; 1 December 1821, p. 2c; *LL*, 7 August 1821; *Trial* (1821); *Murder*.

36. *Trial* (1820); *Times*, 28 August 1819, p. 3d; 3 January 1820, p. 3c; 7 March 1820, p. 3c; 1 April 1820, p. 3c.

37. The background discussion for this section is drawn mainly from Pitcairn Jones, Clogg, Woodhouse, Lemos.

38. Pitcairn Jones, p. 4; ADM 1/445, 25 March 1826; ADM 1/445, 23 April 1826.

39. ADM 1/446, 11 September 1826.

40. ADM 1/3995, 26 April 1827.

41. ADM 1/3995, 7 July 1826; Pitcairn Jones, pp. 232, 281–90.

42. *Times*, 18 December 1827, p. 2f.

43. ADM 1/3995, 7 July 1826.

44. *Journal*, p. 41; *Times*, 28 August 1827, p. 2d; Pitcairn Jones, p. 100.

45. Crane, pp. 148, 93.

## Chapter Twelve: An End to Piracy

1. Numbers of ships here and below from ADM 8/101.
2. Pitcairn Jones, pp. xxiv–xxv.
3. Lloyd (1949), p. 70 and *passim*; ADM 1/1573, Commodore Bullen to Admiralty, 15 September 1826.
4. ADM 1/277, 24 August 1825.
5. ADM 8/15, 1 May 1721.
6. Wright and Fayle, pp. 71–8, 285, 330–1.
7. Robinson.
8. *Times*, 23 September 1817, p. 2e.
9. *Times*, 25 July 1818, p. 2e.
10. Whitaker, pp. 278–86; Allen (1929), pp. 17–21.
11. For example, *LL*, 4 February, 1 September 1820, 31 July 1821, 29 January, 8 February, 28 May, 4 June 1822.
12. For some examples of acquittal, see *Times*: 23 July 1818; 4 February 1820, p. 2d; 9 February 1829, p. 3f.
13. For this war, see Vale.
14. ADM 1/30, 29 May 1827, Otway to Admiralty.
15. ADM 1/30, 28 August 1827; ADM 1/280, 24 December 1828; Vale, p. 227.
16. *Times*, 9 February 1829, p. 3f; 14 February 1829, p. 4c; 7 April 1729, p. 6e; Vale, p. 227; ADM 1/280, 24 December 1828, 16 January 1829.
17. ADM 1/30, 2 April 1829, Otway to Admiralty; Vale, p. 230.
18. ADM 1/1566, letters from Blacker to the Admiralty, 20 January, and 26 June 1819; ADM 1/3846, Consul Benjamin Moodie to the Admiralty, Charleston, 4 June 1819.
19. Battis, p. 44 and *passim*; Ellms, pp. 121–42.
20. Smith, p. 70.
21. *NA* i, #207, p. 787.
22. Goodrich, pp. 88–95, 316.
23. Ibid., p. 490.
24. For example, *The Pirate Hunter* (1866).
25. ADM 1/273, 7 October 1822.
26. Goodrich, pp. 317–18.
27. Thomas, pp. 9–13.
28. Goodrich, p. 316; *LL*, 8 February 1822.

29. *Times*, 24 July 1822, p. 3c; 1 August 1822, p. 3a-c; 8 August 1822 p. 2d; *LL*, 19 November 1822; *Times*, 18 November 1822, p. 2d.

30. *Times*, 7 September 1822, p. 2e.

31. ADM 1/272, 5 September 1822.

32. ADM 1/273, 23 December 1822.

33. Ibid., 17 February 1823.

34. *NA* i, 822, #215; Goodrich, p. 491.

35. Porter, p. 282; *NA* i, 822; Allen (1929), p. 41; *LL*, 20 May 1825.

36. Goodrich, pp. 973–4.

37. *NA* i, 1121.

38. ADM 1/277, 26 April 1825; *NA* ii, 107.

39. ADM 1/275, 26 September 1823.

40. ADM 1/273, 23 December 1822; Allen (1929), pp. 54–5.

41. *NA* i, 1049–50.

42. *Times*, 28 May 1823, p. 3c.

43. *Times*, 30 August 1823, p. 2c; 5 September 1823, p. 2c; 10 September 1823, p. 2d; *NA* i, 1113–14; Allen (1929), p. 52; Porter, p. 290.

44. *NA* ii, 104–5; Allen (1929), pp. 82–3.

45. ADM 1/3995, 23 May 1829, enclosing a cutting from the *New York Gazette* of 20 April.

46. Bradlee, p. 23, although he is not a very reliable writer.

47. *Times*, 5 September 1827, p. 3d.

48. On Britain in the Ionian Islands, see Pratt.

49. ADM 1/448, 6 July 1827; for general background to the Greek anti-piracy campaign, see Pitcairn Jones.

50. Pitcairn Jones, p. 33.

51. ADM 1/448, 4 April 1827.

52. Pitcairn Jones, pp. 35–6.

53. ADM 1/448, Commander Davies of *Rose* to Hamilton, 14 June 1827.

54. ADM 1/3995, 26 July 1827.

55. ADM 1/446, 31 July 1826; ADM 1/3995, 25 July 1826.

56. ADM 12/248, #75, 9 November 1827.

57. Pitcairn Jones, pp. 109–13.

58. Woodhouse, pp. 140–1 and *passim*.

59. Pitcairn Jones, pp. 217–18.

60. Pitcairn Jones, pp. xxxi–xxxiii.
61. Allen (1905), ch. 15.
62. Bono, pp. 69–70; Wolf, p. 331.
63. Lane-Poole, pp. 294–9; Spencer, pp. 141–4; *LL*, 7 October 1817.
64. Tatton, p. 51.
65. Spencer, pp. 148–66; Bono, p. 76; Wolf, pp. 335–8; Lane-Poole, pp. 300–3.
66. For a general survey, see Course.
67. For recent piracy, see Villar, Ellen, Gottschalk, and the annual reports of the International Maritime Bureau's Piracy Reporting Centre.
68. *Times*: 12 December 1846, p. 7b; 15 December 1846, p. 8d; 12 May 1847, p. 6c; 27 August 1847, p. 2e.
69. *Times*: 30 November 1848, p. 3d; 7 April 1896, p. 3f.
70. Gosse (1932), p. 298; *Times*, 4 September 1919, p. 11d.

# Bibliography

*Abbreviations used in endnotes*

| | |
|---|---|
| Add. | Additional Manuscript, British Library |
| ADM | Admiralty Records, Public Record Office |
| AGI | Archivo General de Indias, Seville |
| *APC* | *Acts of the Privy Council* |
| BL | British Library |
| CO | Colonial Office Records, Public Record Office |
| *CSPAWI* | *Calendar of State Papers, America and West Indies* |
| *CSPD* | *Calendar of State Papers, Domestic* |
| *CSPI* | *Calendar of State Papers, Ireland* |
| *CSPV* | *Calendar of State Papers, Venetian* |
| *EHR* | *English Historical Review* |
| HCA | High Court of Admiralty Records, Public Record Office |
| HMC | Historical Manuscripts Commission |
| IG | Indiferente General section, AGI |
| *LL* | *Lloyd's List* |
| *MM* | *Mariners' Mirror* |
| *NA* | *U.S.A. Documents of Congress, Naval Affairs:* vol. 1, 1789–1825; vol. 2, 1824–7 (Washington, 1834, 1860) |
| NRS | Navy Records Society |
| OIOC | Oriental & India Office Collections, British Library |
| PRO | Public Record Office |
| SP | State Papers, Public Record Office |
| *TRHS* | *Transactions of the Royal Historical Society* |
| *VCH* | *Victoria County History* |

There is a huge literature on piracy and the works listed here include just those which have been referred to in the Notes. Place of publication is London unless otherwise stated. Where there is a second publication date in parentheses, the second one has been consulted.

Alexander, J.E., *Transatlantic Sketches* (1833).

Allen, Gardner W., *Our Navy and the Barbary Corsairs* (Boston, 1905).

Allen, Gardner W., *Our Navy and the West Indian Pirates* (Salem, Mass., 1929).

Anderson, M.S., 'Great Britain and the Barbary States in the Eighteenth Century', *Bulletin of the Institute of Historical Research* xxix (1956).

Andrews, K.R., *Drake's Voyages* (1970).

Andrews, K.R., 'The expansion of English privateering and piracy in the Atlantic, *c.* 1540–1625' in Mollat (1975), vol. i, 196–230.

Andrews, K.R., 'Sir Robert Cecil and Mediterranean plunder', *EHR* lxxxvii (1972).

Andrews, K.R., *The Spanish Caribbean: trade and plunder, 1530–1630* (New Haven, Conn., 1978).

Atkinson, Geoffroy, *The Extraordinary Voyage in French Literature before 1700* (New York, 1920).

Atkinson, Geoffroy, *The Extraordinary Voyage in French Literature from 1700 to 1720* (Paris, 1922).

Barbour, Violet, 'Privateers and pirates of the West Indies', *American Historical Review* xvi (1911).

Barendse, R.J., *The Arabian Seas: the Indian Ocean World of the Seventeenth Century* (New York, 2002).

Barker, Andrew, *A Report of Captaine Ward and Danseker, pirates* (1609; Amsterdam facsimile, 1968).

Barlow, Edward, *Journal of his Life at Sea* (ed., B. Lubbock, 1934).

Barnby, H., 'The Sack of Baltimore', *Journal of the Cork Historical and Archaeological Society* lxxiv (1969).

Battis, Edward C., 'The brig *Mexican* of Salem, captured by pirates and her escape', *Historical Collections of the Essex Institute*, vol. 34 (1898).

Baugh, Daniel A., *British Naval Administration in the Age of Walpole* (Princeton, 1965).

Baugh, Daniel A., 'Maritime strength and Atlantic commerce: the uses of a "grand marine empire"' in Lawrence Stone (ed.), *An Imperial State at War: Britain from 1689 to 1815* (1994).

Baumber, Michael, *General-at-Sea: Robert Blake and the 17th-century revolution in naval warfare* (1989).

Belhamissi, Moulay, *Histoire de la marine algérienne* (Algiers, 1983).

Beraza, Agustín, *Los corsarios de Artigas* (Montevideo, 1978).

Berckman, Evelyn, *Victims of Piracy in the Admiralty Court, 1575–1678* (1979).

Betagh, *A Voyage round the World* (1728).

Biddulph, John, *The Pirates of Malabar* (1907).

Billingsley, Edward Baxter, *In Defence of Neutral Rights* (Chapel Hill, 1967).

Black, Clinton V., *Pirates of the West Indies* (Cambridge, 1989).

Bolster, W. Jeffery, *Black Jacks: African American seamen in the age of sail* (Cambridge, Mass., 1997).

Bono, S., *I corsari barbareschi* (Turin, 1964).

Bourne, Ruth, *Queen Anne's Navy in the West Indies* (Yale, 1939).

Bradlee, Francis B.C., *Piracy in the West Indies and its Suppression* (Salem, Mass., 1923).

Bromley, J.S., 'Outlaws at sea, 1660–1720: liberty, equality and fraternity among Caribbean freebooters' in J.S. Bromley, *Corsairs and Navies* (1987).

Bruijn, Jaap R., and Gaastra, Femme S. (eds), *Ships, Sailors and Spices: East India Companies and their shipping in the 16th, 17th and 18th centuries* (Amsterdam, 1993).

Burg, B.R., 'Legitimacy and authority: a case study of pirate commanders in the seventeenth and eighteenth centuries', *American Neptune* xxxvii (1977).

Burg, B.R., *Sodomy and the Perception of Evil: English sea rovers in the seventeenth-century Caribbean* (New York, 1983).

Callander, John, *Terra Australis Cognita*, 3 vols (Edinburgh, 1766–8).

Capp, Bernard, *Cromwell's Navy: the fleet and the English Revolution, 1648–1660* (1989).

Caulfield, R. (ed.), *The Council Book of the Corporation of Youghal* (Guildford, 1878).

Cavaliero, Roderic E., 'The decline of the Maltese *corso* in the XVIIIth century', *Melita Historica* (1955).

Céspedes del Castillo, Guillermo, 'La defensa militar de istmo de Panamá a fines del siglo XVII y comienzos del XVIII', *Anuario de Estudios Americanos* ix (Seville, 1952).

Charlevoix, Pierre-François-Xavier, *Histoire de l'Isle Espagnole ou de S. Domingue* vol. ii (Paris, 1731).

Chaudhuri, K.N., *The Trading World of Asia and the English East India Company* (Cambridge, 1978).

Clifford, Barry, *The Black Ship: the quest to recover an English pirate ship and its lost treasure* (2000).

Clogg, Richard, *A Short History of Modern Greece* (Cambridge, 1986).

Coindreau, Roger, *Les Corsaires de Salé* (Paris, 1948).

Corbett, Julian S., *England in the Mediterranean, 1603–1713,* 2 vols (1904).

Cordingly, David, *Life Among the Pirates: the romance and the reality* (1995).

Course, A.G., *Piracy in the Eastern Seas* (1966).

Crane, David, *Lord Byron's Jackal: the life of Edward John Trelawny* (1998).

Craton, Michael, *A History of the Bahamas* (1962).

Creighton, Margaret S., and Norling, Lisa (eds), *Iron Men, Wooden Women: gender and seafaring in the Atlantic world, 1700–1920* (Baltimore, Md., 1996).

Crouse, Nellis M., *The French Struggle for the West Indies, 1665–1713* (New York, 1943).

Currier, Theodore S., *Los Corsarios del Rio de la Plata* (Buenos Aires, 1929).

Dampier, William, *A New Voyage round the World* (1927).

D'Aranda, Emanuel, *Relation de la captivité et liberté du sieur Emanuel d'Aranda, jadis esclave à Alger* (Brussels, 1662).

Davis, Ralph, 'England and the Mediterranean, 1570–1670' in F.J. Fisher (ed.), *Essays in the Economic and Social History of Tudor and Stuart England* (Cambridge, 1961).

Davis, Ralph, *The Rise of the English Shipping Industry in the 17th and 18th centuries* (1962).

De Castries, Henry (ed.), *Les sources inédites de l'histoire du Maroc,* vol. ii (Paris, 1909).

Defoe, Daniel, *A General History of Discoveries and Improvements* (1725–7).

De Lussan, Raveneau, *Journal of a Voyage into the South Seas in 1684* (tr. and ed., Marguerite Eyer Wilbur, Cleveland, Ohio, 1930).

De Paradis, Venture, *Alger au XVIIIe siècle* (Algiers, 1898).

Des Boys, Le Sieur du Chastelet, 'L'Odyssée', *Revue Africaine* x–xiv (1866–70).

Deschamps, Hubert, *Les pirates à Madagascar aux XVIIe et XVIIIe siècles* (Paris, 1972).

Dow, George Francis, and Edmonds, John Henry, *Pirates of the New England Coast, 1630–1730* (Salem, Mass., 1923).

Dumont, Jean [Le Sieur du Mont], *A New Voyage to the Levant* (1696).

Earle, Peter, *Corsairs of Malta and Barbary* (1970).

Earle, Peter, *Sailors: English Merchant Seamen, 1650–1775* (1998).

Earle, Peter, *The Sack of Panamá* (1981).

Earle, Peter, *The Wreck of the Almiranta: Sir William Phips and the search for the Hispaniola Treasure* (1979).

Edwards, R.D. (ed.), 'Letter-book of Sir Arthur Chichester, 1612–14', *Analecta Hibernica* No. 8 (March 1938).

Eisenbeth, M., 'Les Juifs en Algérie et en Tunisie à l'époque turque, 1516–1830', *Revue Africaine* xcvi (1952).

Ellen, Eric (ed.), *Piracy at Sea* (Paris, 1989).

Ellms, Charles, *The Pirates' Own Book* (Philadelphia, 1837).

Engel, Claire Eliane, *Knights of Malta: a gallery of portraits* (1963).

Ewen, C. L'Estrange, *The Golden Chalice* (Paignton, 1939).

Ewen, C. L'Estrange, 'Organized piracy round England in the sixteenth century', *MM* 35 (1949).

Exquemelin, Alexander Olivier, *The Buccaneers of America* (1684–5; n.d. reprint by Broadway Translations).

Ferro, Carlos A., *Vida de Luis Aury* (Buenos Aires, 1976).

Fisher, Sir Godfrey, *Barbary legend: war, trade and piracy in North Africa, 1415–1830* (Oxford, 1957).

Flavel, John, *Navigation Spiritualised: or, a new compass for sea-men* (1682).

Fontenay, Michel, 'Corsaires de la foi ou rentiers du sol? Les chevaliers de Malte dans le 'corso' Méditerranéen au xviie siècle', *Revue d'Histoire moderne et contemporaine* xxxv (1988).

Fontenay, Michel, and Tenenti, Alberto, 'Course et piraterie méditerranéennes de la fin du moyen-âge au début du XIXème siècle', in Mollat (1975), vol. i, 78–136.

Friedman, Ellen G., *Spanish Captives in North Africa in the early modern age* (Madison, Wisconsin, 1983).

Furbank, P.N., and Owens, W.R., *The Canonisation of Daniel Defoe* (New Haven, Conn., 1988).

Furber, Holden, *Rival Empires of Trade in the Orient, 1600–1800* (Minneapolis, 1976).

Gauci, Perry, *The Politics of Trade: the overseas merchants in state and society, 1660–1720* (Oxford, 2001).

Gerhard, Peter, *Pirates on the west coast of New Spain, 1575–1742* (Glendale, Cal., 1960).

Goodrich, Rear Admiral Caspar F., 'Our navy and the West Indian pirates', *United States Naval Institute Proceedings,* vols 42, 43 (1916–17).

Gosse, Philip, *A Bibliography of the Works of Captain Charles Johnson* (1927).

Gosse, Philip, *The History of Piracy* (1932).

Gottschalk, Jack A., *Jolly Roger with an Uzi: the rise and threat of modern piracy* (2000).

Graham, Gerald S., and Humphreys, R.A., *The Navy and South America, 1807–1823* (1962).

Grandchamp, Pierre, 'Une mission délicate en Barbarie au XVIIe siècle: J.B. Salvago, drogman vénitien à Alger et à Tunis', *Revue Tunisienne* xxx (1937).

Grandidier, Alfred, *Collection des ouvrages anciens concernant Madagascar: tome v, (1718–1800)* (Paris, 1907).

Grey, Charles, *Pirates of the Eastern Seas, 1618–1723* (1933).

Griffin, Charles C., 'Privateering from Baltimore during the Spanish American Wars of Independence', *Maryland Historical Magazine* xxxv (1940).

Griffin, Nicholas, *The Requiem Shark* (2000).

Hamilton, Alexander, *A New Account of the East Indies* (Edinburgh, 1727).

Hannay, David, 'The Pirate' in *Ships and Men* (1910).

Haring, C.H., *Buccaneers in the West Indies in the seventeenth century* (New York, 1910).

Harte, Bret, *The Queen of the Pirate Isle* (1886).

Haugaard, Erik Christian, *Under the Black Flag* (Niwot, Colo., 1995).

Hebb, D.D., *Piracy and the English Government, 1616–1642* (Aldershot, 1994).

Hepper, David J., *British Warship Losses in the Age of Sail, 1650–1859* (Rotherfield, 1994).

Hickeringill, Edward, *Jamaica View'd* (1661).

Hill, S.C., *Episodes of Piracy in the Eastern Seas, 1519–1851* (Bombay, 1920).

Hill, S.C., *Notes on Piracy in Eastern Waters* (Bombay, 1923).

Hornstein, Sari R., *The Restoration Navy and English Foreign Trade, 1674–1688: a study in the peacetime use of naval force* (Aldershot, 1991).

Howat, J.N.T., *South American Packets, 1808–1880* (York, 1984).

Howison, John, *Foreign Scenes and Travelling Recreations* (Edinburgh, 1825).

Hughson, S.C., *The Carolina Pirates and Colonial Commerce, 1670–1740* (Baltimore, Md., 1894).

Jameson, John Franklin, *Privateering and Piracy in the Colonial Period: Illustrative documents* (New York, 1923).

Johnson, Captain Charles, *A General History of the Robberies and Murders of the most notorious Pirates* (1724–6, 1955).

*Journal kept by John Tatton Brown, Lieutenant, Royal Marines, aboard HMS Sybille*, vol. i, July 1823 to January 1825 (1993).

Keay, John, *The Honourable Company: a history of the English East India Company* (1991).

Kemp, P.K., and Lloyd, Christopher, *The Brethren of the Coast: the British and French buccaneers in the South Seas* (1960).

Labat, Jean-Baptiste, *Memoirs, 1693–1705* (tr., John Eaden, 1931).

Lane-Poole, Stanley, *The Barbary Corsairs* (1890).

Larsson, Björn, *Long John Silver* (tr., Tom Geddes, 1999).

Le Golif, Louis A.T., *Memoirs of a Buccaneer* (eds, G. Alaux and A. t'Serstevens, 1954).

Leibbrandt, H.C.V. (ed.), *Précis of the Archives of the Cape of Good Hope: journal, 1699–1732* (Cape Town, 1896a).

Leibbrandt, H.C.V. (ed.), *Précis of the Archives of the Cape of Good Hope: letters received, 1695–1708* (Cape Town, 1896b).

Lemos, Andreas G., *The Greeks and the Sea* (1970).

Leslie, Charles, *A New History of Jamaica* (1740).

Lewis, W.H., *Levantine Adventurer, the travels and missions of the Chevalier d'Arvieux, 1653–1697* (1962).

Lloyd, Christopher, *English Corsairs on the Barbary Coast* (1981).

Lloyd, Christopher, *The Navy and the Slave Trade: the suppression of the African slave trade in the nineteenth century* (1949).

Lorimer, Sara, *Booty: Girl Pirates on the High Seas* (2002).

Low, Charles Rathbone, *History of the Indian Navy (1613–1863)* (1990).

Lyon, David, *The Sailing Navy List: all the ships of the Royal Navy – built, purchased and captured – 1688–1860* (1994).

Macintyre, Ben, 'A war of noble retaliation', *The Times*, 19 September 2001, pp. 2–3.

Mainwaring, Sir Henry, 'Of the beginnings, practices, and suppression of pirates' in Manwaring (1922).

Manwaring, G.E., and Perrin, W.G. (eds.), *The Life and Works of Sir Henry Mainwaring* (NRS vols 54, 56, 1920–22).

Marley, David F., *Pirates and Privateers of the Americas, 1654–99* (Santa Barbara, Cal., 1994).

Marryat, Captain Frederick, *The Pirate* (1836, 1889).

Mathew, David, 'The Cornish and Welsh pirates in the reign of Elizabeth', *EHR* 39 (1924).

Mathiex, Jean, 'Sur la marine marchande barbaresque au XVIIIe siècle', *Annales* xiii (1958).

Mattingly, G., 'No Peace beyond the Line', *TRHS* 5th ser. 13 (1963).

May, W.E., 'The Mutiny of the *Chesterfield*', *MM* 47 (1961).

Middleton, W.E. Knowles (ed.), *Lorenzo Magalotti at the Court of Charles II* (Waterloo, Ont., 1980).

Milford, Elizabeth, 'The Navy at peace: the activities of the early Jacobean navy, 1603–1618', *MM* lxxvi (1990).

Mollat, Michel (ed.), *Course et Piraterie,* 2 vols (Paris, 1975).

Molloy, C., *De jure maritimo et navali: or, a treatise of affairs maritime and of commerce* (2nd edn, 1682).

Moore, H. Kingsmill, 'The pirates of Leamcon', *Blackwood's Magazine* cxcii (1912).

Moore, John Robert, *Defoe in the Pillory and other studies* (Bloomington, Ind., 1939).

*Murder and Piracy; particulars of the murders of Capt. Johnston and the steersman of the ship* Jane (Edinburgh, 1821).

*Narrative of the Capture, Sufferings and Escape of Capt. Barnabas Lincoln and his Crew* (Boston, 1822).

Newton, A.P., *Colonising Activities of the English Puritans* (New Haven, Conn., 1914).

Newton, A.P., *The European Nations in the West Indies, 1493–1688* (1933).

Nuñez Jiménez, Antonio, *Piratas en el archipiélago cubano* (Havana, 1986).

Oppenheim, M., *A History of the Administration of the Royal Navy* (1896).

Panzac, Daniel, 'La guerre de course à Tripoli de Barbarie dans la seconde moitié du xviiie siècle' in Vergé-Franceschi (1991) pp. 255–78.

Parish, James Robert, *Pirates and Seafaring Swashbucklers on the Hollywood Screen* (Jefferson, N.C., 1995).

Pawson, Michael, and Buisseret, David, *Port Royal, Jamaica* (Oxford, 1975).

Penn, C.D., *The Navy under the Early Stuarts* (1970).

Pennell, C.R. (ed.), *Piracy and Diplomacy in 17th-century North Africa: the journal of Thomas Baker, English consul in Tripoli, 1677–1685* (1989).

Pennell, C.R., 'Who needs pirate heroes?', *The Northern Mariner* viii (1998).

Pérez-Reverte, Arturo, *The Nautical Chart* (New York, 2000).

Pérotin-Dumon, Anne, 'La contribution des *corsarios insurgentes* à l'indépendance américaine: course et piraterie dans la golfe du Mexique et la mer des Antilles (1810–1830)' in Mollat (1975), ii, 666–75.

Philip, Maxwell, *Emmanuel Appadocca or Blighted Life: a tale of the Boucaneers* (Amherst, Mass., 1997).

Pignon, Jean, 'Un document inédit sur la Tunisie au début du XVIIe siècle', *Cahiers de Tunisie* ix (1961).

*The Pirate Hunter: a story of the ocean* (1866).

Pitcairn Jones, C.G. (ed.), *Piracy in the Levant, 1827–28* (1934).

Porter, Admiral David D., *Memoir of Commodore David Porter of the United States Navy* (Albany, New York, 1875).

Pratt, Michael, *Britain's Greek Empire: reflections of the history of the Ionian Islands* (1978).

Rediker, Marcus, *Between the Devil and the Deep Blue Sea* (Cambridge, 1989).

Rediker, Marcus, 'Hydrarchy and Libertalia: the utopian dimensions of Atlantic piracy in the early eighteenth century' in Starkey (1997).

Rediker, Marcus, 'Liberty beneath the Jolly Roger: the lives of Anne Bonny and Mary Read, pirates' in Creighton and Norling (1996).

Rediker, Marcus, '"Under the Banner of King Death": the social world of Anglo-American pirates, 1716 to 1726', *William & Mary Quarterly* 3rd ser. 38 (1981).

Risso, Patricia, 'Cross-cultural perceptions of piracy: maritime violence in the western Indian Ocean and Persian Gulf region during a long eighteenth century', *Journal of World History* xii (2001).

Ritchie, Robert C., *Captain Kidd and the War against the Pirates* (Cambridge, Mass., 1986).

Ritchie, Robert C., 'Government measures against piracy and privateering in the Atlantic area, 1750–1850' in Starkey (1997).

Ritchie, Robert C., *Pirates: myths and realities* (Minneapolis, 1986).

Roberts, Captain George, *The Four Years' Voyages of Captain George Roberts* (1726).

Robinson, Howard, *Carrying British Mail Overseas* (1964).

Rodger, N.A.M., *The Safeguard of the Sea: a naval history of Britain. Vol. i, 660–1649* (1997).

Rodger, N.A.M., *The Wooden World: an anatomy of the Georgian Navy* (1986).

Rogoziński, Jan, *Honor among Thieves: Captain Kidd, Henry Every, and the pirate democracy in the Indian Ocean* (Mechanicsburg, Pa., 2000).

Rogoziński, Jan, *Pirates! An A–Z Encyclopedia* (New York, 1995).

Saiz Cidoncha, Carlos, *Historia de la piratería en América española* (Madrid, 1985).

Sebag, Paul, *Tunis au XVIIe siècle: une cité barbaresque au temps de la course* (Paris, 1989).

Senior, C.M., 'The confederation of deep-sea pirates: English pirates in the Atlantic, 1603–25' in Mollat (1975), vol. i, pp. 331–59.

Senior, C.M., *A Nation of Pirates: English piracy in its heyday* (Newton Abbot, 1976).

Senior, C.M., 'Robert Walsingham: a Jacobean pirate', *MM* lx (1974).

Sharpe, Bartholomew, *Voyages and Adventures* (1684).

Shaw, T., *Travels and observations relating to several parts of Barbary and the Levant* (2nd edn, 1757).

Shelvocke, George (the elder), *A Voyage round the World* (1726, 1928).

Shepherd, James F., and Walton, Gary M., *Shipping, Maritime Trade and the Economic Development of Colonial North America* (Cambridge, 1972).

Smith, Aaron, *The Atrocities of the Pirates* (1824).

Snelgrave, William, *A New Account of some parts of Guinea and the Slave-trade* (1734).

Spencer, William, *Algiers in the Age of the Corsairs* (Norman, Okla., 1976).

Stanley, Jo (ed.), *Bold in Her Breeches: Women Pirates across the Ages* (1995).

Stark, Francis R., *The Abolition of Privateering and the Declaration of Paris* (New York, 1897).

Starkey, David J. (ed.), *Pirates and Privateers: new perspectives on the war on trade in the eighteenth and nineteenth centuries* (Exeter, 1997).

*State Trials, A Complete Collection of,* (1730).

Steele, Ian K., *The English Atlantic, 1675–1740* (Oxford, 1986).

Steele, Ian K., *Politics of Colonial Policy: the Board of Trade in Colonial Administration, 1696–1720* (Oxford, 1968).

Stirling-Maxwell, Sir John, *Don John of Austria* (1883).

Stow, John, *Annales* (1615).

Tenenti, Alberto, *Piracy and the Decline of Venice, 1580–1615* (1967).

Thomas, Hugh, 'Cuba, c.1750–c.1860' in Leslie Bethell (ed.), *Cuba: a short history* (Cambridge, 1993).

Thomson, Janice E., *Mercenaries, Pirates, and Sovereigns: state-building and extraterritorial violence in early modern Europe* (Princeton, 1994).

Thoreau, Henry David, *Cape Cod* (1865, 1987).

Thornton, A.P., 'Agents of Empire: the Buccaneers' in *For the File on Empire: Essays and Reviews* (1968).

Thornton, A.P., 'The Modyfords and Morgan', *Jamaican Historical Review* ii (1952).

Thornton, A.P., *West-India Policy under the Restoration* (Oxford, 1956).

*The Trial of Charles Christopher Delano and others* (1820).

*Trial of Peter Heaman and François Gauthiez ... for piracy* (Edinburgh, 1821).

Turbet-Delof, Guy, *L'Afrique Barbaresque dans la littérature française aux XVIe et XVIIe siècles* (Geneva, 1973).

Turley, Hans, *Rum, Sodomy and the Lash: piracy, sexuality, and masculine identity* (New York, 1999).

Tyng, Charles, *Before the Wind: the memoirs of an American sea captain, 1808–1833* (1999).

Uring, Nathaniel, *Voyages and Travels* (1726).

Vaissière, Pierre de, *Saint-Domingue: la société et la vie créoles sous l'ancien régime* (Paris, 1909).

Vale, Brian, *A War betwixt Englishmen: Brazil against Argentina on the River Plate, 1825–1830* (2000).

Vergé-Franceschi, Michel, *Guerre et commerce en Méditerranée, IXe–*

*XXe siècles* (Paris, 1991).

Villar, Roger, *Piracy Today: robbery and violence at sea since 1980* (1985).

Wagner, Kip, *Pieces of Eight* (1967).

Westergaard, Waldemar, *The Danish West Indies under Company rule, 1671–1754* (New York, 1917).

Whitaker, Arthur Preston, *The United States and the Independence of Latin America, 1800–1830* (Baltimore, Md., 1941).

Wilkinson, Henry C., *Bermuda in the Old Empire* (Oxford, 1950).

Wilson, Arthur M., 'The logwood trade in the 17th and 18th centuries' in Donald C. McKay (ed.), *Essays in the History of Modern Europe* (New York, 1936).

Wilson, Peter Lamborn, *Pirate Utopias: Moorish corsairs and European renegadoes* (New York, 1995).

Wolf, John B., *The Barbary Coast: Algiers under the Turks, 1500 to 1830* (New York, 1979).

Woodhouse, C.M., *The Battle of Navarino* (1965).

Woodward, Donald (ed.), 'Sir Thomas Button, the *Phoenix* and the defence of the Irish coast, 1614–22', *MM* lix (1973).

Wright, Arnold, *Annesley of Surat and his times* (1918).

Wright, Charles, and Fayle, C.E., *A History of Lloyd's* (1928).

Zahedieh, Nuala, 'A frugal, prudential and hopeful trade: privateering in Jamaica, 1655–89', *Journal of Imperial and Commonwealth History* 18 (1990).

# Index